HORSE

♦

THE
COMPLETE GUIDE

♦

Mary Gordon Watson
Russell Lyon
Sue Montgomery

BARNES
&NOBLE
BOOKS
NEW YORK

Horse – The Complete Guide
was conceived, edited, and designed by
Team Media Limited
Masters House
107 Hammersmith Road
London W14 0QH

Authors

Mary Gordon   What is a Horse?
Watson   Caring for Horses
                         Horse and Pony Breeds
R. Russell Lyon   Your Horse's Health
Sue Montgomery   Equestrian Sports
                         The Noble Horse

Consultant
Amanda J. Waters

Senior Editor   **Antonia Cunningham**
Art Editor   **Thomas Keenes**
Design Assistants   **Max Newton**
                       Zoe Quayle
Picture Researchers   **Veneta Bullen**
                       Sarah Moule
Illustrators   **Linden Artists**
                       David Ashby

Team Media
Editorial Director   **Louise Tucker**
Managing Editor   **Elizabeth Tatham**
Art Directors   **Eddie Poulton**
                       Paul Wilkinson

1999 Barnes & Noble Books

ISBN 0-7607-1720-6

Book design by Team Media, Ltd.

Printed and bound in China

00 01 02 03 M 9 8 7 6 5 4 3

LFA

Mary Gordon Watson, MBE, a former member of the British Three-day Event team, won the European Three-day Event in 1969, the World Championship in 1970, and was a gold medallist at the 1972 Olympics. Mary now teaches riding, judges dressage, show hunters, and Connemara ponies, and writes for equine and broadsheet publications.

R. Russell Lyon BVM&S, MRCVS is a working vet, specializing in horses. He writes on equine health, and broadcasts on Radio Norfolk in the UK.

Sue Montgomery is a freelance sports journalist, specializing in racing. She works for the UK equine and broadsheet press, including the *Independent*, *Independent on Sunday*, *Horse and Hound* and *Racing Post*, and contributes regularly as Senior England Correspondent to Italy's daily racing newspaper, *Lo Sportsman*.

Amanda J. Waters BSc (Hons), MSc, MIBiol, CBiol is Senior lecturer in Equine Science at Hartpury College, Herefordshire, one of the UK's foremost equine colleges.

Mary Ratlcliffe writes and designs a regular newsletter for the nonprofit Thoroughbred Retirement Foundation, which provides a lifetime haven to racehorses who no longer compete. She is also a freelance writer, editor, and designer.

Contents

Introduction

Horses and ponies provide millions of people of all ages with great pleasure, whether they are directly involved with them as riders, owners or handlers, or are armchair enthusiasts who admire the sheer beauty of the animal without feeling the need to get up and ride one. For those who have a one-on-one relationship with these beautiful animals, they are a source of true, loyal friendship once trust has been established on both sides.

UNDERSTANDING HORSES

Horse – The Complete Guide is a book for anyone who loves horses. Written by a team of experts, it is filled with sound information and practical advice based on years of experience handling, riding, and caring for horses on a professional level. It focuses on providing an understanding of how the horse functions, both biologically and psychologically, and discusses how a new horse owner should approach the responsibilities involved in buying and owning a horse. The book also discusses the place of the horse in sports, history, and culture.

The book divides into six parts. Part 1 introduces the reader to the ancestor of the horse, a small mammal living in the marshy forests of the American continent millions of years ago, and explains its evolution to the modern horse and pony breeds of today. The anatomy of the horse, how its body systems work, how it moves, breathes, and processes food, is followed by a discussion of the horse's natural behavior in the wild and the adaptations that are made in a domestic environment.

Part 2 deals with horse care, covering all the factors that need to be considered in order to provide a horse with a happy environment and proper care. This section also discusses whether owning a horse is suitable in the first place, gives advice on assessing horses, stables and grazing, and provides information on horse care and basic tack, including what to do in circumstances such as traveling or when a mare is pregnant.

Part 3 deals with what to do if a horse becomes sick, describing the causes and symptoms of many common problems and explaining the treatment that the vet will advise. Information on first aid and nursing ensures a knowledge of what to do in an emergency and how to care for a horse once the vet has visited and diagnosed the problem.

SPORTS, BREEDS, HISTORY AND CULTURE

Part 4 enters the world of sports, describing the rules of various equine disciplines. Whether discussing an international showjumping course or explaining the dressage arena, this section will be a constant source of interest, enhancing your understanding and enjoyment as spectator or rider. Famous sporting horses receive concise, lively biographies.

Part 5, divided into light horses, heavy horses, and ponies, examines over 120 breeds, explaining the histories, characteristics, and uses of each.

The final part looks at the ways in which the horse has featured in the imagination and history of humanity – its role in making and breaking empires, the magical powers it possesses in mythologies and religions across different cultures, the heroic part it has played in the lives of great commanders, and its place in literature and the arts all over the world.

Horse – The Complete Guide is a book for the entire family – a practical guide for use in the stable and an armchair treasury of horse history and facts to be enjoyed at leisure.

Below: Two horses stand together in a field. Horses are naturally sociable animals and are happiest in the company of other creatures, particularly of their own kind. If possible, you should try to stable and graze your horse with other horses, which will prevent it from becoming bored and lonely.

HORSES IN THE WILD

Horses and their ancestors have run wild over the earth for thousands of years. Short and sturdy to withstand the cold, or fine-boned and thin-skinned to deal with extreme desert heat, most of them have now been domesticated and cross-bred to serve the purposes of humanity. Today, only the Mustang and the

Brumby can be classed as true wild horses. However, others, such as some of the British ponies, the horses of the Camargue or the Steppe horses in the former USSR, although managed and bred in controlled circumstances, live all year in the open, moving and feeding at will where their ancestors roamed before them.

... he was wild,
Wild as the wild deer,
and untaught,
With spur and bridle undefiled ...

Lord Byron, Mazeppa's Ride, 1819

Now the great winds
shoreward blow;
Now the salt tides
seaward flow;
Now the wild white
horses play,
Champ and chafe and
toss in the spray.

*Matthew Arnold,
The Forsaken Merman,
1892*

*When God wanted to make
the horse, he said to the South Wind,
"I want to make a creature of you.
Condense." And the Wind condensed.
The Archangel Gabriel . . . took a
handful of the stuff and presented it
to God who made a brown bay, or
burnt chestnut, upon saying "I call
you Horse . . . You shall be the Lord
of the other animals."*

EMIR ABD EL-KADER (1808–83),

IN A LETTER TO A FRENCHMAN,

GENERAL DAUMAS

He looks upon his love and
neighs unto her;
She answers him as if she knew
his mind;
Being proud, as females are,
to see him woo her,
She puts on outward strangeness,
seems unkind,
Spurns his love . . .

WILLIAM SHAKESPEARE,
ADONIS'S TRAMPLING COURSER, 1593

Who in the garden-pony
carrying skeps
Of grass, or fallen leaves,
his knees gone slack,
Round belly, hollow back,
Sees the Mongolian Tarpan
of the Steppes?

DOROTHY WELLESLY,
DUCHESS OF WELLINGTON,
HORSES, C.1930

A thousand horse, the wild, the free,
Like waves that follow o'er the sea
Came thickly thundering on . . .

LORD BYRON, MAZEPPA'S RIDE, 1819

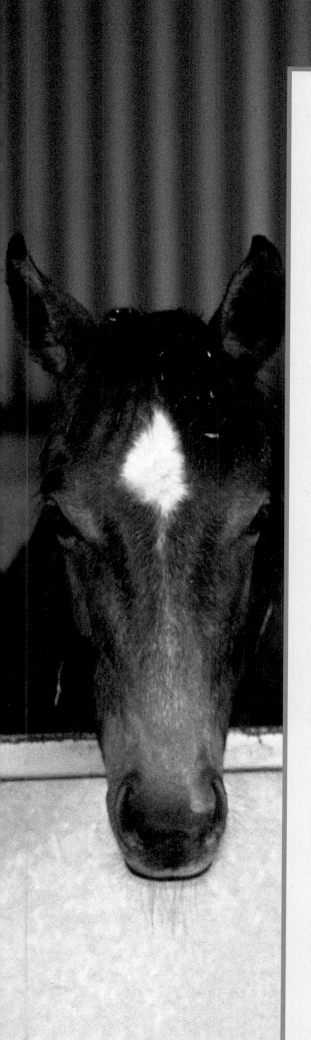

PART I

WHAT IS A HORSE?

*T*he horse is a hoofed, herbivorous mammal of the Equidae family, genus *Equus*, which includes the domestic horse and pony, the wild Przewalski's horse, and the zebra. Horses and ponies are quick-moving, plains-dwelling, herd animals with teeth adapted to grinding coarse vegetation. Although equid species can interbreed, the offspring are almost always sterile. The horse began to evolve on the American continent over 60 million years ago and spread to other parts of the world, where it evolved to suit the local habitats, whether cold and damp or hot and dry. It became extinct in America about 8,000 years ago, three thousand years before horses were first domesticated – probably by Asian nomads in the the third millenium BC. This marked the beginning of the relationship between the horse and humankind that has lasted for thousands of years, as partners in agriculture, warfare, transportation and, more recently, in competitive sport and leisure activities.

Evolution of the Horse

Eohippus to Pliohippus ✦ *Equus caballus* ✦ *Early horses* ✦ *Other equines*

The horse has evolved over more than 60 million years, adapting to changing climates and habitats. Its earliest known ancestor, according to fossils found in southern parts of North America, was a small quadruped, the size of a fox. This creature is known as the "Dawn Horse," or Eohippus, a name derived from the Eocene geological era, 50 million years ago, and from *hippos*, the Greek word for horse.

EARLY DEVELOPMENT

Eohippus had four toes on its front feet and three on its back feet. There was a soft pad at the base of the toes and at the end of each toe a horny, hoof-like nail. Eohippus stood just 10in (25cm) high at the shoulder (although some individuals may have been slightly bigger) and its back was arched and ran down to a tail set lower than its shoulder. It had small, sharp teeth, eyes set centrally in its head and bore little resemblance to the modern horse. An inhabitant of swampy forests, it browsed on leaves and was probably camouflaged with a striped or blotchy coat. It evolved on the American continent and then spread east and west over the land bridges that linked America, Europe, and Asia. It disappeared between 40 and 35 million years ago.

The next significant stage was Mesohippus, a sheep-sized creature that appeared in the Oligocene era, between 40 and 26 million years ago. Mesohippus retained Eohippus' soft foot pad, but now had just three toes on each foot. The middle toe was larger than the side toes and bore the most weight, suggesting that the swampy forest floor of the earlier period was giving way to slighty harder ground. Mesohippus continued to browse on soft, leafy vegetation and may also have had a camouflaged coat.

Over the next fifteen million years or so, during the Miocene era (26–10 million years ago), the climate, and consequently the environment, continued to change. The climate became drier, forests gave way to open grasslands, and "horses" travelled further and faster, developing longer legs. In the early part of the period, Mesohippus was superseded by Miohippus, a larger type not unlike the modern

Eohippus stood 10–14 in (25–35cm) at the shoulder, on a level with low-level foliage. It had four toes on its front feet and three on the back feet, which all took weight. There were soft pads at the base of each toe, each with a horny, hoof-like nail at the end. The back was arched, the coat striped and rough textured like a deer's. The eyes were set centrally in the head.

Mesohippus stood 18in (45cm) at the shoulder. It had three toes on each leg – the central toe had become more prominent. It still had an arched back, but the legs, neck, ears and muzzle were longer than those of Eohippus. The coat pattern was less marked.

Miohippus was similar to Mesohippus. It stood 24in (60cm) at the shoulder; the neck, ears and muzzle were longer and the eyes were beginning to move farther apart

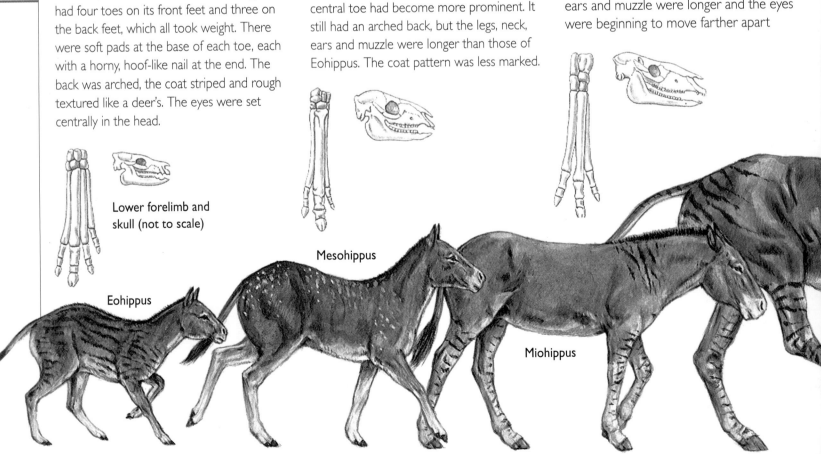

Lower forelimb and skull (not to scale)

Eohippus

Mesohippus

Miohippus

pony, although it was still very small, had low-crowned teeth for browsing and three-toed feet.

Gradually, as the environment changed, the "horse" began to eat grass, its teeth changing and its neck lengthening to adapt to grazing. The eyes moved farther apart, allowing a wider field of vision, and the ears lengthened, enabling the "horse" to pinpoint accurately the source of distant sounds. By now there were many varied lines of horse-like creatures, and six distinct main groups in North America, of which the most significant, Merychippus, appeared about 20 million years ago.

Merychippus probably overlapped with Miohippus and other types such as Megahippus (which was bigger than any horse known today) for a few million years. But eventually all the browsing horses became extinct, unable to adapt to the changing environment. Merychippus, however, was adapted to its open grassland environment. It had longer legs, allowing it to flee predators more easily, and although it still had three toes, the side toes were increasingly vestigial and only the central toe bore any weight. The soft pads had gone, and flexible ligaments had evolved to control and support the greatly increased action of the limbs. Merychippus had a flat, longer back and a heavier skull.

Pliohippus was the last stage in the evolution of the modern horse, Equus. It appeared about six million years ago, during the Pliocene age, and was the first to have a single horn-covered toe, or hoof. A leggy, grass-eating creature, it was well suited to living on the plains, steppes and prairies, where there were fewer hiding places, requiring it to have the ability to evade predators swiftly. The teeth were now larger and longer, for cutting or tearing off coarse grasses, and an elaborate pattern of ridges developed on the molars, for grinding down the tough cellulose of grasses. As a result, the muzzle was longer. Pliohippus stood at about 48in (1.22m) at the shoulder; it was also the progenitor for zebras and asses.

THE MODERN HORSE

Equus caballus, the horse as we know it, was established one million years ago. It spread into South America, Asia, and then Europe and Africa. All other branches of horse-like creatures became extinct.

By the end of the Ice Age, in about 9000 BC, there were three related equine groups, found in different areas, that had all evolved from Pliohippus: horses, all of which had

Merychippus stood 36in (90cm) at the shoulder. The side toes were increasingly vestigial and only the central toe bore weight. The soft toe pads had disappeared, the neck and legs were longer and the back longer and flatter. The skull was bigger and heavier.

Pliohippus stood 48in (1.22m) at the shoulder, and had the general proportions of a horse. It now had a single horn-covered toe, eyes placed high on its

head, and teeth suitable for grazing. The back was straight with no discernable withers and the quarters sloped. It had a dorsal stripe and may have had markings on its legs.

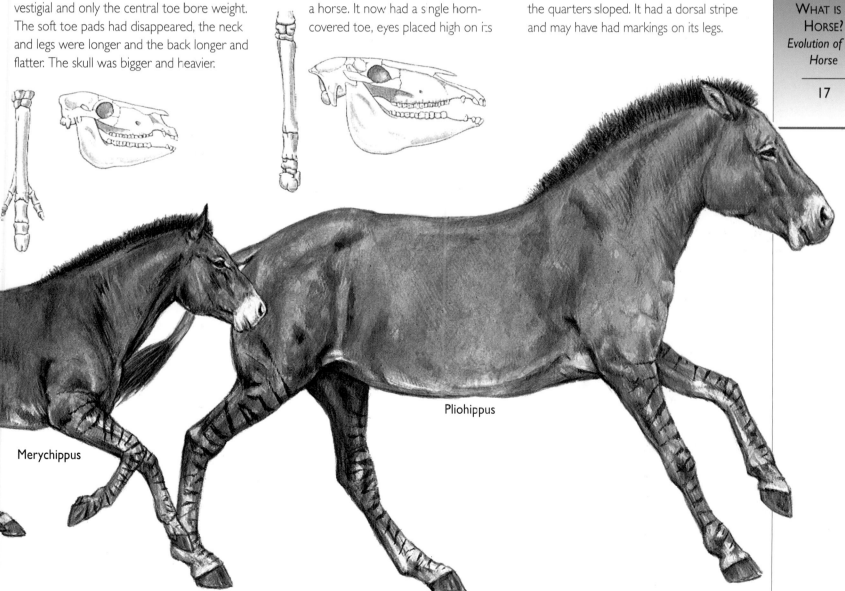

Pliohippus

Merychippus

Evolution of the horse

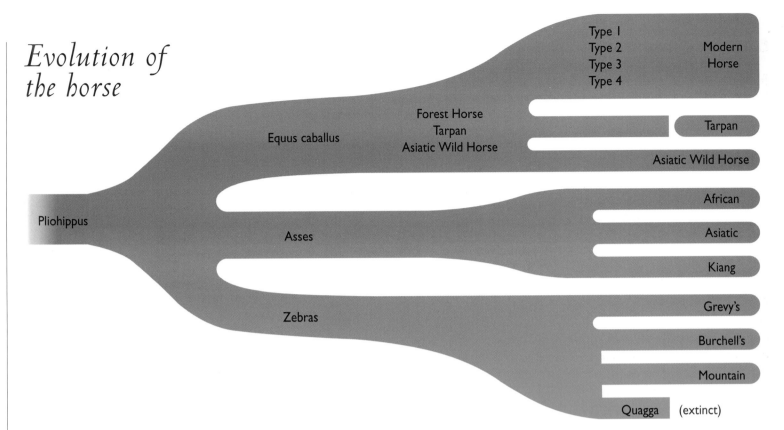

			Type 1 Type 2 Type 3 Type 4	Modern Horse
Pliohippus	Equus caballus	Forest Horse Tarpan Asiatic Wild Horse		Tarpan
				Asiatic Wild Horse
	Asses			African
				Asiatic
				Kiang
	Zebras			Grevy's
				Burchell's
				Mountain
			Quagga (extinct)	

Above: This diagram shows the relationship between Pliohippus, *Equus caballus*, the ass and the zebra groups and the modern equines. Note the four types giving rise to the modern horse, the extinction of the Quagga; the reappearance of the Tarpan after reconstruction by selective breeding; and the range of equid species that exist today – with over 300 breeds of horse.

evolved from Pliohippus. Horses inhabited Europe and western Asia, zebras, eastern and southern Africa, and asses and onagers lived in northern Africa and the Middle East respectively. The horse died out in the Americas about 8,000 years ago, a circumstance for which experts can offer no explanation. It was reintroduced by the Spanish when they landed in Mexico for the first time in 1519 (see page 242).

ORIGINAL TYPES

The progression of the wild horse from these early days is debatable. However, it seems likely that although there were numerous forms of the horse at this time, the modern horse probably derived initially from three particular types: the Forest Horse, a slow-moving hairy creature standing about 15 hands that lived in the then-swampy forested lands of northern Europe; the Asiatic Wild Horse (still in

Above: The Exmoor pony, a native of northern England is the closest modern equivalent to Pony Type 1. Like Pony Type 1 it has a distinctive jaw formation and the beginnings of a seventh molar and a double-layered coat, which is ideal as protection against cold and damp.

Above: The Highland Pony is the nearest modern equivalent to Pony Type 2, which lived in northern Eurasia, resembled the Asiatic Wild horse and was resistant to cold. It was bigger than Pony Type 1. The modern Highland may be a cross between the two Pony types.

Above: The Akhal-Teke, an ancient desert breed, best represents Horse Type 3. Horse Type 3 lived in Central Asia, was resistant to drought and heat and may have been influenced by the Tarpan. The Akhal-Teke has very thin skin and a fine coat, a characteristic of desert-bred horses.

Above: The Caspian is the equivalent of Horse Type 4, which was a small, fine-boned, desert horse, resistant to heat. It has several unusual characteristics, including a seventh molar and a vault-shaped skull. It may the ancestor of the Arab and, with the Asiatic Wild Horse, is the oldest breed in existence.

Above: The African ass (*Equus africanus*) is the ancestor of the domestic ass (*Equus asinus*). The Asiatic ass, above, of which there are four types, belongs to the subgenus *Hemionus* (*Equus hemionus onager, khur, luteus,* and *hemionus*), and has horse and ass features as well as its own distinctive characteristics. The Kiang is a separate branch of the ass family.

Above: The Mountain zebra and Burchell's zebra are the two species most closely related to horses and asses. They are grouped under the sub-genus *Hippotigris*, while Grevy's zebra, the largest of the three, standing at 13.2 hands (1.37m), was the first to break away from Pliohippus and is classified under the subgenus *Dolichohippus*.

existence and also known as "Przewalski's horse" (see page 230); and the Tarpan, a lighter horse that existed on the Russian Steppes until the late 19th century (see page 228). From these three types, it is postulated that four further types, two ponies and two horses, evolved, which are the basis for all of today's breeds.

The first, a pony type, sometimes called the Celtic or Atlantic pony, evolved in northwest Europe. It thrived in wet, harsh conditions, and fossils and cave drawings show a close resemblance to the Exmoor and Icelandic ponies (see pages 215 and 227).

The second pony type lived in northeast Europe and Asia, and was larger than the first type. It was a coarser, heavier, slow-moving animal and was the probable ancestor of the present-day heavy horses. It did not migrate, but grew a long, thick coat in winter, had a large body for extra fat storage, and large feet to cross swamps. It is thought to have been dun colored with a dorsal stripe and to have looked similar to the Asiatic Wild Horse. The modern Fjord and Highland ponies and the Noriker horse (see pages 226, 217, and 209) are likely descendants.

The third type, from Central Asia, was a fine, small horse, at about 14.3 hands standing slightly taller than the second Pony type. This first horse type was light framed and narrow, with a long neck, long ears, and a very fine coat. It resembled the Akhal-Teke (see page 186), which can exist in extreme heat on very little water. The Karabakh and Andalucian (see pages 189 and 170), and the Sorraia pony (see page 224), probably derive from this type.

The fourth type of horse inhabited western Asia. It was a smaller horse (standing at about 12 hands) and was lighter than Type 3, with a finer head, high-set tail, and fine coat. Like Type 3, it was resistant to heat. Clearly influenced by Tarpan stock, the Arab (see page 184) would have derived from this type, although the Caspian pony (see page 229) is the closest equivalent today.

The great diversity shown between the types, such as hair growth and bone density, is due predominantly to the horse having migrated to, and evolved in, varying climates. Terrain, soil, and forage were all important influences on the evolution of each type. The process accelerated once horses began to be domesticated (probably in Central Asia about 5,000 to 6,000 years ago), when Mongolian and other tribesmen put their horses to work. Once selective breeding was introduced, stronger, faster and more athletic animals were created and great breeds, such as the Arab horse, were founded that have endured and thrived up to the present time.

EQUINE RELATIONS

Zebras and asses evolved from the Asinus branch of the Equus family, and also have just one "toe" on each foot.

The zebra evolved and originated in Africa. There are now three species of zebra distributed through eastern and southern Africa, Grevy's zebra, Burchell's zebra, and the Mountain zebra. The Quagga, a semi-striped species, died out in the 19th century. The zebra, unlike other equines, has not been widely domesticated.

The two groups of wild asses (Asiatic and African) also evolved in the Old World and live in the desert and scrublands of central Asia, the Middle East and North Africa. They are sure-footed, and usually live in small groups or alone. Like zebras, they can survive for long periods without water and travel great distances. The domestic donkey descends from the ass.

CROSSBREEDING

◆

The breeding of different horses or ponies results in fertile offspring that inherit characteristics from both parents. But breeding of different branches of the equine family, which does not occur in the wild, results in infertile offspring. The combination of sire and dam also affects the offspring.

Mule: the progeny of a male donkey and a female horse, it has a horse-like body and donkey-like ears, legs and feet.

Hinny: the progeny of a female donkey and a male horse, with a donkey-like body and horse-like ears, legs and feet.

Zebrinny: the offspring of a male horse and a female zebra.

Zebrula: the offspring of a male zebra and a female horse.

Zedonk: the offspring of a zebra and a donkey.

The History of the Horse

Domestication ✦ Warfare ✦ Glorification ✦ Place in society ✦ The horse in peacetime

The history of horse breeding has evolved alongside human need and ambition. In the centuries before domestication, the relationship was that of the hunted and the hunter. Timid and easily frightened, whole herds could be driven into blocked spaces and clubbed to death or possibly chased off cliffs.

Around 4000–3000 BC, probably as a result of experience in herding semi-wild animals such as sheep or goats, Asian nomadic tribes north of

Above: The nomads of Kyrgyzstan continue to milk their Novokhirghiz mares, as they have done for centuries. They ferment the milk to make *kumiss*, the national alcohol.

Below: The Assyrian horses of the ninth century BC were small, light animals, not unlike the Caspian horse of Iran (see p.232).

the Black Sea began to tame wild horses, keeping them in herds for milk, meat, and skins. Gradually, these same tribes began to ride the horse and recognized the advantages of its strength and speed, for drawing sleds, herding on horseback, and travelling to distant feeding grounds.

The wheel was invented around 3500 BC, in Mesopotamia (which later became a center for horse breeding). This made trading increasingly easy and tribes gained status and wealth by dealing in horses. Over the next millenium far-reaching trade networks were established, especially in western Asia and southeastern Europe.

Elsewhere, horses were being used in warfare by nomadic, horse-riding peoples, such as the Kassites, Elamites, and Hittites, who all conquered neighboring peoples in about 3000 BC.

By about 2000 BC, chariots were being used in warfare. Egypt, for example, not yet in possession of the wheel, was overrun about this time by the chariot-driving Hyksos, who remained in power until 1542 BC. Within 400 years, Egypt had sophisticated chariots, and in China, to the east, they were perfected by 1300 BC.

Chariots continued to be the primary vehicle of war, until mounted armies, or cavalry, became more widely used. As weaponry and tools improved, the cavalry developed and proved very effective in combat, having the advantages of speed, height, and surprise over opponents. It could also be used in areas unsuitable for chariots. Gradually, larger horses were sought to carry armored men. Bits, reins, and spurs came into use, to control the horses' speed and direction. Initially, these were made of wood, bone or hide, but by *c.*1500 BC, bronze was used, later replaced by iron. Saddles (other than a cloth) were not invented until the late Roman period (*c.*4th–5th century AD) and stirrups did not appear until even later.

GLORIFICATION
Without the horse, the history of humankind would have lacked the fast and efficient transportation of men, goods, and weapons necessary for far-flung commerce, exploration, and conquest. As a result, from early on, the horse was regarded as an important part of political life. The

Assyrians, a martial people whose empire was at its height from the mid-eighth century BC, regarded fine horsemanship as their ultimate aim, a tradition continued by the Persians who conquered their empire in 612 BC. Cyrus the Great, for example, the Persian ruler who took Babylon in 539 BC kept 8,000 stallions and 6,000 mares in his stables in Babylon alone.

The Chinese glorified the horse in art (see page 239), particularly their war horses, which were also adopted in Korea and Japan. The horse earned increasing respect and value and was even fought over as a coveted charger, or to improve imperial studs. For peoples such as the Turks, Huns, and Mongols, the horse was so vital to their success and survival that it was considered a friend, and warriors were buried with their chargers. In many countries, horses meant prestige, and knights on both sides of the endless religious wars and crusades were expected to breed and provide fine horses to ride against the infidel.

THE HORSE IN PEACETIME

Over the centuries, horses have been bred to suit different purposes and changing demands.

Between about AD 600 and 1500, heavy horses began to be used on the land and were economically important by the 18th century. In the 17th century, with the rise of coach travel, strong, fast horses were bred to pull heavy public coaches. The 18th century saw Arab and Barb blood transform racehorses and hunters in England as gambling and sport became increasingly popular. This laid the foundation for the Thoroughbred (see page 160), the most influential modern breed.

When pulling horses were largely replaced by tractors, and driving horses by cars, the demand for horses declined in the developed world, although they are still used extensively for transport and agricultural tasks in less developed places.

However, since World War II, the demand for recreational and sports horses has increased, and selective breeding for sport is now an important industry in many countries.

Above: Although this 16th-century Flemish scene shows horses, they were not widely used in agriculture until the 18th century, when new machines meant that the horse was better suited to farm labor than the ox.

Below: Racing between private individuals was increasingly in vogue from the 18th century in England, once the technology for horse-drawn vehicles became more sophisticated. Trotting races became popular in the US.

Structure

Points of the horse ✦ Colors and markings ✦ Skeletal frame ✦ Internal structure of the feet ✦ Teeth development ✦ Muscles, tendons and ligaments

Horses have been adapted and developed to suit the changing needs of the human race since they were first domesticated. Yet despite human interference and cross-breeding, resulting in over 300 current breeds, the structure and bone formation of the "domestic" horse has remained the same. From the smallest Shetland pony to the largest work horse, all belong to the species *Equus caballus*. All share a common body structure and have a constant 64 chromosomes in each cell.

The horse is uniquely designed for strength, size, and speed. Its lower limbs are light, with minimal bone and no muscle. They are propelled forward and backward, by highly developed muscles attached to the bones of the upper limbs and body. To

COAT COLORS
✦

Horses are described by their coat colors and markings. No two horses are identical, and colors vary within a category. The main colors are: bay (light, bright, dappled or dark); brown; black; gray (light, dark, dappled, flea-bitten, iron-gray); chestnut (liver, bright, sorrel); roan (strawberry, red, blue); cream; dun; palomino; piebald (black and white); skewbald (any other color and white); or spotted (see p.244).

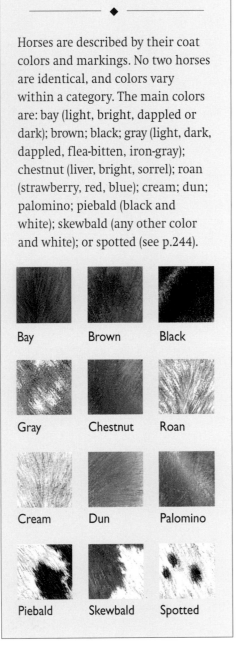

Bay Brown Black

Gray Chestnut Roan

Cream Dun Palomino

Piebald Skewbald Spotted

Right: Conformation is the way in which a horse is put together, or structured. The horse's shape when standing is its "static conformation," and when in motion, it is the "dynamic conformation;" each body part plays an important role.

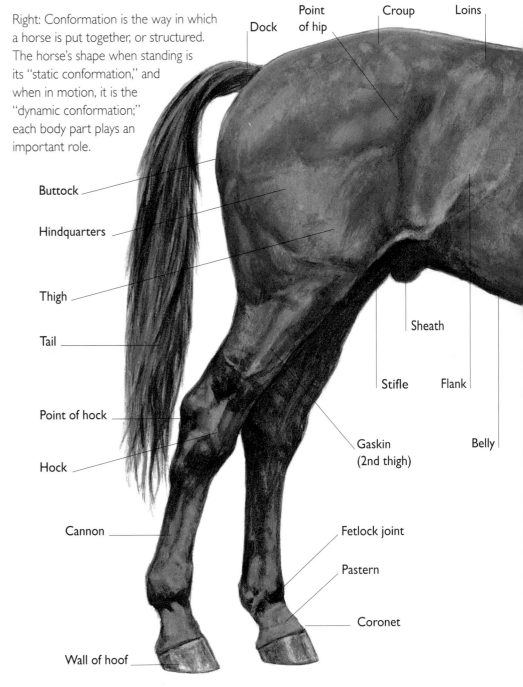

Dock · Point of hip · Croup · Loins · Buttock · Hindquarters · Thigh · Tail · Point of hock · Hock · Cannon · Wall of hoof · Sheath · Stifle · Flank · Gaskin (2nd thigh) · Belly · Fetlock joint · Pastern · Coronet

understand the physical and mental capabilities of a horse, and the limitations of both, it is important to have some knowledge of its conformation and build: how its body functions; how the mind and senses work; and its life cycle.

DESCRIBING A HORSE

The various points, or parts, of a horse need identification, since every one of them has a particular role. It is also useful and important to know and describe the conformation accurately when veterinary help is needed.

The left side of the horse is described as the "near" side and the right as the "off" side. The parts of the horse's body are attached to a frame, or skeleton, made of bone and cartilage, which give it strength. The lower legs and feet are the most vulnerable parts as they provide support for a large body and are often subjected to considerable weight and concussion, especially when the horse jumps while carrying a rider. The forelegs fold backward at the knee and the fetlock joint, while the hind legs fold under the horse when the hocks bend. They never fold back.

A horse's performance and usefulness depend on good conformation (see page 46); structural weaknesses (see pages 47–8) can undermine its soundness and overall strength.

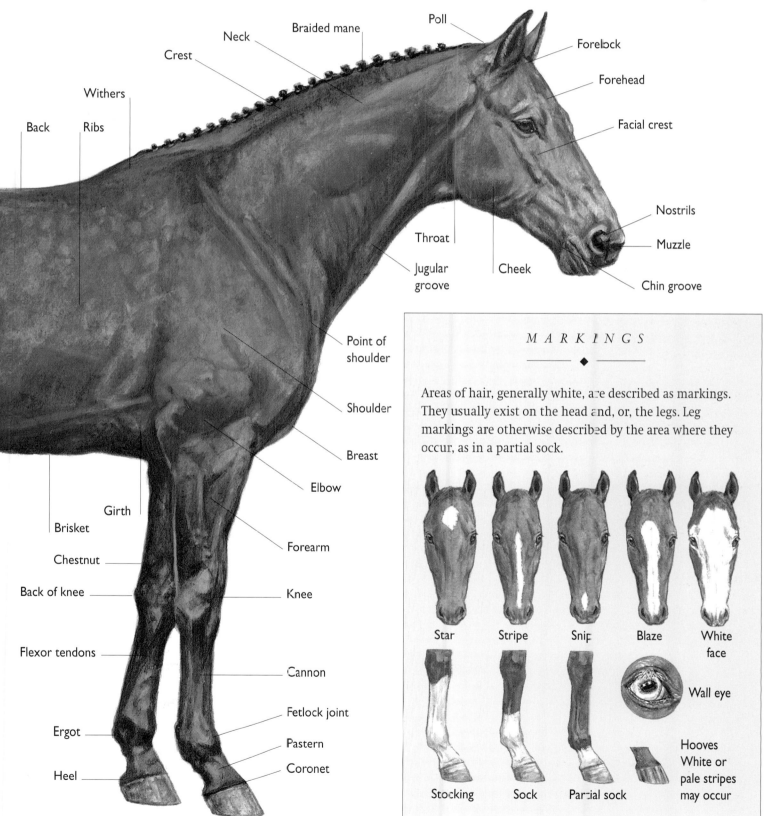

Poll
Braided mane
Neck
Crest
Withers
Back
Ribs
Forelock
Forehead
Facial crest
Nostrils
Throat
Muzzle
Jugular groove
Cheek
Chin groove
Point of shoulder
Shoulder
Breast
Elbow
Forearm
Girth
Brisket
Chestnut
Back of knee
Knee
Flexor tendons
Cannon
Ergot
Fetlock joint
Pastern
Heel
Coronet

MARKINGS
◆

Areas of hair, generally white, are described as markings. They usually exist on the head and, or, the legs. Leg markings are otherwise described by the area where they occur, as in a partial sock.

Star
Stripe
Snip
Blaze
White face

Wall eye

Stocking
Sock
Partial sock

Hooves White or pale stripes may occur

Structure

THE SKELETON

The skeleton of a horse is made up of approximately 205 bones. It provides a frame for the muscles and tendons, as well as protecting the internal organs. The back and ribs have a fixed framework with minimal movement, but some of the joints, particularly those in the legs, have a great deal of flexion. All the joints are capped with cartilage, which nature preserves by regeneration and by releasing synovial fluid, a lubricant stored in joint capsules. The bones are given strength by connecting ligaments, which also allow or limit their movements.

Below: The equine foot is the equivalent of the human middle finger. It has four bones: the long pastern; the short pastern; the pedal bone; and the navicular bone. The pasterns meet at the pastern joint; the short pastern is separated from the pedal bone by the coffin joint. The lower surface of the foot is slightly concave. It has a sole, a frog – a V-shaped region between the sole and the heel – and bars to absorb concussion and to grip.

Right: The teeth provide a cutting and grinding system. The incisors at the front are used for cutting and the molars at the back for grinding. Foals have milk teeth, which are replaced by permanent teeth at between three and five years old. The molars have a wide, patterned surface of enamel for efficient grinding as the horse's jaws move from side to side when it chews. The grinding keeps the surface even, but the lower jaw is narrower than the upper, so wear may be uneven and cause sharp edges.

Below: The horse's skeleton consists of bones, joints, cartilage and ligaments. It has two portions: the axial skeleton – the skull, back bones, and ribs; and the appendicular skeleton – the limbs and limb girdles, such as the shoulder and pelvic girdle, which connect the limbs to the axial skeleton.

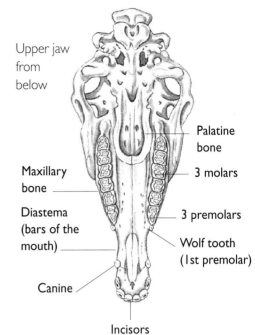

Upper jaw from below

Palatine bone
3 molars
Maxillary bone
3 premolars
Diastema (bars of the mouth)
Wolf tooth (1st premolar)
Canine
Incisors

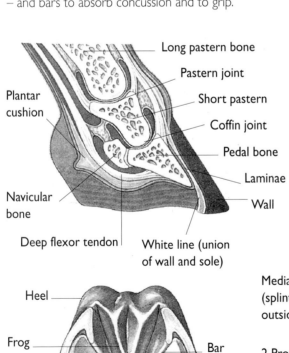

Long pastern bone
Pastern joint
Short pastern
Coffin joint
Pedal bone
Laminae
Wall
Plantar cushion
Navicular bone
Deep flexor tendon
White line (union of wall and sole)

Heel
Frog
Sole
White line
Bar
Wall
Toe

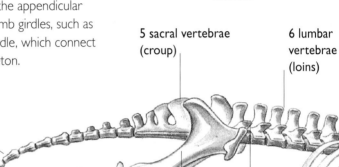

5 sacral vertebrae (croup)
6 lumbar vertebrae (loins)
Coccygeal vertebrae (usually 18 to 21)
Ilium
Point of hip
Ischium
Pubis
Hip joint
Femur
Patella
Fibula
18 pairs of ribs, forming the wall of the thorax
Tibia
Stifle joint
Point of hock
Tarsal (hock) bones
Medial metatarsal (splint-bone) on outside of limb
Lateral metatarsal (splint-bone) on inside of limb
Cannon bone (middle metatarsal)
Long pastern bone
2 Proximal sesamoid bones
Pastern joint
Fetlock joint
Short pastern bone

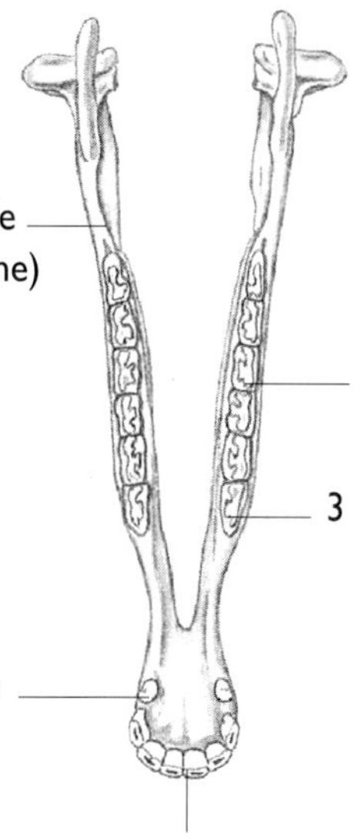

Lower jaw from above
Mandible (jaw bone)
3 molars
3 premolars
Canine
Incisors

ARAB RIBCAGE

The Arab horse (see p.184) and other types of Eastern descent differ from most other breeds in the structure of the ribs and vertebrae. Instead of the usual 18 ribs and 6 lumbar vertebrae, they have 17 ribs and 5 lumbar vertebrae.

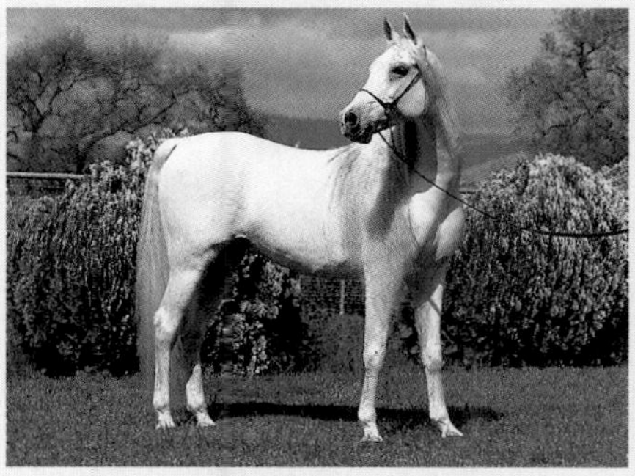

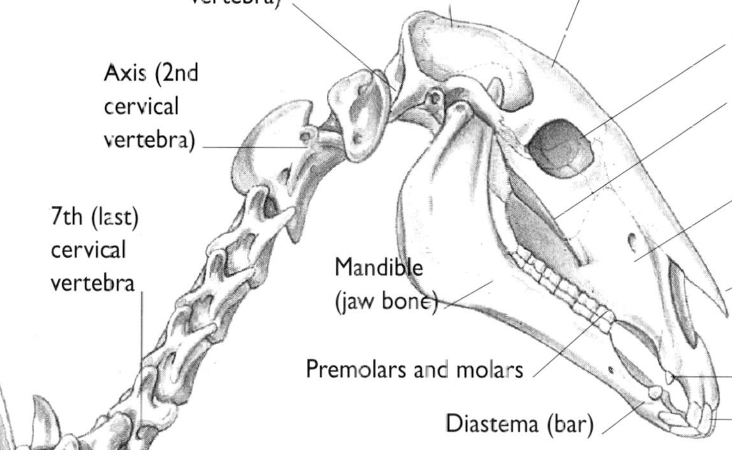

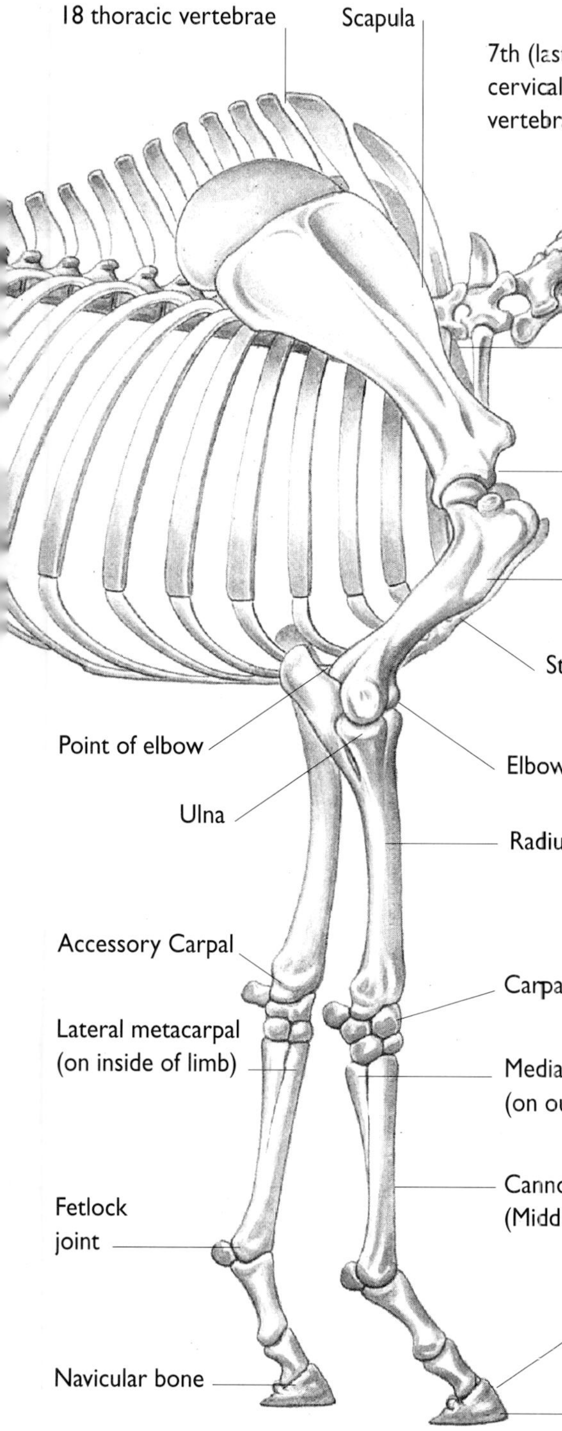

Atlas (1st cervical vertebra)
Poll
Cranium
Orbit (eye socket)
Facial crest
Maxillary bone
Nasal bone
Axis (2nd cervical vertebra)
Mandible (jaw bone)
Premolars and molars
Canine teeth
Diastema (bar)
Incisors
18 thoracic vertebrae
Scapula
7th (last) cervical vertebra
Scapular spine
Shoulder joint
Humerus
Sternum
Point of elbow
Elbow joint
Ulna
Radius (forearm)
Accessory Carpal
Carpal joint (knee joint)
Lateral metacarpal (on inside of limb)
Medial metacarpal (on outside of limb)
Cannon bone (Middle metacarpal)
Fetlock joint
Coffin joint
Navicular bone
Pedal bone

AGEING TEETH

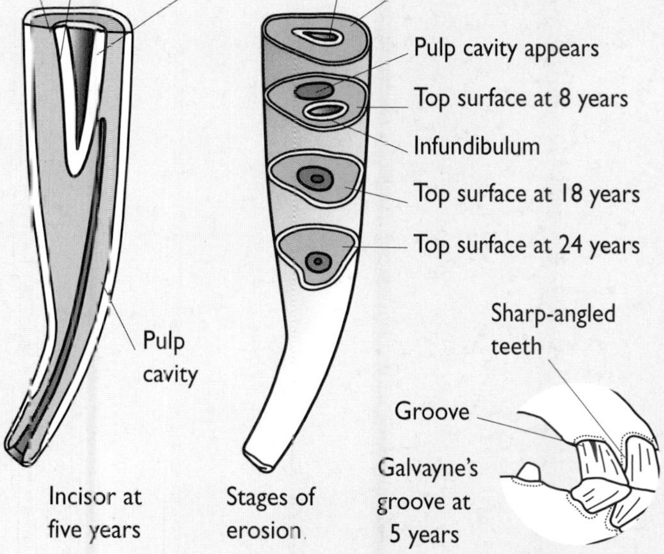

Cement and enamel
Dentine
Infundibulum
Top surface at 5 years
Pulp cavity appears
Top surface at 8 years
Infundibulum
Top surface at 18 years
Top surface at 24 years
Pulp cavity
Sharp-angled teeth
Groove
Galvayne's groove at 5 years
Incisor at five years
Stages of erosion

A horse's teeth can be used to estimate its age. Under five years, a horse will have some of its milk teeth. From six, the teeth become increasingly angled and the incisors gradually wear down to reveal a changing cross-section of the inner structure, which is a guide up to the age of about eight. At 10, a small notch (Galvayne's groove) appears at the top of the upper corner incisors. It grows, reaching the lower edge by 20. It then starts to disappear from the top.

Structure

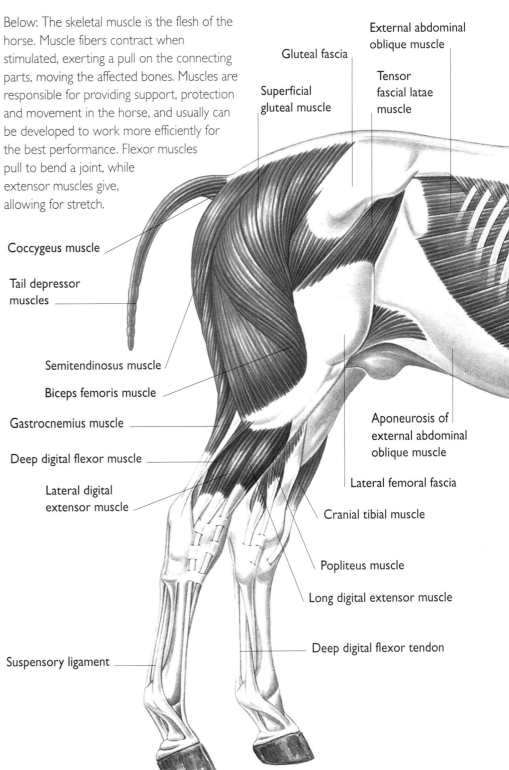

Above: In jumping a fence a horse uses a wide range of muscles. The deltoideus, latissimus dorsi, trapezius supraspinatus and brachiocephalicus are important for controling shoulder action during jumping. The biceps brachii, brachialis, and triceps, act in flexion and extension of the elbow joint. The gluteus medius, biceps femoris, and semitendiosis are involved in hip extension and stifle flexion, while the gastrocnemius controls hock extension. The digital flexor and extension muscles affect lower limb movement throughout the jump sequence.

MUSCLES

Muscles govern movement. Skeletal muscles are joined to bone at one end and to tendons at the other. By extending or contracting to varying degrees, they allow or inhibit actions at a wide range of speeds, and enable a horse to lie down, roll, and graze. Cardiac muscles pump the heart, and smooth muscles drive the digestive system. Muscles are connected to the nervous system. They can be bulky, especially when well developed, but are sometimes confused with fat, a separate substance. When a horse is unfit, sudden strenuous activity at speed or prolonged submaximal work is likely to cause lasting damage to skeletal muscles, tendons or ligaments.

TENDONS

A tendon sheath is a thin casing of fiber lubricated by synovia, or tendon oil, that encapsulates the tendon fibres in vulnerable areas, such as behind the knee and over the fetlock joint. This provides protection against friction with bones or cartilage.

Below: The skeletal muscle is the flesh of the horse. Muscle fibers contract when stimulated, exerting a pull on the connecting parts, moving the affected bones. Muscles are responsible for providing support, protection and movement in the horse, and usually can be developed to work more efficiently for the best performance. Flexor muscles pull to bend a joint, while extensor muscles give, allowing for stretch.

Coccygeus muscle

Tail depressor muscles

Semitendinosus muscle

Biceps femoris muscle

Gastrocnemius muscle

Deep digital flexor muscle

Lateral digital extensor muscle

Suspensory ligament

Gluteal fascia

Superficial gluteal muscle

External abdominal oblique muscle

Tensor fascial latae muscle

Aponeurosis of external abdominal oblique muscle

Lateral femoral fascia

Cranial tibial muscle

Popliteus muscle

Long digital extensor muscle

Deep digital flexor tendon

LIGAMENTS

Ligaments complete the structure that enables a horse to function in so many ways. Ligaments are fibrous bands connected to the bones, close to the joints, which maintain and strengthen structure and mobility. Important ligaments include the suspensory and check ligaments, the latter are accessory ligaments to the knee and hock joints and prevent the over-extension of the lower limbs. A strain of either of these ligaments can cause serious lameness.

LEG MOVEMENT

The horse's leg joints act like hinges, moving to and fro without rotation. Only the stifle joint has some lateral movement. The shoulder and the lower limbs work together almost like a pulley system, while the joints, tendons, and ligaments of the limbs are designed to conserve energy, whether at rest or moving. For example, a horse can sleep standing up, without any muscular effort because of the structure and mechanics of this "stay apparatus" system. As the spine is fairly rigid, it is the limbs, particularly the structures of the distal (lower) limb segments, that absorb most of the concussion caused by movement and ground reaction forces when the horse is traveling fast or jumping.

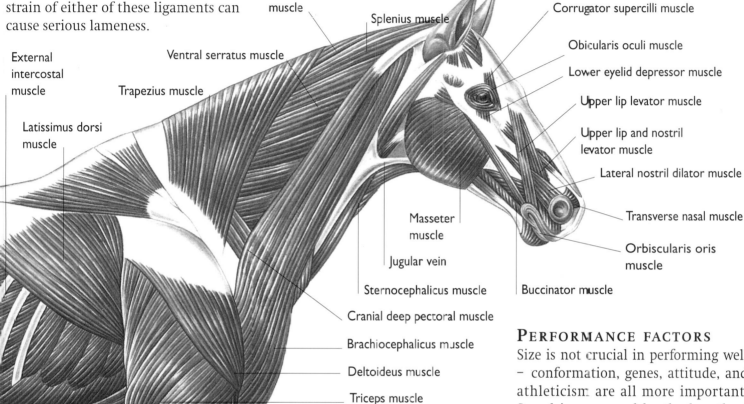

Cervical rhomboideus muscle

Auricular muscles

Splenius muscle

Corrugator supercilli muscle

Obicularis oculi muscle

Lower eyelid depressor muscle

Upper lip levator muscle

Upper lip and nostril levator muscle

Lateral nostril dilator muscle

Transverse nasal muscle

Orbiscularis oris muscle

Masseter muscle

Jugular vein

Sternocephalicus muscle

Buccinator muscle

Cranial deep pectoral muscle

Brachiocephalicus muscle

Deltoideus muscle

Triceps muscle

Cranial superficial pectoral muscle

Biceps brachii

Brachialis muscle

Radial carpal extensor muscle

Common digital extensor muscle

Lateral carpal flexor muscle

Lateral digital extensor muscle

Oblique carpal flexor muscle

Common digital extensor tendon

Lateral digital extensor tendon

Superficial digital flexor tendon

Suspensory ligament

Ventral serratus muscle

Trapezius muscle

External intercostal muscle

Latissimus dorsi muscle

External abdominal oblique muscle

Caudal deep pectoral muscle

Deep digital flexor muscle

Ulnar carpal flexor muscle

Radial carpal flexor muscle

PERFORMANCE FACTORS

Size is not crucial in performing well – conformation, genes, attitude, and athleticism are all more important. Speed is measured by the length of stride multiplied by the number of strides per minute. Larger, longer or heavier bones need stronger muscles to support and propel them, so the mechanism of a big horse can be more vulnerable and subject to strain than that of a small, strongly made horse. The hock is equivalent to the human heel, with the lower limbs and feet developed for greater propulsion and speed – equivalent in a human to the toes becoming a third of the leg structure over evolutionary time. Below the knee, the limbs are very light and easy to maneuver, since they carry no muscle and are made up solely of bone, ligament, and tendons; the upper limbs are well covered with muscle. To compensate for the greater impact on the legs and body as speed increases, a horse will change to a smoother, less jarring gait.

Body Systems

Breathing and circulation ✦ *Processing food* ✦ *Brain and nerves*

The body systems of a horse are those that enable it to function, allowing it to move, breathe, eat, grow, heal, and react to stimuli.

RESPIRATION AND CIRCULATION

Oxygen is vital for a horse's body system to work correctly. The amount of oxygen, and the speed with which it is delivered to the working areas, depend largely on the rate and strength of the heart beat. Respiration and circulation are, therefore, interdependent.

The "normal" respiration of a horse at rest is 6 to 12 breaths per minute and the average heart rate 32 to 40 beats per minute. This doubles at a walk, and triples at an energetic trot. A fit horse might record 100 beats per minute on completing an endurance ride, but a racehorse at full stretch could register 250. Old horses have a much higher heart rate at exercise than young but mature horses, while young ones may also have high readings, although this can be due to excitement, anxiety or stress.

The body temperature of a horse is normally 38°C (100.5°F). This can rise to 40.6°C (105°F) in hot, stressful conditions, but would be unacceptably high in any other situation.

The horse's breathing apparatus is a series of tubes to the lungs. Air is drawn in through the nostrils, via the pharynx in the head and the mobile larynx in the throat, and down the windpipe (trachea), which divides into two bronchi. These supply the bronchioles, alveoli and, ultimately, blood vessels of the lungs.

A horse's heart, a muscular organ that pumps blood through the body by expanding then contracting, has four chambers. Blood is oxygenated in the lungs and supplied to the rest of the body by arteries. The main artery, the aorta, carries blood full of nutrients and oxygen from the heart to the body and large intestine. Blood returns to the lungs via the heart, through intricate veins, disposing of waste as it goes. It then emits carbon dioxide, to be exhaled, collecting oxygen in its place. The jugular vein carries blood from the head and neck back to the heart.

The circulatory system also assists in controlling body temperature, adapting to very cold or hot conditions.

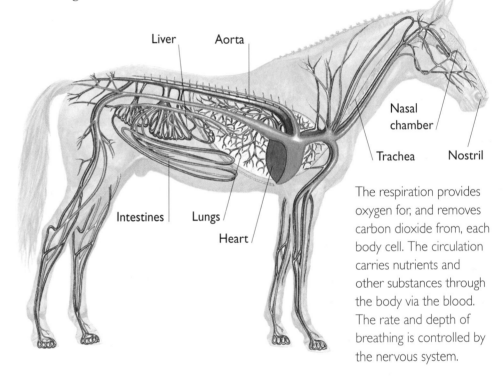

Liver Aorta

Nasal chamber

Trachea Nostril

Intestines Lungs

Heart

The respiration provides oxygen for, and removes carbon dioxide from, each body cell. The circulation carries nutrients and other substances through the body via the blood. The rate and depth of breathing is controlled by the nervous system.

Below: The heart pumps deoxygenated blood (blue) from its right ventricle to the lungs, where it becomes oxygenated (red). It then returns to the left heart ventricle and is pumped through the arteries to the rest of the body, passing into the capillaries, where the body cells take up the oxygen and release carbon dioxide and other waste. The blood, now deoxygenated, returns through the veins to the heart, and the cycle continues.

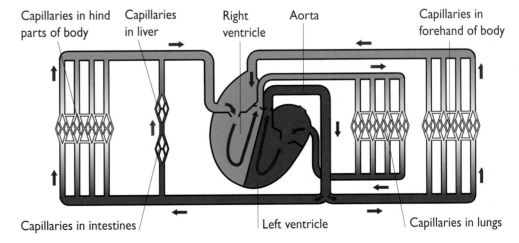

Capillaries in hind parts of body   Capillaries in liver   Right ventricle   Aorta   Capillaries in forehand of body

Capillaries in intestines   Left ventricle   Capillaries in lungs

The lymphatic system, a network of vessels carrying lymph, a clear fluid, protects the circulatory system and connective tissues by flushing out impurities. Lymph nodes help to destroy harmful bacteria. The flow of lymph is stimulated by circulatory and muscular activities.

DIGESTION

Horses are natural browsers, eating a little most of the day and night. This relates to the structure of the digestive tract. Horses ferment food in their hind gut and should only hold a little food in the stomach at any time. It is important to understand this when feeding in an artificial environment.

Horses have an alimentary tract – a tube that passes from the mouth to the anus. Food is bitten off by the front teeth, sent to the back teeth by the tongue and chewed and ground up. Salivary glands secrete digestive juices, and the food enters the esophagus; then passes to the stomach, small intestine, caecum, large colon, and small colon, to the rectum. The liver and pancreas supply bile and juices that break down food into energy or fat for storage or warmth.

The horse has no gall bladder. The digestive organs, the caecum and colon are located in the hind gut. It is here that the final breakdown of food by bacterial fermentation occurs. A weakness is that intestinal obstructions are not unusual, sometimes causing colic (see pages 90–2).

NERVOUS SYSTEM

The brain, protected by the skull, is the center of the nervous system. It is connected to the spinal cord, from which pairs of nerves branch out.

The sensory nerves have endings that are sensitive to pain, pressure, heat or cold, as well as to pleasant sensations. These are interpreted by the brain in reflex or voluntary actions. Nervous tissue damaged by pressure may cease to relay messages, while an impaired nerve supply may cause muscles to waste, or atrophy. The nerve endings in the nose, eyes, and ears, conduct sensations of smell, sight, and hearing to the brain.

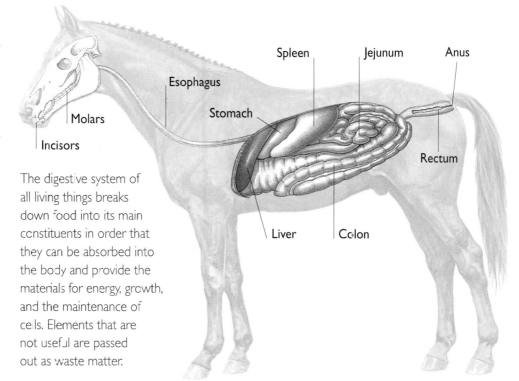

The digestive system of all living things breaks down food into its main constituents in order that they can be absorbed into the body and provide the materials for energy, growth, and the maintenance of cells. Elements that are not useful are passed out as waste matter.

Below: Food enters the stomach through the esophagus, is broken down by gastric juices and passes into the small intestine (duodenum, jejunum and ilium) the caecum and the colon, where it continues to be broken down by bacterial fermentation. The products of digestion are absorbed into the blood mainly from the small intestine and caecum, although fluids are chiefly absorbed from the colon. Waste products pass out as feces.

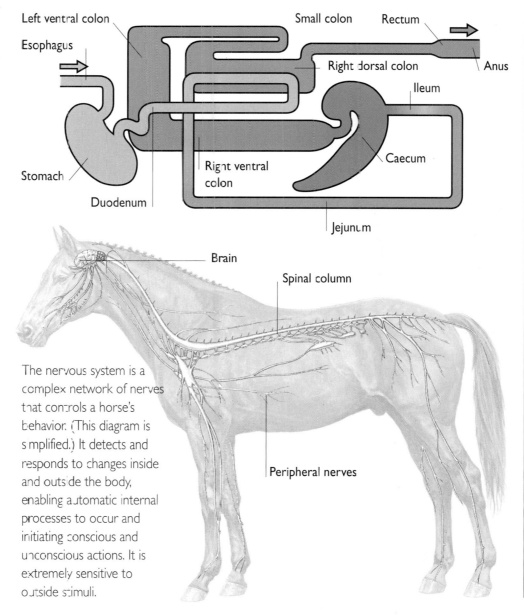

The nervous system is a complex network of nerves that controls a horse's behavior. (This diagram is simplified.) It detects and responds to changes inside and outside the body, enabling automatic internal processes to occur and initiating conscious and unconscious actions. It is extremely sensitive to outside stimuli.

Horse Senses

The five senses ✦ *Expression of emotion* ✦ *Sensitivity to atmosphere*

The horse has highly developed senses, coordinated with its basic instincts. Its sense of taste is similar to that of other animals, but its sight and hearing are unique.

EYES AND SIGHT

The eyes of a horse are set wide apart at the sides of its head. This means that when the head is raised, the horse has almost complete all-round vision without turning its head, an advantage developed in order to give protection from predators in the wild. This is why you must always approach a horse within its range of vision in order to avoid scaring it (see page 57).

A horse's eyes, which are generally kind and trusting, can also express a range of reactions, from curiosity, suspicion, fear, and aggression, to courage, pleasure, and contentment. They also reveal signs of health or, as when dull and listless, illness.

EARS AND HEARING

Horses have acute hearing, with a far wider range than human beings. Their ears are constantly mobile, twitching to pick up sounds, and turning forwards, sideways, and backward, like antennae.

The ears express diverse reactions, among them, interest, enthusiam, boredom, reluctance, irritation, weariness or aggression.

Highly responsive to sound, horses soon learn to associate the various tones of the human voice with praise or scolding, warning or commands. This is a useful aid when a horse is undergoing training.

Above: Touch is a common form of communication. Grooming occurs between two friendly animals, which begins by sniffing. It is often initiated by the weaker of the two.

Below: The horse can see through 340 degrees, but because the eyes are set deep on each side of its head, it does not see everything in depth (have binocular vision).

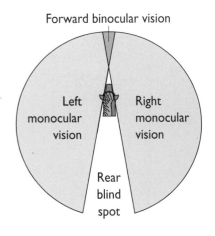

Forward binocular vision

Left monocular vision

Right monocular vision

Rear blind spot

SMELL

The horse has a strong sense of smell with well-developed nostrils designed to take in air at great speed, or when under stress. Horses are able to detect fear in humans via sweat, and are sensitive to the smell of blood. They show their suspicion or dislike of new smells by sniffing or snorting and backing off, and they may refuse to eat food that smells strange to them. Many horses dislike the smell of pigs.

TASTE

Horses are selective feeders, and would starve rather than eat unpalatable vegetation. A field that appears to be evenly covered by healthy grass can be left ragged and patchy by a group of horses, which simply pick out the grasses they like, leaving coarse, rancid or fouled areas. Highly bred Thoroughbreds tend to be more sensitive to unfamiliar tastes than other breeds with stout constitutions. Horses that are difficult to catch can often be lured by tasty "tidbits" such as carrots, mints or sugar lumps.

Below: There are 16 muscles in the external ears of a horse, which can be rotated through 130 degrees. Pricked ears, as here, are typical of horses that are interested, startled or alert to danger. The ears of a tired horse will flop out sideways, with the openings facing down.

TOUCH

As horses are physically very sensitive, especially to pain, they respond well to patting and stroking. A whip is sometimes used as encouragement or correction when riding and as a training aid when lunging (see pages 76–7), to keep the horse moving forwards, or to stop it coming inward. Some horses react more strongly than others to the whip, especially those with fine skin. Horses seem to be reassured if they can touch a strange object with their muzzle.

ATMOSPHERE

Horses pick up and respond to human emotion and can be easily influenced by atmosphere. A nervous or frightened rider, for example, will make a horse hesitant, while a bold, confident one will often inspire boldness in a usually timid animal.

Horses are also affected by new surroundings or by new people. They often show their unease by refusing their feed, sweating, pacing the stall, neighing, and generally being tense. A happy horse, which trusts its owner, will willingly submit to the demands made upon it.

Above: A young foal needs frequent contact with its mother for reassurance and to feel secure. By three to four months it may be mutually grooming with another foal. Here the foal is showing curiosity in its mother's headcollar, nibbling at it playfully.

Below: This horse knows that a tasty morsel may be forthcoming, and its senses of smell, sight, and taste are aroused. It is not afraid to touch in its eagerness to receive the expected treat. Smell is also an important form of identification between mares and foals.

Gaits

Walk ✦ Trot ✦ Canter Gallop ✦ Rein back

There are four basic paces, the walk, trot, canter, and the gallop. Some types or breeds excel in a particular pace. The American Standardbred and French and Russian Trotters (see pages 191, 167, and 180) for example, trot at speed and race in this gait; the Thoroughbred (see page 160) is bred to race and trained to gallop to its maximum ability. Showjumpers are trained mainly at the canter, from which pace they are asked to jump the biggest fences.

Highly schooled horses with powerful paces show variations of each gait. The walk can be of medium length of stride, collected or extended. The trot ranges from the working trot, to collected, medium or extended. The working trot is the basic gait on which the others are based for greater collection or extension. The canter, too, is working, collected, medium, and extended. There is no real variation at the gallop.

REINING BACK

When reining, or stepping, back, the legs, unlike in the walk, are moved in pairs with the left hind and left fore moving together, followed by the right hind and the right fore together.

The gallop
The gallop is a four-time pace. It is an extension of the canter, but with four separate footfalls, which increases the fluency and smoothness of the gait. With the right foreleg leading, the sequence of footfalls is as follows: left hind, right hind, left fore, right fore, followed by a moment of suspension. As with the canter, the horse gallops with a "leading" leg, to left or right, which allows it to turn at this speed yet keep its balance. When changing direction, it will change the lead naturally.

The walk
The walk is a four-time marching pace and the footfalls are well marked in a definite and regular sequence. If the walk begins with the left hind leg, the sequence in which the horse places its feet is as follows: left hind, left fore; right hind, right fore; left hind and so forth. A horse can walk all day and expend very little energy. It is the easiest pace for a beginner rider, while learning how to turn, stop, and start again. It should be comfortable, regular, but active.

The trot
The trot is a two-time pace in which the horse moves on alternate diagonals, left hind and right fore together, followed by a moment of suspension before the right hind and left fore make ground contact. The trot is hardest for a rider to learn because the horse bounces from one diagonal to the other, but it is the most used pace, since the horse trots over long distances. The rider should change from one diagonal to the other at regular intervals to put equal weight on both pairs of legs.

The canter
The canter is a three-time pace: left hind, right hind and left fore leg together, followed by the right fore and a moment of suspension when all four legs are in the air before the sequence is repeated. On the inside of a bend, or circle, the fore and hind legs will "lead" the outer pair. A well-balanced horse can change leads at the canter, called a "flying change," while those less well trained must go into a trot before picking up the opposite leading leg.

The left hind is down, the left fore is coming down. The right hind is up, the fore is down.

The left hind/right fore pair are on the ground. The left fore/right hind pair are coming forward.

The left hind is down, the other three feet are in the air, coming down.

The left hind is down, the three other limbs are raised. The right hind will come down next.

The right hind is down, the left hind is still down, the fore limbs are coming down.

The left fore is down and the right fore is coming up. The right hind is coming down.

The right hind is down. The left hind is about to rise, the right fore is descending.

The right fore is down, the left has risen, the left hind is about to come down.

All four limbs are suspended in the air before the left fore/right hind pair hit the ground.

The left fore/right hind pair are down. The right fore/left hind pair will move forward.

All four limbs are suspended in the air before the right fore/left hind hit the ground.

The left fore/right hind pair has come down. The right fore is still descending.

The right fore has come down and the three other limbs have been raised.

The right fore has come up. All four limbs are suspended before the left hind comes down.

The left fore is down, the left hind has been raised, the right fore is coming down.

The right fore is down, the left fore has been lifted and the hind limbs are fully raised.

The right fore is raised so that all four limbs are suspended before the left hind lands again.

Horse Behavior

Sociability ✦ Group dynamics ✦ Natural instincts ✦ Interpreting signs and building trust

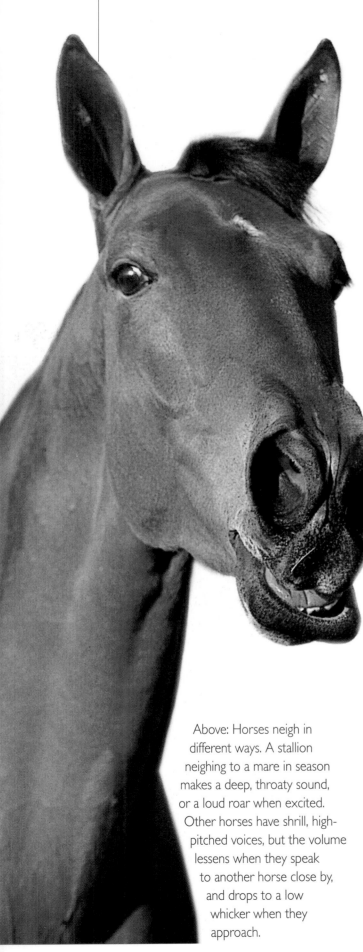

Above: Horses neigh in different ways. A stallion neighing to a mare in season makes a deep, throaty sound, or a loud roar when excited. Other horses have shrill, high-pitched voices, but the volume lessens when they speak to another horse close by, and drops to a low whicker when they approach.

Horses are sociable animals. In their wild state, they live in herds or small groups, known as harems, and the domesticated horse often displays the same inherent behavior. With few exceptions, horses love the company of others, and are unhappy when isolated in a field or stable with no others in sight.

ONE-ON-ONE COMMUNICATION

The voice is an important way for horses to communicate with each other, neighing loudly, and often repeatedly or even frantically, to attract a response, especially when recently separated from paired companions, members of a bonded family, or when they feel insecure or lonely.

The horse will neigh or give a quieter nicker when greeting a friend, or calling to its foal.

Two horses meeting for the first time approach each other warily, before touching noses, which often provokes high-pitched squeals, particularly from females, or lower sounds and a shake of the head. Aggression is rare in the domestic horse, but two colts or stallions kept together may fight, and a mare defending her foal may see an outsider as a threat and attack, producing a roar or screaming noise.

Friends recognize each other by sight and smell. Smell is an important factor in herd life, especially when a mare's scent sends sexual messages to a stallion.

Touch is also important. Horses often greet familiar animals by touching noses, and companions will rub, lick, or nuzzle one another. Young colts may nip and grab each other in play. When two horses stand head to withers, and scratch or nibble each other, it is known as mutual grooming.

HIERARCHY

Just as a hierarchy develops naturally in a herd (see pages 38–9), domestic horses in a field tend to establish a "pecking order." The leader will assert itself with intimidating behavior, such as chasing, biting, kicking or simply making threatening gestures, such as laying back its ears or baring its teeth. A dominant horse may drive away a newcomer, try to separate two friends, or even turn against an old companion in favor of a new one. A

Below: Two males playing – a natural pastime. They rarely damage each other, although horses turned out together should have their hind shoes removed in case they kick out at each other.

timid horse may be a victim of bullying. It can be cornered, kicked, bitten or chased, especially if the animals are being fed together, and it will starve to death rather than approach food that is guarded by a threatening horse. A horse that stands aloof, clearly showing a desire to be left alone, will be respected.

NATURAL INSTINCTS

The natural behavior of a horse must be adapted or subdued to suit a domestic environment and the demands made upon it. This is achieved by establishing security and trust, based on an understanding of the horse's natural pattern of eating, energy, and behavior, all of which are crucially important to its physical and mental well-being.

Flight

Despite domestication, the horse remains a flight animal. It will react to fear by kicking out, or by running away. Loud bangs, strange sights and sounds, a half-dislodged rider or a slipped saddle may cause sudden flight, as may flapping sheets. Shying, spinning round, or rearing are all natural reflex actions. Scared horses may also quiver and shake, show the whites of their eyes or sweat.

Rolling and pawing

Horses roll either for pleasure, to scratch an itch, or to remove sweat or shedding hair. They enjoy rolling in mud, sand, dust, and snow. An energetic roll is generally a healthy sign.

Pawing the ground may be an act of impatience or irritation, when the horse is restrained against its will, for example, or waiting to be fed. Horses also scrape at the ground to dig up minerals, or to scuff up the earth where they want to roll.

A impatient horse may also pace up and down the fence, perhaps galloping and neighing, or bang against the gate. If stabled, it may pace the stall and rush the door.

Kicking

A horse kicks in self-defense, when threatened or startled from behind. Fighting horses will use their heels, and, when loose, an aggressive horse might back into another to kick it. Some horses may kick when groomed in sensitive areas, girthed up too tightly, or when touched unexpectedly.

Biting

Biting is natural among wild horses, when asserting superiority or showing aggression, but it is considered a vice in domestic horses. It is sometimes a reaction to ill-treatment from humans, or to other kinds of physical discomfort or pain. Too many tidbits, given at random, can also cause biting. Sheer exuberance may also be the

Above right: Horses often pair up in a field to groom each other, which they seem to enjoy. This takes the form of rubbing or scratching the other's withers or croup, as here, using the teeth, but not biting.

Right: The gray horse has made advances to the mare on the left, but she has responded with aggression, baring her teeth as a warning. The gray is wary and will keep his distance for a time, but will only be put off temporarily.

Horse behavior

cause, but biting needs correction before it becomes a bad habit. A happy horse is unlikely to bite.

High spirits

Horses are more easily excited in herds. High spirits are infectious, and lead to galloping, bucking, and kicking, rearing up, and playing. When excited, the horse's head and neck are held erect, the ears are sharply pricked and mobile, and the nostrils flare, while the whole body may quiver, appearing to grow taller. The horse might toss its head, snort, and paw or stamp the ground. It might gallop wildly, tail carried high, and become lathered with sweat.

BAD HABITS

Shying, napping, bucking, rearing and bolting are bad habits, or vices, which could develop in the ridden horse. A horse is said to "shy" when it jumps sideways, or swings away from a real or imagined sight. If it then refuses to pass the obstacle, by standing still, running backward, or even rearing, it is said to be "napping." A horse may "buck" from high spirits or when it is over-fresh. It puts its head down low, arching its back, and leaping into the air, coming down with stiff forelegs. It may repeat this several times, until the rider is dislodged. This can develop into an unpleasant

Above: This horse, rearing from pure high spirits, demonstrates the natural movements and abilities upon which high-school, or *haute école,* movements are based.

vice if it is not cured, or the cause for it removed. Rearing is a nervous reaction to fear or excitement, or a refusal to move in the direction asked. Young horses may stand up on their hind legs when startled, when playing with others, or in acts of aggression. However, it can be dangerous if the horse rears very high when ridden, losing its balance and possibly falling on the

rider. A horse is said to "bolt" when it runs away, with no response to the aids, ignoring the bit and reins. It is a frightening experience for a rider, since the horse becomes oblivious to any danger ahead as it flees, perhaps across roads and through fences or hedges.

HUMAN RELATIONS

An understanding between horse and man has existed since long before history was recorded. It is evident in carvings, cave drawings, and ancient burial grounds, where horses were buried in state with their masters. Throughout the centuries, the versatility and servile nature of the horse have been adapted to use for survival, war, transportation, work, and pleasure. Its physical and mental character have not altered, however.

Horses are highly sensitive. An unhappy horse may indicate its mood by unusually slow movements and reactions, loss of interest and appetite, dull eyes, still ears, and by hanging its head.

An owner must learn to interpret the signs and gauge the horse's mood so as to respond appropriately. The voice, for example, is an important training aid because the horse is sensitive to sound. Loud, aggressive voices, therefore, provoke alarm and often a defensive reaction, whereas a soothing but confident tone will be well received. Horses that respect their trainers will respond to a corrective growl, an encouraging click of

Below: "High tailing" in a field, this horse is excited and demonstrating naturally the elevated paces of the highly schooled dressage horse.

Below: If this horse were bucking with a rider on its back, it would be difficult to remain seated. However, bucking is a sign of well-being when a horse is turned loose.

Below: A stallion flares his nostrils, flattens back his ears and shows aggressive body language that makes clear his irritability with another horse.

the tongue or to praising tones. They learn to respond to vocal commands, such as "halt," "trot on,"and "steady."

Ears, too, are indicative of mood. Laid-back ears could mean, "Leave me alone," "I'm bored/irritated/tired," or "This is uncomfortable." Ears forward might be a friendly greeting or curiosity, "That have you got? That smells/tastes/looks/sounds interesting."

A horse's eyes also express many things, including boldness, timidity, interest, lethargy, anger, wariness, submission, and confidence. Dull or lackluster eyes may also indicate poor health, low spirits or tiredness. To form a relationship of mutual respect and confidence, an owner must try to interpret all these signs.

Below: A horse rolls in the snow for sheer pleasure and exuberance. It is usually very obvious if a horse is rolling for fun or if it is doing so as a result of pain (see pp.90–2).

The strongest training aid for horses is touch. However, as touch includes pain and a horse's instinctive reaction to aggression or pain is to run away, the accepted method of reward and punishment must be used with skilful tact and care, in order to build up the horse's trust and confidence so that it submits willingly. The best horsemen have learned to communicate their wishes within the boundaries of the horse's sensibilities. When a horse performs a sequence of "flying changes," or the *passage*, with little visible movement from the rider, it is a fine example of human/equine communication. At the other extreme, an insensitive or ignorant interpretation of a horse's nature can result in a physical battle. When scared, the horse may panic, kicking and thrashing, or bucking or rearing, in its attempts to escape, injuring itself or the rider. If the trust between horse and rider is once destroyed, it may take all the skill of an experienced rider, and a very long time, to rebuild it.

Herd Behavior

Natural habits ✦ *Herd mentality* ✦ *Concessions to domestic life*

Horses and ponies in the wild live in groups or herds, which can vary in size, depending on the vegetation and habitat available. Being a browser, the horse is constantly on the move in search of food and water for its survival. It has an in-built defense mechanism and finely developed senses (see pages 30–1 and 34–7), which enable it to react and move fast, away from danger. Such alertness makes the horse a quick, highly strung animal that can be nervous and excitable. "Cold-blooded," heavy horses are a slower-moving type, less prone to flight, than the typically more fiery "hot-blooded" horses, such as the Arab and Spanish horses (see pages 184 and 170-1).

HERD INSTINCT

The herd instinct in horses is deep-rooted. They feel secure in large groups, and happily follow each other. This is reflected in domestic life, when horses that work together in a monotonous routine (as in army service, at riding schools or in racing stables) feel insecure if separated from their home, and may show strong reluctance to leave the stable yard alone. Even horses reared in isolation, which have never lived in a herd, revert to basic instincts and become excited, at shows for example, when exposed to active groups of horses. Horses enjoy racing with others, indulging their natural instinct of flight – a characteristic long exploited

by sport-loving humanity. Animals will also jump more difficult obstacles than they would when not carried along by the excitement of being in a group, as on cross-country rides. This instinct can be exploited in training horses to jump or gallop by using an experienced horse to provide a "lead,"or incentive. Going towards "home" is another incentive. For most horses today, the security of the herd has been replaced by the stable, source of food, safety and possibly the

Below: This stallion is acting as "caretaker", herding his group and keeping alert to danger. Wild-living groups usually range from two to twenty-one horses. A typical group is a stallion, his mares and their foals.

Above: Horses follow natural instincts when racing, although they are trained to jump safely at speed. If one loses its rider, it will normally stay with the racing field.

Right: Foals stay close to their mothers, which are always watchful for possible threats and danger. Foals start to be more independent at about eight weeks old.

company of other horses. This strong influence is an important factor in understanding a horse's behavior.

PECKING ORDER

In the herd, a hierarchy is established. Those with the strongest urges to survive, eat and reproduce tend to take precedence over the rest. This may not be a male. Often a strong-minded mare leads the order, putting any challenger in its place. This order continues to the last herd member, and is accepted. The horse is not naturally a fighter, except over food and mates. As in the wild, when there is a constant supply of food, horses prefer to eat little and often. In a field, they graze on and off, resting for much of the time. But when food is controled as when horses are fed in a field, character plays a strong role. Unless the food is widely spread and feeding time well supervised, the most timid characters may end up with nothing.

NATURAL GROUPS

In the wild, families tend to stay together. A mare will reject the colt foals as they mature, but may keep a filly foal with her for several years.

Right: These yearling Anglo-Arabs at the Pompadour State Stud, France, are play fighting – a common occurence in young animals learning the skills that they may need in later life.

In a herd, ungelded male horses usually start fighting over mares from the age of two. An older, dominant male, may drive them away. Mares rarely fight, and as they are sexually available for only limited periods, herd life is mostly a peaceful one. When they have foals afoot, mares are naturally protective, whickering to bring them back if they stray too close to another horse, and threatening others with ears and teeth to protect foals. They are usually very attentive mothers.

As a group, horses are more alert and nervous, reacting quickly to new situations. If one horse is frightened by lightning, for example, it can cause a chain reaction, the whole group galloping in blind panic. Fleeing is their natural response to danger.

INDIVIDUAL TEMPERAMENTS

Each horse has a different character and temperament. In a herd, they can range from placid to neurotic, cowardly to brave, contented to irritable, or from sensible to foolhardy, with many other variations. Private breeders have the opportunity to select and combine the best temperamental and physical characteristics in a single horse – a constant challenge.

DOMESTIC LIFE

Domestic life requires certain concessions. A stabled horse's hooves grow and need regular checks. Grazing the same land increases worm reinfestation and regular worming is vital. Constant feeding is also difficult to maintain for stabled horses, although a haynet may help (see page 96).

Life Cycle of the Horse

Life expectancy ✦ Aging a horse ✦ Birth to death development

Above: On day two, as soon as George can coordinate his movements well enough, he and his mother have been turned out.

Below: At one month old, George is much stronger but still dependent for security on his mother, who does not let him stray far.

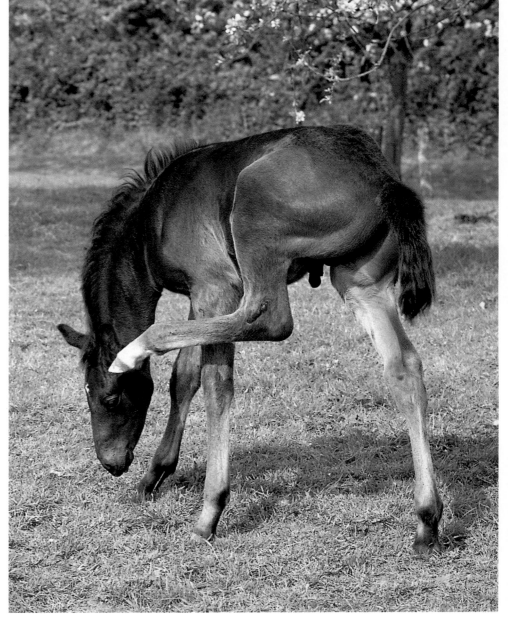

Above: At two months, George is starting to eat grass more, think for himself, and play with other horses rather than just his mother.

Most horse breeds have a life expectancy of at least 20 years. Ponies tend to live longer, but for all types, much will depend on soundness, good health, and their way of life.

In the northern hemisphere, most breeds are aged from January 1, regardless of their actual date of birth. Hence, a two-year-old Thoroughbred (see page 160) born in January that races in March has a huge advantage over its immature rival born in June, which is officially the same age. Horses in the southern hemisphere are aged from July 1.

A natural existence at grass, adjusting to the seasons and different ground conditions, is ideal preparation for a horse's healthy, useful life ahead. It should be handled, perhaps groomed, and have its feet trimmed regularly, as well as being vaccinated and wormed (see pages 99 and 95). It may need extra food in winter or when grazing is poor or scarce, but should never be overfed or encouraged to grow unnaturally quickly, so putting strain on the joints and

Above: At seven months, George has been weaned from his mother. He is a healthy individual, alert, active and well grown.

Above: George is now a boisterous yearling, but has been gelded. He is well-fed and developing into a promising young horse.

Above: At four years old, George is virtually mature. He is ready to be trained as a riding horse, and is growing with good condition.

inviting future problems. Foals need plenty of exercise and will benefit from being with other youngsters.

PHASES OF LIFE

A horse is described as a foal during its first year. A female is called a filly until the age of four, and is then a mare. Males are colts until their fourth birthday, and then become horses or stallions. Once their testicles have appeared, colts may be castrated at any time, and are then described as geldings.

Year 1: The foal has a downy "milk" coat, and the mane and tail are fluffy and soft. The legs are long in relation to the body frame. Foals are usually weaned from their mothers at between six and eight months old.

Year 2: The "milk" coat will have disappeared. Fillies come into "season" for the first time. This then occurs every 18–21 days, from early spring to autumn, the season lasting 5–7 days. The filly can be mated during this time, but the two-year-old is generally too immature in growth and development, and should be left for at least another year. In the wild, nature makes such decisions. Some mares can continue breeding into their 20s.

Years 2–3: Many young horses are broken in, backed, and even ridden, at two years. The less mature start to be trained on the lunge (see page 76) and ridden at three or four years, and go on to their job in life after that. Immature horses, forced to work too soon, may suffer bone and muscle damage, which causes unnecessary pain and will shorten their lives, and their usefulness. Well-reared, healthy horses

that develop naturally, often work well into their 20s, whereas many racehorses, broken in as yearlings and raced at two years, finish their active lives the very same year, through unsoundness. Horses can learn to jump at three years, but rarely compete before the age of four. They often continue to work until they are 20.

Years 3–4: Young horses grow steadily until they reach full height, at about four years old, although undergrown or underfed individuals can continue to grow until they are five or six. The mane and tail grow heavier and coarser, and muscles develop to give the animal strength over the neck, back and loins, while the chest broadens and the body deepens at the girth. Meanwhile, the bones are hardening and maturing. Some breeds, such as heavy ones, mature faster than others.

Feeding, habitat and lifestyle are also factors that affect the rate of their development. Age is best recorded by the teeth, which alter continually until the horse is eight years old (see page 25), and provide a fairly accurate guide thereafter, as well.

Years 6+: Most horses mature at around 6 years old, and have a useful working life until about 16 when some stiffness and wear may start to slow them down physically. When a horse is no longer enjoying life, or is losing condition and not thriving, it is often time to have it humanely destroyed with the dignity that this animal deserves.

Below: Older horses spend more time resting and conserving energy, although all horses need the opportunity to relax for periods during the day.

Part 2

Caring for Horses

Since prehistoric times, when horses were first domesticated and deprived of their freedom, their wild instincts have been subdued and they have become dependent on their masters for their physical and mental welfare. Even horses that still enjoy life in a herd are subject to breeding controls, and many depend on humans for their feed and water supply. The domesticated horse relies on humans to maintain good standards of health care. Apart from the essentials of water, food, and exercise, keeping a horse in a happy, healthy condition requires knowledge, understanding, time, commitment, and the means to provide and maintain a suitable environment. Horses thrive on a regular routine. They must learn to trust their handlers and respect them. This respect must be mutual and be carefully maintained.

Choosing Your Horse

Things to consider ✦ *What questions to ask* ✦ *Measuring* ✦ *Trying a horse*
✦ *A well-made horse* ✦ *Things to avoid*

Owning a horse is a major commitment in terms of time and money: a poor horse takes as much time and costs as much to keep as better one. Before committing yourself, you should consider whether it is cheaper and more practical to pay to ride a horse that belongs to a riding school or private establishment.

THINGS TO CONSIDER

When deciding whether to buy, hire or borrow, you need to consider your requirements and ask yourself the following questions:
✦ How experienced are you?
✦ What type of horse do you need?
✦ How often will you ride?
✦ What do you want the horse to do?
✦ Must it be fit for competitive work, light activities or long-distance rides?
✦ Do you have somewhere suitable to keep the horse? Will it be stabled, live in a field, or a combination of both? Horses that live "out" must be hardy.
✦ Will it live alone, or in company? Most horses do not thrive when lonely.
✦ How much will it cost to buy, keep and transport? Can you afford farrier and veterinary expenses and any necessary equipment?
✦ Do you have time every day to feed, exercise, groom, and muck out a stall? If you do not do it, who will?

✦ Who will look after the horse if it is sick, lame, or confined to its stall?

A BUYER'S QUESTIONS

If you decide to buy, ask the following questions before going to try a horse.
The price: If in doubt, consult a knowledgeable third party. You should always try out a horse before agreeing a price and having it examined by a vet.
Type: A riding horse or pony can be categorized, from the up-to-weight heavy pulling or cob type, likely to be slow but steady and reliable, to the strong but active warmblood and the lightweight, highly bred Arab or Thoroughbred type. These variations occur at every size.
Sex: Mares can be more difficult than geldings, but they may also be used for breeding. A colt or young stallion needs expert handling and is not suitable for the average owner.
Height: A horse that is too tall for its rider is harder to manage. A horse that is too small is less likely to perform well and remain sound if "overloaded." Build and conformation are more important than height for carrying weight. A small horse with good bone and correct conformation is likely to be stronger than a taller horse that is less well made.

Above left: A Cob is strongly built, with stout limbs, and will carry the average adult despite its lack of height. Center: A small pony may look the right size for a particular child, but needs careful assessment as to its reliability and suitability. Right: The temperament, experience, and ability of a lightweight horse for the task required also need assessing.

Below: This rider, his legs hanging below the belly, is much too tall for this pony. This makes it difficult for the rider to remain in balance.

Weight: Horses may be categorized as lightweight, middleweight, or heavyweight, according to their size, build, and the amount of bone measured around the foreleg, just below the knee. Weight should not be confused with condition, since fat does not necessarily mean strong.

Age: First-horse buyers usually need a riding horse with experience and should avoid a 4- or 5-year-old unless it has been very well trained and has an excellent temperament. An old horse, over the age of 12, may well have many more useful years, but will need a thorough veterinary inspection.

Experience: A brief history, the horse's current standard in training and jumping, and any special achievements, will indicate a horse's ability. Also ask about previous owners.

Breeding: The breeding is important when buying a mare that might be used to breed later. Competition riders look for the most successful bloodlines within selected breeds, and for horses that have been bred to excel in a particular sphere. Some crossbreeds, such as the larger native ponies crossed with Thoroughbreds

or Anglo-Arabs, are very popular. Different breeds are favored for different sports.

Temperament: A horse described as "lively" may be nervous and excitable; a "quiet" one may be lazy or sluggish. Ask about the type of bit that is used. A simple snaffle (see page 68) suggests an uncomplicated horse, but a severe bit may mean that it is a badly schooled or strong ride.

Vices: Do not go to see a horse that is reported to rear or bolt. Occasional bucking, from high spirits, or shying, are more acceptable "vices." Avoid horses that weave, crib-bite, windsuck, or pace the stall (see pages 48–9 and 110–11). Kicking or biting are also undesirable habits.

Soundness: Find out if the horse has ever been lame, injured, or sick, and whether there are any physical defects that could lead to problems. Ask if the horse has curbs (a sprain resulting in a bony enlargement at the back of the leg below the hock), worn joints, windgalls (soft swellings that bulge just above the fetlock), splints (a bone formation when the splint bone, attached to the cannon,

Above: This Morgan is wearing a fixed cheek curb bit. Part of a dress bridle, it is a severe bit and should be used by the rider with care.

becomes inflamed from a blow or jarring), wind problems or other weaknesses.

Finally, if you are still interested, ask if the horse, or pony, is easy to shoe, behaves well in traffic (see page 77), loads and travels well in a horse trailer (see pages 78–9), and whether it is good to clip (see pages 66).

GOING TO SEE A HORSE

Regardless of your experience, if you visit a horse, take an expert with you. Start by inspecting the horse in its stable. Look for good feet and well-balanced conformation. Feel the legs for soft swellings or irregular heat and any bony growths. See the horse led out and standing still, from all angles, then watch it walk away and trot past, in hand, to see how straight and freely it moves. Next, see the horse ridden. Note the tack fitted, any gadgets for greater control, and brushing or overreach boots. Observe the horse's attitude, obedience and paces, trotting and cantering in both directions and watch it jumping. Is it willing, careful, athletic, and agile? Or is it excitable? Does it rush?

If you still like the horse, ride and jump it yourself, then ask to take it for a hack, away from home. If possible, test the horse both alone and in

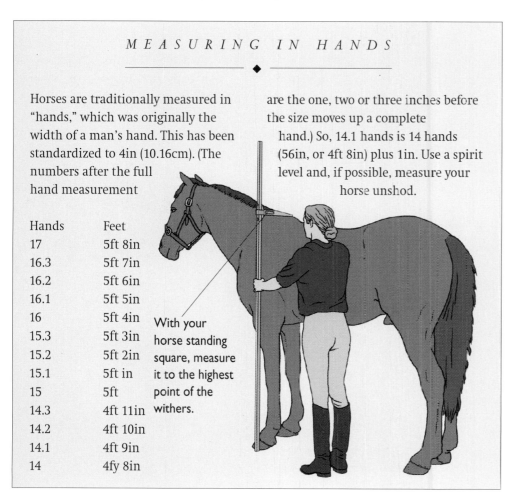

MEASURING IN HANDS

◆

Horses are traditionally measured in "hands," which was originally the width of a man's hand. This has been standardized to 4in (10.16cm). (The numbers after the full hand measurement are the one, two or three inches before the size moves up a complete hand.) So, 14.1 hands is 14 hands (56in, or 4ft 8in) plus 1in. Use a spirit level and, if possible, measure your horse unshod.

Hands	Feet
17	5ft 8in
16.3	5ft 7in
16.2	5ft 6in
16.1	5ft 5in
16	5ft 4in
15.3	5ft 3in
15.2	5ft 2in
15.1	5ft in
15	5ft
14.3	4ft 11in
14.2	4ft 10in
14.1	4ft 9in
14	4fy 8in

With your horse standing square, measure it to the highest point of the withers.

Head

The head should be in proportion to body size. If too large, it may affect the horse's balance. The eyes should be large and prominent and the jaw line clearly defined at the angle of the head and neck, allowing for natural flexion. There must be ample space between the two branches of the jaw for the larynx and its attachments to function well without interfering with the breathing.

Neck

The neck should be arched, long, and run smoothly into the shoulders. A short, thick, straight neck will have limited flexion and may affect balance. An overlong neck may cause breathing problems. A "ewe" neck with muscle development along the bottom of the neck instead of at the crest, is ugly and uncomfortable for a rider, as is a straight, upright shoulder, which limits foreleg movement.

Choosing your horse

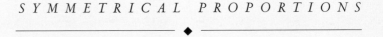

Above: Sound forelegs are a priority when choosing a horse, whether for riding or driving. Weak or defective bone is often hereditary in breeding.

company with other horses. You should feel safe and comfortable. If not, do not assume you can change the horse's temperament or behavior.

CONFORMATION

Conformation is the way in which a horse or pony is formed or "put together." If a horse or pony has correct conformation, there is less risk of weakness and injury, and it is more likely to move freely and be a comfortable, athletic, agile performer. Strongly formed hind legs, for instance, with well-developed muscle and powerful hindquarters, will propel a horse forward or upward for better galloping or jumping.

Perfect conformation is not essential, and good performers come in all shapes and sizes. But while minor defects may be acceptable, others are a more serious threat to a horse's potential usefulness and soundness. Good natural balance, free action, and boldness are more important than mere shape, but a correctly made horse can withstand more hard work, with less effort, than a poorly formed one. It may also have better movement, although this is not guaranteed.

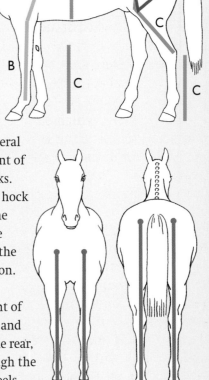

SYMMETRICAL PROPORTIONS

Correct conformation allows the horse to be naturally well balanced, and to perform with optimum efficiency.
Even so, there are exceptions and many horses with almost perfect conformation have poor "dynamics," with limited, slow or defective paces, and lack agility. But if the proportions match as shown, the horse is more likely to perform well.

Above: The length of lines A and B should be equal, as should all lines marked C. An equilateral triangle (D) should be formed between the point of the hip, the stifle, and the point of the buttocks. The point of the buttocks and the point of the hock should align to the ground. The depth from the top of the wither to below the elbow should be equal to, or exceed, the remaining distance to the ground, to allow ample room for lung expansion.

Right: A vertical line should run from the point of each shoulder, through the center of the knee and foot. Deviations may cause crooked action. At the rear, a vertical should run from the buttocks, through the hocks and fetlock joints to the center of the heels.

Withers should be not so high that the saddle is hard to fit, but not so low that they interfere with the freedom of the shoulder. Flat withers allow the saddle to slip forwards or around.

Chest

A broad, deep chest is better than a narrow one, when the forelegs are too close together. Depth at the girth gives plenty of heart and lung space. Flat-sided horses tend to lack stamina. The ribs should be widely sprung, and be wider behind the girth.

Back and hindquarters

A short back can be stronger than a long one, but may lack elasticity. A racehorse needs more length and range, but in all cases, the loins, a source of power, should be short, muscular, and broad. Long, narrow loins are weak and should be avoided. The hindquarters should be rounded and muscular, with ample distance between hip and hock. Very sloping quarters, with undeveloped thighs, or gaskins, denote weakness, although many good jumpers have a prominent croup, or "goose rump," which slopes down to the tail. The points of the hips should be symmetrical and the quarters rounded beneath them.

Forelegs

The forelegs take about 60 per cent of a horse's weight when standing, and must be correctly formed. The forearm should be long and muscled on the outside, broad at the elbow, which must stand clear of the body, and taper to the knee, which should be broad and flat from the front and deep from front to back. Knees with a concave profile, "back at the knee," put extra strain on the tendons. The cannons should be straight and short, appearing wide from the side but narrow from the front, never fleshy or rounded. The ligaments and tendons should be visible, with clean, hard lines. Bent or bowed forelegs are serious defects, causing uneven stress to joints and ligaments, and small, rounded joints will not stand up to hard work for long. Fetlocks should be clean lined, not rounded or worn.

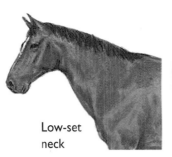

Low-set neck

Bull neck

Ewe neck

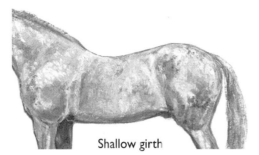

Shallow girth

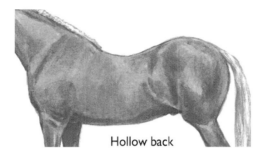

Hollow back

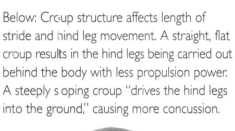

Straight back

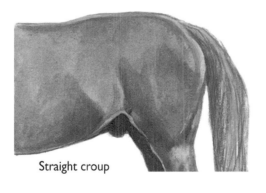

Straight croup

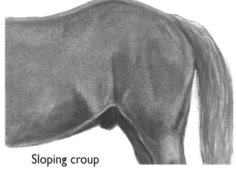

Sloping croup

Above: A low-set neck hinders good balance. A thick, crested, or "bull," neck is strong but may lack flexibility. A "ewe" neck, dips in front of the withers, has more muscle on the under-side than at the top, and makes riding uncomfortable.

Left: A shallow girth denotes a lack of strength and restricted lung space. The horse is likely to have limited endurance, speed and athleticism.

Above: A hollow back, which often appears in old horses, lacks elasticity, requires a special saddle, and the horse tends to lack strength through the body, and depth through the heart. A straight back need not affect performance, but is considered a weakness.

Below: Croup structure affects length of stride and hind leg movement. A straight, flat croup results in the hind legs being carried out behind the body with less propulsion power. A steeply sloping croup "drives the hind legs into the ground," causing more concussion.

Windgalls are a serious sign of weakness, while scar tissue can cause unsoundness later on. Long, sloping pasterns are weak, but absorb the shock of landing at speed better than very short or upright pasterns.

Hind legs

The hind legs are important for propulsion. The second thighs should be prominent, long and muscular, and the hocks wide, large, and well developed at the point, which should be directly below the point of the

buttocks when standing. Weaknesses include "Cow hocks" (see below), which cause the limbs to move outward instead of forwards on a straight line; "bowed hocks," which cause the feet to twist outwards as they touch the ground; and "sickle" or "bent" hocks, which can produce curbs.

Feet

Good feet are vital. They should be "a pair," with wide heels, clearly defined frogs and arched soles. The surface should be smooth and the slope even.

Choosing your horse

The heels should be deep and wide enough to provide shock absorption for the foot; turned-out toes can cause brushing; and flat soles are prone to bruising and lameness.

Movement

Good conformation usually produces straight, balanced movement. The walk will be indicative of the faster paces, and should have long, sweeping strides rather than short, quick steps. The hind feet should overtrack the prints of the fore feet.

Right: "Brushing," "dishing" (as here) and "plaiting," can all cause damage and are accentuated at trot and should be avoided.

Below: Splayed front feet may cause the fetlocks to brush and the elbows to turn tight against the body; pigeon toes put strain on the fetlock joints. Both hinder straight action. A horse "back at the knee," puts greater strain on the tendons. Being "over at the knee" increases the pressure on the knee joint.

Bottom: Bowed and cow hocks are weak and prevent straight movement, placing strain on other parts of the legs or feet. Hocks too far behind the body lose their power to support and propel the horse, while a very bent hock joint puts the cannon bone at an angle to the ground, instead of it being vertical and strong.

Splay-footed

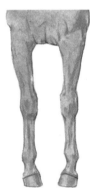
Pigeon-toed

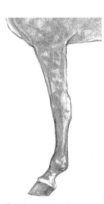
Back at the knee

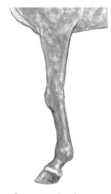
Over at the knee

Bowed hocks

Cow hocks

Hocks too far
behind the body

Bent or sickle
hocks

Just as a house would be good for nothing if it were very handsome above but lacked the proper foundations, so too a war-horse . . . would yet be good for nothing if he had bad feet; for he could not use a single one of his fine points.

XENOPHON (430–355 BC)

HORSES WITH "VICES"

When choosing a horse, a "kind" temperament should be a priority. Look for large eyes, and an honest expression. A friendly horse that approaches willingly, ears forward, pleased to see you, is more fun to own than one that turns its back. A suspicious horse, whether it has been abused, misused, or simply misunderstood, is a challenge, but it will require much time and patience to gain its confidence, which may never be total.

Bad stable habits

Find out if a horse behaves in any of the ways listed below, since this may greatly reduce its value.

✦ Biting, kicking or aggression, whatever the cause, are best avoided.
✦ Crib-biting, wind-sucking and weaving (see pages 110–11) are virtually incurable and may cause management problems.
✦ Excitable horses may pace the stall, or move around the stable incessantly.
✦ A horse that is reluctant to be caught is a nuisance, but can usually be cured with tact and guile.
✦ Horses that are difficult to bridle are curable, using careful, gentle means.
✦ A horse that puts its ears back and tries to kick or bite when saddling up, and when the girth is tightened, may be feeling pain. The initial cause may have been discomfort, and a habit formed, but problems in the region of the back should be taken seriously.

Problems when riding

✦ A horse that kicks out, even if provoked, is a danger to other horses and riders. Kickers can be difficult to manage and may cause problems when they are ridden out in company, causing tension for the riders.

✦ Jogging against other horses is a bad habit that usually occurs when a horse is ridden in company and becomes excited, but it can be very difficult to cure, using a combination of tact, patience, and skill.

✦ A horse that will not stand still to be mounted is also curable with training, but a bad case should be avoided since it may be symptomatic of a highly strung character. However, if the cause is a cold or sore back, this problem can be eradicated.

✦ Shying can be a vice if it becomes a persistent habit, and if the horse learns to "whip around" violently, without warning. It is usually cured by strong riding and anticipation. However, a horse that shies a lot cannot be recommended except to highly experienced riders.

✦ Bucking can also develop into a persistent habit if not corrected early. When a horse learns to dislodge its rider by bucking, it is likely to try it again. If not stopped, it can become a dangerous vice. The cause may be over-freshness, a cold back, or discomfort. But if it becomes a habit, it needs urgent correction by a secure rider, and must be cured before the horse can be ridden by anyone less experienced.

✦ Pulling is a bad habit caused by faulty training and an excitable, keen temperament. Bolting, galloping out of control and ignoring the rider's efforts to stop or turn, is much more serious. It becomes a vice if repeated, and is dangerous, whatever the cause. Persistent bolters should not be ridden.

✦ Rearing is another potentially dangerous vice. Whether it becomes a habit or happens just occasionally, such a horse is unlikely to be enjoyed by any rider, and is unsuitable to be offered for sale as a good riding horse.

✦ Napping, when a horse refuses to go in a certain direction, or to leave other horses, its stable or field, is a disheartening vice that may recur at any time and can become dangerous. The horse may rear, run backwards, or plant its legs and refuse to move. Napping takes many forms, some very unpleasant and unseating, and the vice must be cured before offering such a horse on the open market.

✦ A rider should be wary of a horse that persistently refuses to canter on a certain lead even on the smallest circle. While poor training and one-sidedness are probably responsible, there could easily be a deeper physical problem that may take months, even years, to eliminate. In the same way, a horse that flies through the air when trying to escape its rider's demands, may have a valid excuse, but could prove a nightmare to own.

Above: If a horse tries to bite when being saddled, it may associate this with pain or discomfort, or it may be simply thinskinned or ticklish. The cause should be established since an injured back is a serious defect.

Right: A well-schooled horse that goes kindly, enjoys its work and shows loose, active paces and agility, combined with correct conformation, is the ideal riding horse. It would be the ultimate aim of many riders to own a horse of this standard.

Riding Stables

Stable requirements ✦ Stable design ✦ Riding instruction ✦ Stabled horse care ✦ Mucking out

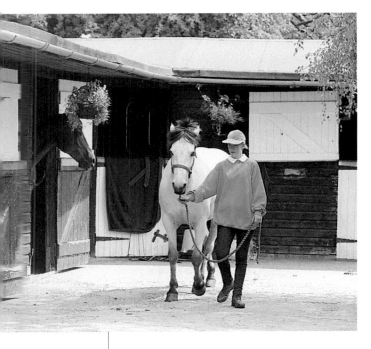

Above: Horses need security, which should be provided by a relaxed, well-ordered environment, and good stable management. They are usually happier and easier to handle when kept with other horses.

Below: Accidents in the stable can be avoided if the stables are safely designed and well maintained, with no sharp protrusions or edges and clean conditions throughout. A high standard of management is essential to a good riding stables. Ask questions about management if you are in any doubt.

A good riding establishment will have been passed by inspectors, who expect high standards of instruction. It should be supervised by a qualified and responsible stable manager. It must have suitable horses and ponies that are in good condition and well stabled; a clean, orderly yard and feed shed; a well-equipped veterinary and first aid closet; suitable tack in good, safe condition; and a definite daily routine.

CHOOSING RIDING STABLES

Unfortunately, you may find when choosing a riding school or stable, for instruction or for hacking, that the one nearest to home may not be the best. To help you make a decision it will help to have a checklist of what to look for, good or bad.

A smart exterior is impressive, but may be misleading. Expensive horses may be spoiled and unsuitable and do not guarantee that instruction is expert and committed. Similarly, ramshackle stables might be better than you think at first, if the horses are well kept, of suitable type, and cared for by experienced, conscientious staff.

A riding establishment should have a pleasant atmosphere. It needs an air of quiet efficiency, no shouting or running, and should be tidy. The state of the muck heap is usually a reliable guide to the way a stableyard is run.

An overhang helps to stop water entering the stables and makes working conditions more pleasant in wet weather.

A clean, covered area is useful for grooming or performing first aid inside, should the weather be bad.

The feed room must be closed to prevent horses going in and to keep out vermin. A rat-control program must be used.

A drainage system that leads water away from the yard, rather than one that relies solely on run-off, is necessary.

A clean, neat yard with dry, non-slip surfaces is a safe environment for your horse.

Gates are in good repair and are kept closed.

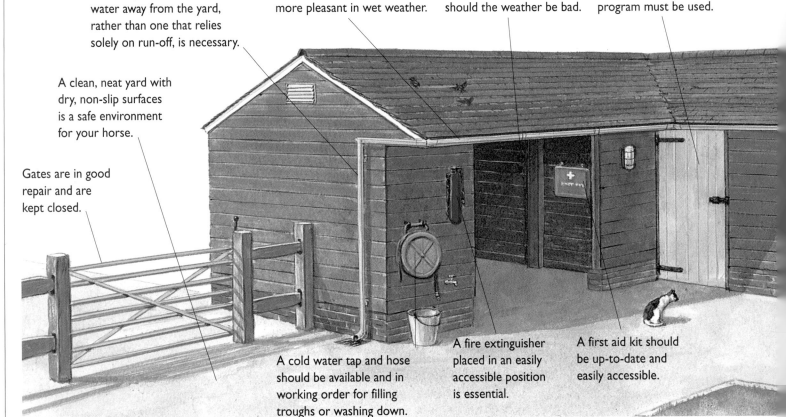

A cold water tap and hose should be available and in working order for filling troughs or washing down.

A fire extinguisher placed in an easily accessible position is essential.

A first aid kit should be up-to-date and easily accessible.

THE BARN SYSTEM

◆

Stables built into a barn, or similar building, with loose boxes facing on to a central aisle have the advantages of being compact and convenient, appealing to a horse's sociable nature, and providing a dry and protected environment for stable staff. They are ventilated by the windows and doors, but can be stuffy and unhealthy if fresh air cannot circulate freely at all times, while drafts must be prevented as well. Many barns have windows, and sometimes doors, that

open onto the outside, as well as on to the stable's central passageway. Thisis useful and provides cooler conditions in hot weather.

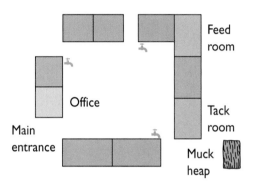

Above: This yard is laid out badly. The muck heap is not easy to reach from the stables and is visible to visitors. There is only one water point and one exit in case of fire. The tack room is easily accessible to thieves and the office is too far from the entrance.

Above: This yard is laid out well. There are several exits in case of fire, and the buildings are widely spaced to prevent fire from spreading. The muck heap, which is flammable, s accessible from the stables, but far enough away in case of fire and is not visible to visitors. The office is close to the entrance, there are several water points, and the tack room is far from the entrance, making it difficult for thieves to enter and escape undetected.

However relaxed a stable may be, certain standards must prevail. There should be constant qualified or experienced supervision, particularly where students are working, and there must be a routine. Horses and ponies should be fed regularly and well, according to the work they do, and none should be neglected or overworked. Water buckets should never be empty or upturned in the middle of the stable, and feed bowls should be cleaned after use. The feed shed should be well organized, clean, and dry, with a clear wall chart, and the bins or containers should have closed lids, keeping the food vermin-free. Open bags, litter, dirty buckets, and spilled grain are bad signs. The tack room must also be dry, with a secure lock if saddlery is inside. The tack should be cleaned regularly, not dry

Stables are well ventilated with plenty of fresh air circulating to keep horses healthy.

Windows must be protected by bars so that they cannot be kicked in and broken.

Automatic lighting is useful as a security measure. Lights must be covered, and designed so that animals cannot accidentally turn them on and off.

The tack room must be securely locked. It should have a warm atmosphere and be far enough away from the yard entrance to make theft difficult.

Mucking out tools should be put away tidily, preferably in a covered area, and never left lying about the yard.

The muck heap should be placed close by, but away from the yard to avoid any odours. It should be easy to remove whenever convenient.

Riding stables

and stiff, or greasy, and the buckles and important items, such as stirrup leathers and girths, should be in good repair. Bridles with simple bits, rather than gadgets, are another good sign.

There should be well-labelled veterinary and human first aid kits (see page 112). Farriery equipment, for the removal of shoes if necessary, would be a bonus: how well the horses are shod, and how regularly, will show the general standard of horse care.

If there is grazing, check it to make sure it is acceptable (see pages 54–5).

The stables are expected to be clean and well ventilated. Bedding should be better than adequate. Sparse, dirty beds, sweating horses covered in flies, unsafe doors and windows, and sharp protrusions, all suggest a low standard of horse care.

Above: A busy riding stables needs a well-organized tack room in a dry, clean atmosphere, as well as good facilities for cleaning the tack and storing extra equipment.

Below: Feeding a large number of horses of different sizes and types is a responsible task. Each one will have different requirements. To avoid mistakes, an accurate an up-to-date wall chart will be needed as a guide.

RIDING INSTRUCTION

Instruction should be enthusiastic and fun, but well founded on sound practical knowledge. Very large classes tend to be boring and unsatisfactory.

A good instructor sets a standard by dressing tidily and always wearing the recommended hard hat when demonstrating an exercise on a horse. Qualifications are expected and preferred, but practical experience, a sense of humour, authority, and sensitivity are equally important assets. A teacher who shows up a pupil, is sarcastic, shouts rudely, or constantly criticises, is unsuitable. Riders receiving constructive help and individual attention will feel the lesson is worthwhile, and are more likely to return. A good lesson is well organized, sets a goal, and, if possible, achieves it.

Horses used in lessons must be of suitable size, type and behavior to perform as the instructor expects. They need to be willing and fit enough to carry the rider with ease during the lesson. Excitable, disruptive horses or ponies will ruin the lesson for everyone: all the horses should respond obediently when the correct aids are given. The tack used must fit correctly and be suitable for the horse wearing it.

Safe horses, safe clothing, and safe teaching methods in a safe environment, are the priorities. If the class consists of beginners, there are more

Above: A group of students is instructed in how to detect problems relating to the health and condition of a horse. A thorough knowledge of conformation is necessary to enable you to recognize ailments.

than five riders, or if the lesson involves jumping, an assistant should help with the lesson.

STABLE NEEDS

Horses or ponies may be confined in small stables for up to 24 hours a day and, therefore, should be kept as safe and comfortable as possible.

✦ There should be enough space to move around and to lie down with minimal risk of becoming cast against the wall or door.

✦ Sharp protrusions such as nails or metal edges are hazardous.

✦ To prevent stable vices developing from boredom or hunger (see pages 110–11), horses should be fed small feeds, often, or given a constant supply of hay.

✦ Horses should be turned out to graze and receive fresh air when possible.

✦ Fresh water must be constantly available in a clean container.

✦ Air should be able to circulate at all times, to prevent fumes and germs.

✦ Bedding needs to be deep and comfortable enough to encourage horses to lie down.

✦ Drains should be cleaned out regularly. If there are no drains, the

Top and above: The pony (top) is in a very cramped and sparsely bedded stable and is unlikely to lie down comfortably, unlike the horse (above), which has a deep paper bed that is well built up at the sides for safety.

bedding should be of absorbent material, to avoid unpleasant odours.
✦ Vermin must be controlled professionally.

Bedding

Bedding can be aired while a horse is away from the stable, or bedding mats can be used to provide an insulated floor that is dust-free, yielding, and quick and easy to muck out. Urine drains away between the mats, but a layer of bedding on top encourages horses to lie down, and is more absorbent. The mats are cleaned periodically with disinfectant.

Straw is the traditional bedding, but tends to be dusty and to contain spores and chemicals that can be harmful if they are eaten in large quantities (see page 91). Good-quality straw is also difficult to obtain.
✦ Wheat straw, which is light and drains well, is best, but can be cut short and is less durable than in the past.

✦ Barley straw can be used, but is irritating to the skin.
✦ Oat straw is very absorbent but rather expensive.
✦ Shredded paper is absorbent, dust-free, and ideal for preventing allergies to dust or chemicals, although the ink occasionally reacts on horses' legs. But the paper must be kept deep, and it needs constant renewal, Some stables use shredders, but should beware of staples and paperclips. Paper bedding tends to make a yard messy.
✦ Wood shavings drain well and are easy to handle, although, like paper, they spread everywhere. A screened product is safest, to avoid the nails or other sharp objects found at saw mills.
✦ Hemp bedding, made from flax, is expensive but popular, efficient, and comparatively economical, since it is extremely absorbent. It is dry and easy to maintain, and eliminates odours naturally. Horses will not eat it, and there is no dust or mold.

MUCKING OUT

◆

The mucking-out equipment needed will depend on practicality and the type of bedding being used.

Large wheelbarrow, small wheelbarrow: A large, light barrow is useful in large stables; a two-wheeler is more stable than a single-wheeled barrow.

Two-pronged fork, four-pronged fork: A two-pronged or four-pronged fork shakes out and beds down a straw bed.

Wire rake: A wire rake separates droppings from a shavings or hemp bed, and evens out the bedding.

Shovel, broom: A large, lightweight shovel, and a wide, tough broom are essential for clearing bedding.

Muck bucket: A plastic, bucket-like container used for removing manure.

Plastic buckets: These may be used in place of a muck bucket.

Plastic muck sheet: A waterproof sheet is used for moving soiled bedding out or carrying straw into a stable.

Before mucking out, remove or tie up the horse and take out any water or feed

containers from the stable. If straw is used, use a fork to remove the droppings into a barrow or on to a muck sack. Next, separate the soiled bedding from the clean, and fork it into a wheelbarrow, piling the clean straw into the corners. Clean the floor, using the shovel and broom, and leave it to air and dry. Replace the bed evenly with a pitchfork. Top up the bedding, as necessary, with an extra layer around

the edges to prevent injury from rolling. For paper or wood shavings, use a rake to collect the dung. Wear rubber gloves to put droppings in a muck bucket over the course of the day. Dispose of waste on a muck heap which should be removed as often as possible. Straw manure is sometimes used as fertilizer once it has rotted down, but paper and shavings rot very slowly, making disposal difficult. Incineration is an option.

Grazing

Rotating grazing ✦ *Grazing season* ✦ *Suitable and unsuitable conditions*

It is natural for horses to prefer being out in a field, to spending most of the day confined in a small stall. A field can be almost equally restrictive if it is small and the only one available. However, if sensibly maintained, it can still provide a healthy environment.

MAINTAINING YOUR FIELD

A small paddock, grazed continuously, soon becomes "horse-sick," with sour, inedible pasture, bare or muddy, poached soil – conditions in which horses do not thrive. If there is no other choice, the paddock should be divided into three parts, to be grazed, treated, and rested, in rotation.

A single horse needs a minimum of one acre (0.4 hectares) of grazing, but preferably at least 3 acres (1.2 hectares), depending on the weather and the quality and condition of the grazing. In winter, grass has no food value. It starts to grow in spring and is at its most nutritious between May and July. In summer, weeds and unwanted vegetation must be removed, the tufts of coarse grass should be topped, and the field harrowed. In autumn, the grass fades, and horses may look for extra hay or feed, to avoid losing condition. It is a good idea to rest a field, and fertilize it, or to allow cattle to graze it off whenever possible.

A SUITABLE FIELD

A suitable field has a good supply of fresh water, nutritious grass, companionship, preferably with other horses,

Right: The difference between a good field and a bad one will make the difference between having a healthy, happy horse and a miserable one in poor condition, which might suffer from injury or become clinically ill.

Above: It may look idyllic, but it is best not to use grazing with lots of buttercups as, if eaten, they can have a cumulative toxic effect, similar but less virulent than ragwort poisoning.

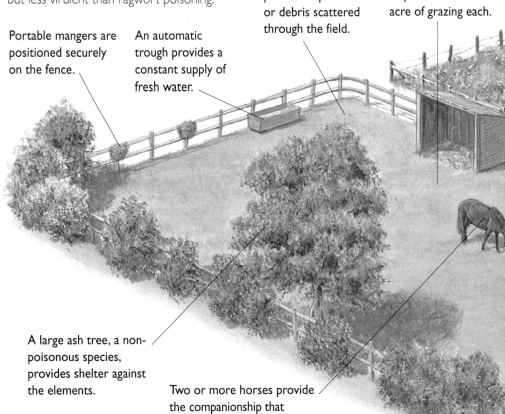

Portable mangers are positioned securely on the fence.

An automatic trough provides a constant supply of fresh water.

The grazing is green and palatable, without weeds, poisonous plants or debris scattered through the field.

The field is a reasonable size for a pair of horses, which require at least one acre of grazing each.

A large ash tree, a non-poisonous species, provides shelter against the elements.

Two or more horses provide the companionship that horses need, being naturally sociable, herd creatures.

and sufficient shade and shelter.

The field should be inspected every day, to check the horses, see that gates and fences are safe, and that there are no potential hazards. Ideally, droppings should be removed daily, to minimize worm infestation (see pages 98–101), and weeds should be pulled up and burned. If pasture deteriorates with overgrazing, it can take more than a year to recover and alternative grazing will need to be sought.

AN UNSUITABLE FIELD

A captive horse is dependant on what it can find in a field. Above all, it needs fresh water, which is vital to all its bodily functions. A dirty water container, or stagnant pond, is not acceptable. A neglected water source may contain dead birds, insects, and leaves or bird droppings. If there is no shelter, or shade, a horse will suffer in extreme wet or heat and in cold winds. A bushy hedge is preferable to an unsuitable or unsafe shed.

A sick field has bare, or ungrazed, coarse patches, and rough areas of

Above: Tractors are effective in clearing a field of horse dung. Clean pasture will remain useful for longer periods with less wastage.

unpalatable weeds and grasses. Droppings will have contaminated the pasture and, therefore, the horses, with worms, which are extremely unhealthy. In such conditions, horses are unlikely to be healthy or happy.

A dangerous field is poorly fenced with loose barbed wire or broken rails and unsafe gates. It is littered with jumps or other hazardous objects, such as cans and broken bottles, unguarded pylons or cables. The ground may be stony, boggy or full of holes, or the drainage inadequate.

POISONOUS PLANTS AND SHRUBS

◆

Poisonous plants pose a serious problem to the horse population. Horses will eat toxic plants only if they are extremely hungry, but dead poisonous plants are just as dangerous as living ones and horses may also unknowingly eat the seeds. Dangerous plants should, therefore, be pulled up with their roots, and burned. In badly contaminated fields, they should be destroyed with chemicals, and the field rested for several weeks.

◆ Groundsel (*Senecio vulgaris*)
◆ Foxglove (*Digitalis purpurea*)
◆ Bracken (*Pteridium aquilinum*)
◆ Acorns and oakleaves (*Quercus* spp.)
◆ Privet (*Ligustrum* spp.)
◆ Yew (*Taxus* spp.)
◆ Ragwort (*Senecio jacobaea*) (see page 110)
◆ Deadly nightshade (Bittersweet nightshade) (*Solanum dulcamara*)
◆ Henbane (*Hyoscyamus niger*)
◆ Laburnum (*Laburnum* spp.)
◆ Sheep Laurel (*Kalmia angustifolia*)
◆ Buttercup (*Ranunculus* spp.)
◆ Hemlock (*Conium maculatum*)
◆ Plantain (*Plantago major*)
◆ Oleander (*Nerium oleander*)
◆ Rhododendron (*Rhododendron* spp.)
◆ Larkspur (*Delphinium* spp.)
◆ Buckthorn (*Rhamnus catharticus*)

The field is in poor repair, with broken gates and fencing and no form of shelter for the horse. Debris in the field is an unwanted hazard.

A single horse becomes lonely and may develop behavioural problems.

Weeds and ragwort spoil the field and are potential hazards for a hungry horse. Potholes and very uneven ground are also a danger.

Poor drainage creates boggy patches that could be dangerous.

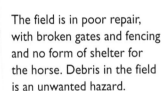

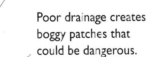

Fences and gates are in good repair and are checked regularly.

The field is too small to support a horse through the summer and the grazing lacks nutrition.

A stagnant pond creates an unhealthy environment and is not a suitable source of drinking water.

Rhododendron

You & Your Horse

The individual horse ✦ Communication ✦ Routine ✦ Skills you need

Every horse has its own distinctive character and temperament, revealed in its actions and expressions. How it reacts to different people and situations varies, since, like humans, a horse can be nervous or brave, happy, suspicious, sensible, stupid, or a combination of these. Learning to interpret the signs, and to understand them, is an important part of horsemanship. No time is wasted in watching horses' behavior, in the field or stable, when being fed, groomed or ridden, in order to know them better and handle them appropriately. Understanding their natural instincts (see pages 34–9) will also help you to anticipate behavior in certain situations. A horse will react differently to a situation when alone or in a group. When solitary, it may be more dependent on its keepers. But however docile a horse may seem, it is always better to know the right and wrong ways to approach and handle it, to establish a good relationship and avoid unnecessary risks.

ROUTINE AND DAILY CHECKS

Horses are creatures of habit, reacting well to a routine and happy environment, where they know what to expect and when. It is your responsibility to make sure that your horse has all the care, exercise, and social contact that it needs. You must create a routine and keep to it and make daily checks for

CARING FOR
HORSES
*You & Your
Horse*

56

HORSE WHISPERING

✦

"Horse whispering" is a way of communicating with horses that has been made famous by the American Monty Roberts. The aim is to behave in ways that your horse understands, using comparable body language to communicate your wishes, and to ensure complete trust and obedience, without using any force. Monty Roberts has achieved amazing results and maintains that "whispering" can be learnt and applied by all horse owners.

Right: This horse is bright and alert: a picture of health. It is important to recognize and interpret the horse's expressions and moods in order to understand its behavior fully and know how it may react in different situations.

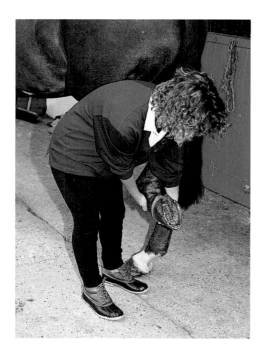

Left: A horse's feet need constant attention, and most are trained from an early age to pick up each foot in turn to have it picked out, with a blunt-edged hoof pick.

Right: Biting is a vice that may develop when sensitive-skinned horses are irritated by rough handling, tight girthing or being rugged up uncomfortably. It is a difficult habit to cure.

any injury and its general well-being, such as taking temperature, pulse, and respiration (see below), and also picking out its feet.

Lifting up the feet

A horse's feet should be picked out regularly to keep them clean and healthy. Once it is used to the routine, the job becomes much easier. It is best to lift up the legs in a regular rotation, starting with the near fore.

✦ Reach down beside the leg, running your hand down to the fetlock joint to pick it up, facing to the rear.

✦ Be ready to move away to avoid being stepped on.

✦ To lift the hind feet, stand slightly in front of the leg to avoid being kicked.

✦ Hold the foot in one hand and, using a blunt-ended pick, remove dirt or stones, working from heel down to toe.

✦ Check that the shoes are secure.

APPROACHING YOUR HORSE

Not all horses are good natured and reliable in the stable, and it is important to know how to handle them safely and to make that practise a habit. Horses should always be approached quietly and confidently. Even the quietest horse must be warned, by seeing and hearing you. Sudden movements and loud voices will startle it. Horses are sensitive to tone, and wary of aggressive or excited voices, people running or waving their arms, unruly dogs, flapping or rustling clothing, or any unfamiliar or careless behavior. Before going behind a horse, warn it by placing your nearest hand along the top of the hindquarters, but avoid touching the sensitive areas, the flank, lower belly or between the hind legs.

Most stabled horses have been trained to "move over" on command, so that they shift their rear end to the other side of the area, allowing you space to inspect, or groom, or adjust rugs or tack. If a horse is not cooperative, rather than standing behind it against the wall to push it over, walk around the front, where there is more space and less risk, then place a hand on the quarters, and ask it firmly to move across the stable, tapping it if necessary. To move a horse backward, again use your voice as you push against its chest.

Persuasion and praise

Horses respond better to persuasion than to force. A timid horse, for example, can be persuaded to enter a stall, but if forced and frightened, may fight and become dangerously strong. The damage can be long lasting, since horses never forget a bad experience. A well-trained horse is easy to lead in

---

HOW TO TAKE TPR
(TEMPERATURE, PULSE, RESPIRATION)

◆

You should check your horse's TPR each day in order to be aware of problems early on. Temperature should be 100–100.5°F (38°C); pulse should be 36–42 beats per minute at rest, respiration should be 8–16 breaths per minute at rest. A veterinary thermometer is safest and easiest to use.

Temperature: Shake the thermometer so that the mercury reads zero. Ask an assistant to hold the horse's head. Stand to one side of the hindquarters, hold the tail to one side and insert a greased thermometer into the rectum, bulb first, using a rotating action. The section inside should rest at an angle against the rectum wall to get a true reading. Hold on to the thermometer firmly and remove it after one minute. Wipe clean and read.

Pulse: Using a finger, press gently against the artery on the the lower jaw or on the inside of the foreleg just inside the elbow (see p.23). Using a

watch with a second hand, count the beats in 30 seconds. Double this figure to get the beats per minute.

Respiration: Watch the horse's flanks to see how many times it inhales (breathes in) and exhales (breathes out). Count an inhalation and exhalation as one. Count the breaths for 30 seconds and double for breaths per minute.

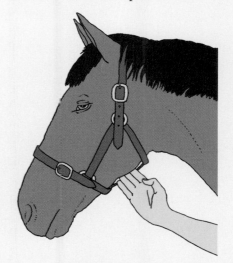

Taking the pulse

You & your horse

hand, but will sense if a person is uncertain and may react negatively by hanging back or refusing to move in a certain direction.

Most horses respond well to praise. They can soon learn that a pat is associated with praise. If patting is used as a training aid, it should be in proportion to the deed. Horses remember good experiences, as well as bad ones. Tidbits should be used sparingly and consistently, for the same reason. A nervous or suspicious horse will benefit from constant attention. Some dislike being pampered, but most respond well to stroking and rubbing along the neck and shoulder areas. This can gradually progress to the head, in the case of a head-shy horse, until it is quite relaxed about contact around the ears or other delicate areas.

Horses have no reasoning powers, which many riders often seem to forget. A smack can be effective if given immediately, to correct biting or kicking, for example, barging in the stable or field, or pawing the ground, but it is always best to look at the cause, to prevent it recurring. A smack in anger is likely to induce fear and a nervous reaction and must be avoided, as must a blow to the head or any sensitive area. Once a horse is head-shy, it is a difficult problem to overcome.

TURNING OUT

All horses enjoy being turned out for a few hours a day and there are good and bad ways of doing this.

To let the horse loose, open the gate wide and lead it through. Turn it round to face the gate, closing it before releasing the horse. If there is more than one horse, let them all go at once, but keep excited horses apart, so they do not kick each other.

CATCHING AND LEADING

Horses are easier to catch if they are brought in at the same time each day, especially if they are expecting a feed. But they can be difficult to catch if they do not want to be ridden, or the grass is more delicious than the tidbit offered. In the latter instance, you will need help, either to remove the horse's companions so that it wants to go with them, or to corner the horse so it submits to being caught.

✦ Always approach from the front and side, the hand raised quietly to the shoulder and neck area, before touching the head.

✦ Do not wave the rope and halter about. Offer food on a flat hand. Take care the horse does not snatch at it.

✦ Take time to pat and talk to the horse without trying to catch it, but avoid touching the more ticklish areas, the flanks and stomach, or the rear end, which might invite a kick.

✦ Never chase the horse if it will not be caught, since this makes it worse. Patience and calmness will be rewarded in the long term.

✦ Pass the free end of the rope around the neck, about midway, to secure the horse, and with the other hand slip the noseband over the nose.

✦ Use the rope hand to reach under the throat to bring the headpiece up behind the ears. Attach it to the buckle.

✦ Stand beside the horse, level with its shoulder, your right hand close to the head collar or halter, and the slack end in your left hand. For safety, never twist the rope around your hand or leave the loose end dangling around your feet.

✦ Start with firm intent, using a click of the tongue or a command, "walk on."

✦ If necessary, flick the rope end behind you, touching the horse's rear, to get it moving. Once in motion, keep level with the horse's shoulder for maximum control.

✦ Speak to the horse in suitable tones, to go slower or more briskly, or to demand its attention.

✦ It is essential to approach a gate or stable doorway straight and carefully, to avoid catching the horse's hip against the side: a damaged hip can be a serious long-term injury.

✦ Ensure the door will not swing shut, and never send the horse in alone, since it may rush in and hurt itself.

✦ Once in, tie up the horse or turn it round to face the door while you secure the bolt. Then release it.

Below: Horses sometimes need persuasion to leave their companions. A firm "walk on," using the rein to encourage it forwards, should succeed but without dragging too much at the head collar, which can have the opposite effect.

Trotting up

When leading a horse out for a veterinary or soundness inspection, use a bridle for the best control. Then stand it up "squarely," with its weight evenly distributed so that it can be checked.

✦ To trot a horse up, choose a level, hard surface, walk the horse away from the observer in a straight line.

✦ Turn the horse, always moving it away from you, for greater control and safety.

✦ Run back at the trot in a straight line, allowing the horse enough freedom to stretch its neck and show a regular rhythm.

Leading in groups

When leading a group of horses, choose a reliable leader and leave a safe space between horses, to avoid any accidents should one take fright. If possible, avoid leading horses along a

busy road, but to minimize the risks, take an extra person. If the road is narrow, go in single file, and use gateways or bays to let traffic pass. Keep a firm hold of the horse's head at all times, speaking calmly when needed. Stay alert to potential hazards. A nervous horse can be escorted by another calm, quiet horse. As when riding on roads, use hand signals well in advance to make your intentions clear. If in a group, the last person must signal, as well as the leader. Follow the rules for riding in traffic (see page 77).

TYING UP

A quick-release knot must be used to secure a horse. It is advisable to tie the horse to a loop of strong twine attached to a wall ring. The knot can be undone quickly if necessary, and the string will break if the horse should panic, preventing injury.

To make a quick-release knot, make a loop with the free end of the rope as shown in step 1. Then make another small loop in the free end of the rope, and thread it under and through the first loop (step 2). Now, pull on

the loop to tighten it (step 3). To release the knot, pull on the loose end. If you want to prevent an unattended horse from undoing the rope, pass the free end through the loop (step 4).

Riding clothes are designed for comfort, practicality, and safety. The most important items are always the hat and boots.
Hat: This *must* conform to approved safety standards, fit perfectly, and be attached with a safety harness.
Boots: Strong footwear is essential. The heels must be defined to stop the foot from sliding through the stirrup iron, and the boot should be without buckles, which might trap the foot. Soft shoes are not suitable. Leather is safer and stronger than rubber.
Loose clothing, scarves, jewellry: Avoid these as they can be dangerous.
Breeches and jodhpurs: These are designed to fit the leg closely and smoothly when it is in contact with the saddle. They are reinforced at the calf and knee and are worn with either long, or jodhpur, boots.
Back protector: All riders should wear these, especially children, or when jumping or riding at speed.
Padded jacket: This will absorb some of the impact of a fall.

Step 1   Step 2   Step 3   Step 4

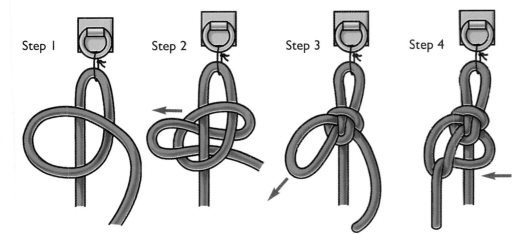

Feeding

Nutritional needs ✦ Rules of feeding ✦ Different foodstuffs

Above: Fresh water should be available at all times. Hay can be fed from a haynet, rack or the stable floor depending on individual preference, although feeding from the floor may encourage dust-related health problems.

Feeding horses is both an art and a science. A skilful, observant horseman will recognize when a horse looks well, and when its diet should be altered to improve its condition, performance, or appearance.

BASIC NEEDS

The basic nutrients required by a horse are water and fiber, to maintain a working digestive system; carbohydrates, which include sugars, starches and fiber, to supply energy; proteins for bone and skin growth and repair; fats and oils for energy and body maintenance; and vitamins and minerals for correct body functioning. Ideally, a horse would receive enough of these from good grass and herbage in the spring and summer to stay healthy all year. However, a stabled horse will not derive all its nutrition from constant grazing and needs careful feeding, according to the work that it does, its condition, size, age, and the time of year. The feeding method should be as natural as possible, since a horse has a small stomach, designed to have a little food in it at all times (see page 29). Hay replaces grass as the chief source of bulk, and "hard" concentrated feed is added gradually, depending on the balance of exercise or individual needs.

Water must be constantly available, since it is 70 per cent of the body weight and is lost by breathing and sweating and via urine and feces.

TYPES OF FOOD

Essential foods for a horse must include roughage – the bulky, fibrous part of a horse's diet, which is based on grass products, and concentrates, which are cereal-based and provide additional energy and variety.

RULES OF FEEDING

✦

✦ Make sure there is a constant supply of fresh water available.
✦ Feed your horse little and often.
✦ Feed plenty of bulk. Hay provides the roughage that is essential to a healthy digestive system.
✦ Feed according to energy used and the size and temperament of the horse. Adapt concentrates to the workload, replacing them with bulk when necessary (see opposite).
✦ Feed at regular times every day.
✦ Feed good-quality, clean foods that are easy to digest.
✦ Avoid sudden changes of diet or routine.
✦ Never work or travel a horse immediately after a full feed, or after heavy grazing.
✦ Treat each horse as an individual.

Roughage

Sources of roughage are hay, chaff, alfalfa (chopped hay) and haylage (grass that has been cut, baled and sealed, before drying out, leaving it dust-free and rich in protein). Hay less than six months old may cause indigestion or colic (see pages 90–1).
✦ Seed hay is a mixture of special grasses grown for horses such as rye, clover, timothy, sanfoin, and cocksfoot. It is crisp and greenish brown.
✦ Meadow hay is taken from permanent pasture, and is generally the softest. Its quality and nutritional value varies, depending on the grasses it contains. Hay with weeds in it should be avoided, and horses will reject moldy or musty hay.
✦ Fresh cut grass and alfafa may also

be fed as a replacement for grazing, and to improve the appetite.

Concentrates and supplements

Concentrates and supplements provide a horse with energy and other nutrients essential for good health. You must be precise in feeding in order to keep the vitamin and mineral intake balanced. An excess or lack of either is potentially harmful.

✦ Oats, the traditional grain feed, can be fed whole but are easier to digest if rolled or bruised. Oats are too rich for ponies, and many horses.

✦ Barley is fed as a substitute for oats, and is rolled, crushed or flaked.

✦ Boiled barley, cooked for several hours, when mixed into a feed can be a nourishing restorative, after hard work or in cold weather.

✦ Corn is fattening, but also very heating. It should be fed sparingly.

✦ Bran adds bulk to feeds, but has little nutritional value.

✦ Beet pulp or pellets are a supplement that must be soaked before feeding. It adds roughage and energy, and is fattening.

✦ Appetizers, such as molasses,

Below: Cereals contain natural nutrients. Digestion works best if the grain is fed in small quantities mixed with roughage. Beet pulp must be soaked (top) and oats (bottom) should be clean and dust-free,

ROUGHAGE / CONCENTRATES RATIO

◆

Your horse's diet depends on the work that it does, its age, weight, and the season. If grass is sparse, more hay is needed simply to maintain condition; if work is required, extra sources of energy will be necessary in the form of concentrates. Each horse must be judged individually, but the chart below gives an approximate guide to the ratio of roughage to concentrates.

	Roughage	Concentrates
Maintenance (no work)	Roughage 100%	
Light work (slow, short hacks)	80-100%	0-20%
Medium work (normal hacking, schooling, riding club activities)	60-80%	20-40%
Hard work (in training for competition, eventing, intensive schooling)	40-50%	50-60%
Ultra fitness (racing, three-day eventing)	30%	70% Concentrates

carrots or apples, are sweeteners and make feeds more appetizing.

✦ Salt is a valuable mineral, fed as a lick or in a feed.

Mixes and compounds

Complete feeds, in cube or coarse mixture form, have been scientifically prepared in a wide range for different types of horse, and should be "safe" and balanced. They are easy to store, and to feed, saving time and the knowledge needed to make up feeds. They also provide a consistent diet,

with added vitamins and minerals. Special mixes are formulated for brood mares, youngstock, foals, convalescent horses, and many others.

Many supplements and herbs are available to promote physical or mental health, or to add variety for a difficult feeder.

Below: The feed room or shed must be kept dry and clean. Bins with lids help keep feed fresh and protect it from vermin or damp. A well-organized feed room reflects good stable care.

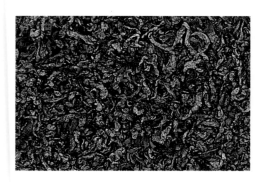

Grooming & Hoof Care

How to groom ✦ Tails and manes ✦ Clipping ✦ Foot care

For the stabled horse, grooming replaces rolling. It also promotes health and circulation, removes sweat and dirt, opens the pores, can tone the muscle, and skin, and improves the appearance.

Stabled horses should be groomed regularly, but a horse kept at grass should not be groomed but simply checked each day, and its feet picked out. If it is ridden, mud or dried sweat can be removed with a dandy brush or rubber curry comb, and the eyes, muzzle, and dock sponged clean. It is generally a mistake to disturb the underlying grease and scurf that acts as protective "waterproofing." The coat of a grass-kept horse should not normally be washed. If preparing for a show, a thorough grooming should be enough. However, if a shampoo is required, keep the horse warm in a stable, away from drafts, and rugged or

Above: A hoof pick is used in the heel-to-toe direction to clean out the foot. Feet should be picked out daily.

dried thoroughly, to avoid a chill. A longer mane and bushier tail helps to protect the horse from cold and wet in winter and from flies in summer.

HOW TO GROOM

Before grooming, tie up the horse. Groom outside, if possible, since it gives you more light and prevents the stable from becoming very dusty. Keep the complete grooming kit close to hand, but safely out of the horse's range. You may also need a small bucket of water. If a rug is worn, undo it and fold it back, or remove it entirely if the weather is warm enough.

✦ First, pick out the feet. Drop the dirt into a skip to avoid having to sweep up the debris later.

✦ Use the dandy brush to remove dirt, mud, and sweat marks. This can be too harsh for thin-skinned horses, so do not use it near the head or on sensitive parts, but only on the tougher areas, especially the legs. When brushing the hind legs and hocks, hold the tail to one side. Never use the dandy brush on the tail – it will break or remove the hairs, which take months to replace.

✦ Remove persistent mud or sweat with the rubber curry comb, using a

---

THE GROOMING KIT

✦

The grooming kit, kept in a box or bag, should contain the following:

Hoof pick: to clean out the feet.

Dandy brush: to remove heavy dirt and dried mud; useful for the grass-kept horse.

Body brush: to remove dust and scurf, lay the coat, and brush the mane and tail.

Metal curry comb: to clean the body brush.

Rubber or plastic curry comb: to clean the body brush and also to help remove stubborn dried mud.

Water brush: to dampen the mane and tail and clean off the feet.

Mane comb: to help when laying, pulling or braiding a mane.

Sponges: one to clean the eyes and nose and one for the dock.

Sweat scraper: to remove excess sweat and water after washing.

Stable rubber: to give a final polish after grooming.

Hoof oil and brush: to replace natural oils, preventing dry, cracked feet.

Tail bandages: to keep the tail neat after pulling or braiding.

Right: Vigorous strokes with a body brush clean the horse and tone the skin and muscles. A rhythmic motion is effective. Make sure that you have removed all the dust and dirt in the horse's coat.

Below: A body brush is used to brush out the tail; separate the strands with care so that the hair does not break.

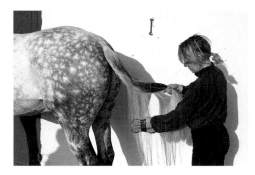

Below: Hoof oil helps to maintain and lubricate the feet, which often become too dry when a horse is stabled.

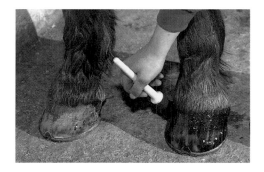

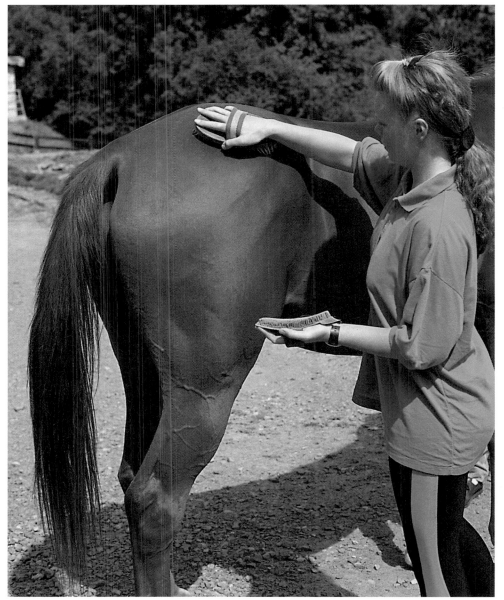

circular motion and brisk strokes.
✦ Use the body brush for deeper grooming. Start near the head and work towards the tail, using firm, sweeping strokes in the same direction as the hair growth, as far down as the skin. When grooming the near (left) side, hold the brush in the left hand and the metal curry comb in the right, and after a few strokes, use the comb to clean the brush. The tools change hands for the other side.
✦ Use the body brush to brush under the mane. Then brush the mane itself, separating the hairs. Repeat this on the tail, standing slightly to one side in case the horse kicks back.
✦ Use the body brush to clean the head, gently loosening or removing the head collar for easier access.
✦ Dampen a sponge and clean around the eyes and then around the muzzle.
✦ Clean the dock with another sponge.

✦ Neaten and "lay" the mane with a damp water brush.
✦ Use the same damp water brush to clean off the hooves.
✦ When the feet are dry, apply hoof oil with the brush, all round the horn and up into the coronet at the heel.
✦ Use a stable rubber for a glossy finish. Dampen the coat in dusty conditions.
✦ Replace the rug. A sheet worn under the rug will help to keep a horse's coat flat and clean. After washing the tail, apply a stable bandage to shape the top of it.

WASHING DOWN
Washing should be kept to a minimum, especially in cold weather. When it is hot, or after sweating heavily, the horse may be washed all over without harm, but otherwise this should be avoided and washing and drying confined to stained areas.

Washing should be done quickly in a well-drained spot, using a bucket, a large sponge or a hose pipe, and a sweat scraper. Use a horse shampoo if desired and cold or tepid water, not warm. Washing is easier with two people.
✦ Start by washing the shoulder and move on over the back, hindquarters and legs; wash the neck area, taking care not to upset the horse.
✦ Sponge the head, including behind the ears, and the more sensitive areas, such as inside the hind legs, very carefully. You may need to loosen the head collar for better access.
✦ Use the sweat scraper to remove the water and encourage drying. Towel the loins and back on cool or windy days.
✦ Walk the horse until dry, using a sweat sheet if it may get cold. Legs, in particular, should be dried quickly.
✦ Apply stable bandages (see page 79) following a bath in wintry conditions.

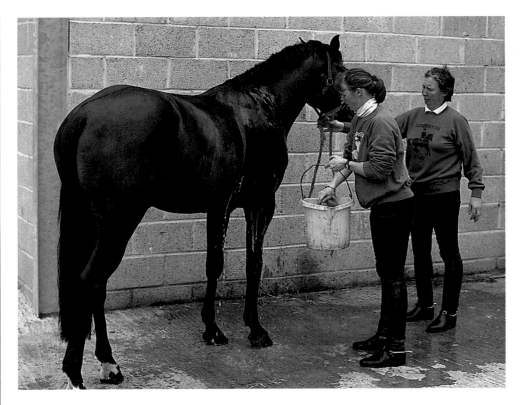

Grooming & hoof care

Washing the mane and tail

Brush out any tangles in the mane and tail first. Use cold or tepid water.
+ Wet the mane with a large sponge.
+ Apply the shampoo with a water brush near the top of the neck. Rub it in well if the hair is very dense or dirty.
+ Rinse the mane thoroughly, until no trace of soap remains, and use a towel to dry it as far as possible.
+ Wet the tail with the sponge.
+ Apply the shampoo using the brush, unless the hair is very fine or brittle.
+ Immerse the tail in a bucket of clean, tepid water, swirling it around.
+ Rinse several times and towel dry.

TRIMMING

Horses are trimmed to smarten their appearance, but horses that live out are best left untrimmed, since their hair protects against mud, wet, and insects. Heels should never be trimmed too closely on any horse. Safety "trimming" scissors should be used.

Head and whiskers

The head can be trimmed to the level of the winter coat when long hairs grow on the jaws and muzzle. If the

Above: After a work-out, or in warm weather when the horse has sweated, it should be washed down with a sponge or hose, to remove all sweat and grime.

Below: Horses with feathering can be trimmed for a neater appearance, especially if they are to be shown. Trimming should be done with care, using a comb and scissors.

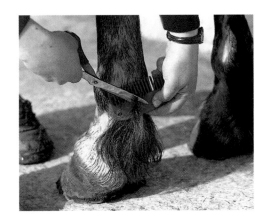

scissors cut into the dense coat, it will leave ugly "steps." Whiskers can be shortened, but they do act as "feelers," and those around the eyes must not be cut. Long hairs protruding from the ears can be trimmed flush with the outside edges, but the inside hair should never be removed, since it forms a barrier to insects, drafts, and driving rain. Long fine hairs on the head can be trimmed by laying a comb against the hair and cutting above it. Long hairs can be plucked.

Legs

Trimming feather on the heels and coronet makes the legs look finer and makes it easier to keep a stabled horse clean. A trimmed horse should still look as natural as possible. A smooth finish is difficult to achieve on very shaggy legs, and should be done little by little, using the comb to lift the hair. Native ponies and heavy breeds are not usually trimmed, but careful trimming can transform most show horses and ponies by accentuating their form. Hand clippers may be used instead of scissors on long, thick hair, but they require skilful handling.

Mane

The mane can be trimmed at the poll, making a bridle path that separates the mane from the forelock. This should be cut short, flat, and about 2in (5cm) wide – any wider and it will be unsightly. The straggly hairs at the wither can also be trimmed, but a rugged-up horse will need these as protection against chafing, which will result in a raw patch.

MANE-PULLING

The purpose of mane-pulling is to shorten and thin it out or to lay it flat so that it is tidier, and easier to braid. A horse living out all the time should retain about 6in (15cm) of mane as protection in bad weather and against flies.

Below: Pulling a mane to keep it tidy and to the required length and thickness is easier for both the horse and the owner if it is done frequently and a little at a time.

Pulling the mane involves plucking out a few strands of hair, methodically. This should be done with a special thinning comb, which prevents the roots from being removed. If you use scissors or clippers, an ugly, bristling ridge of new hair will grow. If the mane is very thick and long, you can pull a little at a time. It will be easier and more comfortable for the horse if this is done after exercise, when the skin is warm and the pores are open.

✦ Comb out the mane before pulling, starting at the top, near the poll.

✦ Take most of the hair that you want to pull from underneath so that the mane will lie flat.

✦ With the comb, separate the longest hairs into small bunches, which can be plucked with a single sharp tug.

✦ Repeat this procedure down the neck until the mane is the required length and thickness.

✦ Correct any unevenness by hand.

✦ Pull the forelock to the same length as the mane.

TAIL-PULLING

Pulling the tail means shaping the top of the tail neatly by removing the side hairs and some of those from the

center. Like mane-pulling, tail-pulling should be kept to a minimum for horses living out.

Some horses are more sensitive to tail-pulling than others, and many owners prefer to leave their horses' tails "full," braiding them instead for shows and competitions. Racehorses rarely have their tails pulled, since a natural, flowing tail suits a young Thoroughbred (see page 160). But, generally, if it is done well, tail-pulling will improve a horse's appearance.

If the tail is very thick, or has never been pulled, do a little over several days, to avoid soreness. If the horse is wary, stand to one side in case it kicks out. It is easier to pull out hair if the horse is warm. The final result should look even and sleek, narrow at the top and widening gradually to fullness. You will need a body brush, water brush, mane comb, and scissors.

✦ Brush the tail.

✦ Comb a section from the side of the dock, holding the longest hairs and combing back the rest.

✦ Pull out these few hairs with a sharp jerk. If the hair is coarse, wrap it around the comb and pull firmly.

✦ Continue evenly to halfway down

Left: A neatly pulled tail has the bushy side hairs removed by hand, leaving the longer central hairs and the lower tail intact.

Above: The mane is much easier to braid if it is first pulled and thinned. Each braid can be secured with an elastic band or tied with thread before finishing off.

the dock on either side. Unless the tail is too thick, leave most of the longer central hair.

✦ When you have finished, dampen the tail with the water brush and put on a tail bandage to lay the hair.

✦ To level off the tail, put an arm under the dock to raise it and measure the desired length, below the hocks. This is because the angle of the tail is different in motion and the tail will seem shorter.

✦ Finally, cut straight across the tail so that the end is parallel to the ground when the horse is moving.

BRAIDING AND CLIPPING

Braiding the mane divides the hair into small, neat bunches along the crest of the neck and smartens the horse's appearance. An unruly mane may also be braided to train it to lie flat, usually on the the right, off-side. A well-pulled mane is much easier to braid than a thick or straggly one. The number of braids is not important, but they should be evenly spaced and sized. Small braids tend to suit an elegant neck best, and larger ones a big or heavy horse type.

Grooming & hoof care

You will need a water brush, comb, braiding thread that matches the mane, large-eyed needles, and scissors. Rubber bands are an alternative to thread and quicker to use, but they may prove to be less secure.

Before starting, if using thread, prepare a number of needles with a knotted length of cotton, about 8in (20cm) long. Pin them to a stable rubber so they are safe and easily seen.

✦ Brush the mane and dampen the section near the poll to be braided – wet hair is easier to control.

✦ Use the comb to make straight partings between each braid, and between the three equally divided strands of each individual braid.

✦ For each braid, take the right strand over the center, then the left over the center, and repeat until finished. Braid tightly, especially at the top.

✦ Holding the end, pass the needle through the braid and wrap the thread around it before passing the needle through again to secure the end of the braid.

✦ Turn under the end hairs and sew around them to make a neat end.

✦ Double the braid under and sew it in place securely.

✦ Fold the braid under again to form a neat, rounded braid, secured neatly and strongly, with as little visible thread as possible.

✦ Cut off the thread underneath.

Below: When the whole coat is removed, leaving only the legs and a saddle patch, it is known as a hunter clip suitable for horses that gallop regularly.

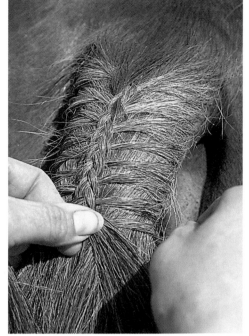

Above: When braided for special occasions, a full tail can become very smart. It also needs considerably less maintenance on a day-to-day basis than a pulled tail.

✦ When using rubber bands, braid as described, then wind the band round the end to secure it. Allow some slack, and pull this over the doubled-up braid. Use a second band to secure the finished braid.

Tail-braiding

Tails are braided as an alternative to pulling them, usually for showing and smart presentation.

✦ Brush out the tail and make sure it is clean and that there is plenty of long, thick hair at the top, which is necessary for braiding.

✦ Dampen and comb the top. Separate

Below: A horse that has most of its coat clipped, but has a blanket-shaped area left on its back to keep it warm in cold or wet weather, is said to have a blanket clip.

some hairs with the finger and thumb, as high as possible on either side, and take a third group from the center.

✦ Holding the braid with one hand, keep it taut, while selecting the next strand to be added; take the strands from alternate sides.

✦ Continue down the dock as far as desired and stop adding hairs from the side.

✦ Continue to braid the long central hairs and sew the braid at the end to secure it.

✦ Turn under the end to double the thickness, and hide it under the braid.

✦ Sew the parts of the braid together, leaving a neat loop if preferred.

✦ The tail braid can be flat, or raised, according to the method used. To protect the braid from rubbing in the stable, and for travelling, dampen it with a wet sponge and bandage it.

Clipping

The horse's winter coat may be shaved off with electric clippers, removing most or part of it, depending on whether it is stabled and how much work it does. Clipping allows the horse to work without undue sweating and discomfort, or losing too much condition. It enables it to dry off quickly after work, preventing a chill, and saves grooming time and effort. Horses that live out or that are ridden only occasionally need not be clipped. A clipped horse needs to be rugged, as well as fed, exercised and groomed.

There are four main types of clip: the "full" clip, when all the hair is

Below: If the coat on the underside of the horse's head, neck and stomach and the lower part of the hindquarters is clipped off, it is called a trace clip.

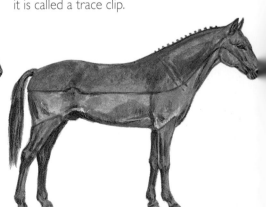

removed; the "hunter" clip, when all but a saddle patch and the legs, up to the elbows and second thighs is clipped; the "blanket" clip, when the legs, the area on the back, loins and rump are left unclipped; and the "trace" clip, which is a compromise for horses living partly outside, or ridden irregularly, which varies from a high trace, unsuitable for those living out, to the very low trace, removing only a strip under the neck, the breast and under the belly.

It is best to clip when the winter coat is fully grown, which is usually around mid-October. Most horses need reclipping, two or more times, until the end of January. Make sure that you use suitable clippers, which

---

A little neglect may breed mischief…
for want of a nail the shoe was lost;
for want of a shoe the horse was lost;
and for want of a horse
the rider was lost.

BENJAMIN FRANKLIN, POOR RICHARD'S
ALMANAC, 1758

---

have been serviced, oiled, and have sharp blades. Small-headed hand clippers are useful for the head, stomach, and any sensitive areas. The coat must be dry and well groomed so that the blades run easily and cut the hairs smoothly. Make sure that the light is good, since mistakes can seldom be rectified. Always clip against the lay of the coat and use a rug to cover finished areas. If the clippers become hot, stop and wait until they have cooled down. Take care to keep the clippers flat, to avoid nicks or unsightly "tramlines." Do not clip the inside of the ears and avoid the hair at the top of the mane and tail.

✦ Mark out the shape of the clip beforehand. Straight lines can be hard to achieve without guide lines, and the saddle area must be accurate and the lines of the fore and hind leg level.
✦ Start to clip at the front, on the shoulder or neck, working in sections

Above: This shoe is very worn and the clenches have risen so that it is probably loose, moving across the foot or coming off. It needs replacing.

towards the rear, but leave the ticklish areas, the head, belly, and inside the hind legs, until the horse is relaxed and an assistant is available.

FOOT CARE

Healthy feet and good shoeing keep a horse sound and useful. Shoes are required if the horse is ridden regularly, especially on roads or rough ground, and for most activities. Shod feet grow as fast as unshod feet so that even if shoes are barely worn, they need to be removed every six weeks or so to trim back the feet. A horse turned out with others, or ridden rarely, may just be shod in front. A well-shod horse will perform better than one that is not well shod.

A lost or loose shoe should be replaced before the foot becomes worn, broken or sore. It is time to re-shoe when the nails, or clenches, become prominent or loose or when any part of the shoe wears thin. Although shoeing is expensive, it should never be neglected.

The rate at which the foot grows varies according to feeding, exercise and environment, and the horn at the toe grows faster than at the heel. A good farrier can improve a horse's action by gradually reshaping its feet.

A horse may be shod "hot", when the farrier heats the metal and fits it to the foot, or cold, when the shoe is ready-made and only small adjustments can be made. The clenches should be aligned and secured, not too high or low, and the heels should support the foot without protruding at the back. Different types of shoe are suitable for different types of work and may need stud holes at the heels if, for instance, the horse will be required to jump on slippery or hard ground. Make sure you use an experienced farrier.

✦ First, one of the existing shoes is removed.
✦ Then the foot is prepared by cutting back the horn and the wall, and trimming the frog and sole if necessary, levelling the underside with a rasp.
✦ The shoe is then measured against the foot and adjusted to fit as required.
✦ The shoe is nailed to the foot with precision.
✦ The nail heads are removed, and the ends knocked down, before the foot is finished off with a rasp.
✦ The same process is repeated for each foot.

Basic Tack

Halters, bridles, bits, saddles, girths, boots, and bandages ✦ *Tacking up* ✦ *Cleaning tack*

Above: A fully tacked-up horse wearing a simple snaffle bridle, a grakle noseband, saddle, numnah, or saddle pad, and brushing boots to protect the legs.

Below: This correctly fitted bridle has a jointed eggbutt snaffle bit with a copper mouthpiece. It has a "flash" noseband that fastens above and below the bit, keeping the horse's mouth closed.

A wide range of tack exists for different types of horse and pony and their various uses. However, its basic purpose has always remained the same. Bridles and saddles are designed to help riders to control their horses and to allow them to ride comfortably, often for several hours a day. Most importantly, tack must be suitable, must fit the horse properly, and be in good condition to avoid injury to horse or rider. Basic tack consists of halter or headcollar; bridle and bit; and the saddle. There are several other items for specific purposes.

HALTERS

A horse wears a rope or head collar to be caught, led or tied up. The halter is an adjustable head harness and rope

Below: This is another variation of a jointed snaffle bit with side bars to help the rider to steer without pulling the bit through the mouth. A drop noseband and colored browband are worn.

combined. A headcollar is also adjustable, but comes in different sizes to fit the smallest pony foal up to a Shire stallion. It is made of either leather or nylon webbing, and the lead rope is normally clipped on to a metal ring at the back of the noseband when the horse is led or tied up.

BRIDLES AND BITS

The bridle and bit are fitted to control the horse's head and are used, in conjunction with pressure from the rider's legs, to convey instructions, via the reins and bit, through varying degrees of contact on the horse's mouth.

The bridle is a harness for the head, with several leather straps. It holds in place a bit, or mouthpiece, to which a pair of reins is attached. The bit lies on the bars of the mouth – between the incisor and premolar teeth (see pages 24–5). It acts on the bars, which are sensitive, and on the lips and tongue, so its design must be as sympathetic as possible.

Types of bit

The basic bits are the snaffle and curb bits, although many variations on each design exist.

✦ The snaffle bit usually has one mouthpiece, often jointed. The rings on either side are attached both to the bridle and to the reins, which have direct action on the mouth, but no leverage.

✦ The curb bit has a straight, arched, or sometimes jointed mouthpiece with a curb chain attached, which lies in the chin groove. The straight side pieces, attached to one or two pairs of reins vary in length, providing leverage on the mouth, chin and at the poll. The Pelham is a typical curb bit.

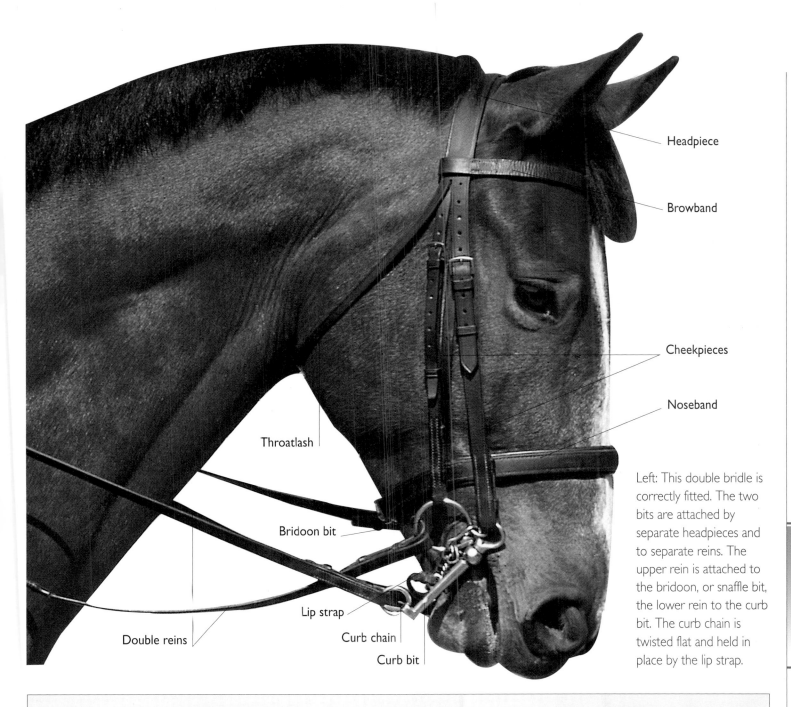

Headpiece

Browband

Cheekpieces

Noseband

Throatlash

Bridoon bit

Lip strap

Curb chain

Curb bit

Double reins

Left: This double bridle is correctly fitted. The two bits are attached by separate headpieces and to separate reins. The upper rein is attached to the bridoon, or snaffle bit, the lower rein to the curb bit. The curb chain is twisted flat and held in place by the lip strap.

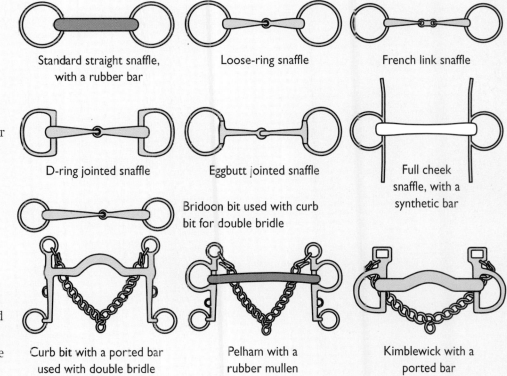

BIT VARIATIONS

◆

Countless bits have been designed since horses first wore bridles. They are mostly made from metals such as stainless steel, copper or aluminum, although vulcanite rubber, soft rubber and synthetic materials are also used. Jointed bits act solely on the mouth while others act on the chin and poll as well, with varying degrees of pressure exerted from the reins. The longer the side pieces on a bit, the greater the leverage that will be exerted. Most horses react better to a smooth simple bit without a curb action. A severe bit can cause pain and resentment in the horse and usually suggests a lack of good training on the part of the rider.

Standard straight snaffle, with a rubber bar

Loose-ring snaffle

French link snaffle

D-ring jointed snaffle

Eggbutt jointed snaffle

Full cheek snaffle, with a synthetic bar

Bridoon bit used with curb bit for double bridle

Curb bit with a ported bar used with double bridle

Pelham with a rubber mullen

Kimblewick with a ported bar

Basic tack

Types of Bridle
✦ The simplest, most common bridle has a snaffle bit. It is either loose-ringed or fixed with smooth side joints, known as "eggbutts."
✦ The double bridle has both a snaffle and a curb bit, and is only for the finest aids in experienced hands. It is often used for showing and dressage and is unsuitable for young, physically immature or uneducated horses.
✦ The "Hackamore" is a bitless bridle, useful for horses with sore mouths or teeth. It works by leverage on the nose, poll, and chin groove and is usually only a temporary gadget.

Nosebands
✦ The cavesson is the standard noseband. It is worn above the bit and inside the cheek pieces. A wide cavesson, done up tightly, is a suitable alternative to a drop noseband or grakle (see below), since it is equally effective in keeping the mouth closed, yet will not interfere with the horse's breathing or the action of the bit.
✦ The drop noseband is lower on the nose than the cavesson and fastens tightly enough under the bit in the chin groove to keep the mouth closed without discomfort. The front portion

Above: Reins are available in a range of styles and materials. The type selected will usually depend upon the discipline for which they are required.

Putting on a bridle
Before putting on a bridle, adjust it to about the right size. Remove the straps from the keepers and undo the noseband and throatlash. Once the bridle is on, make sure the bit is level and at the right height in the mouth, with no sag in the cheek pieces when the reins are applied. There should be only a slight wrinkle at the sides of the mouth. The bit should not be too narrow, pinching the sides, nor too wide so that it can slide or move about.

1. Stand close to the head on the near side. With the bridle over the left arm, and the left hand on the muzzle to keep the head still, put the reins over the head with the right hand.

2. Transfer the bridle to the right hand and hold the bit splayed out below the mouth, using the left hand. Feel the gums at the side, to open the mouth gently.

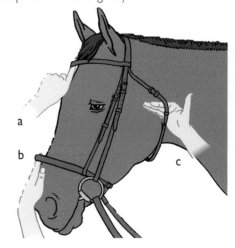

3. Ease the bit into place, lifting the headpiece over the ears, one side at a time, using both hands. Level the browband just below the ears, but not touching them, and bring the forelock over the browband.

4. Do up the throatlash, allowing a hand's width between it and the throat. Close the noseband and fasten it inside the cheek pieces. Check that the buckles are properly fastened and the nose band is level.

5. When the bridle is on, you should be able to slide a finger easily under all the straps (a); insert two fingers underneath the noseband (b); and fit the width of four fingers between the side of the throat and the throat lash (c).

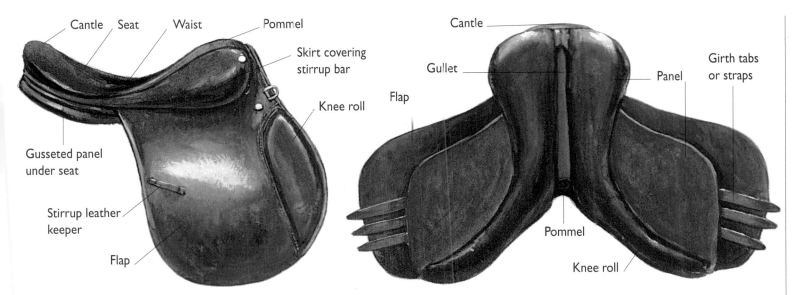

Cantle Seat Waist Pommel

Skirt covering
stirrup bar

Knee roll

Flap

Gusseted panel
under seat

Stirrup leather
keeper

Flap

Cantle

Gullet

Flap

Panel

Girth tabs
or straps

Pommel

Knee roll

should be at least three fingers clear of the nostrils, to prevent it from interfering with breathing.

✦ The "flash" noseband is a cavesson and drop noseband combined.

✦ The "grakle" is a crossed noseband, acting over a wider area, which helps to stop the horse crossing its jaw when trying to evade the action of the bit.

SADDLES

A saddle, like the bridle, should be of strong, good-quality leather and be kept in good condition. It should then last for ever. Synthetic saddles are also

Above: The leather parts of a saddle are built upon the tree. This provides a solid base and should fit th ehorse's back appropriately.

made, which are easy to maintain but are less durable.

A saddle is built around a "tree," or frame, and should be designed to distribute the rider's weight evenly, and to help place the rider into the correct position, without hampering the horse's natural action.

The saddle should help both horse and rider perform comfortably. The girth straps must be checked often for

strength and safety, and the saddle may need to be restuffed after years of use.

A saddle must sit level on the back, and not slope backwards. It should not be too large, but must be clear of the loins, and not too narrow, pinching the withers. The gullet must be high and wide enough to avoid pressing on the spine or withers.

Stirrups

Stirrups are usually made of stainless steel and are often fitted with rubber treads to help keep the rider's feet in the stirrups. (Continued on page 73.)

TYPES OF SADDLE

◆

Saddles are designed for different activities, including racing, endurance riding and riding Western-style, with variations on each design (see pp.122, 151, and 245).

✦ The General purpose is the most versatile saddle. It has an adaptable design and is suitable for most riding activities.

✦ The dressage saddle is very straight-cut, to suit a long leg position, allowing a rider to sit deep and upright.

✦ The jumping saddle has a forward-cut knee flap to allow for shorter stirrup lengths. It often has knee rolls for more stability when jumping and allows the rider to fold into a good position.

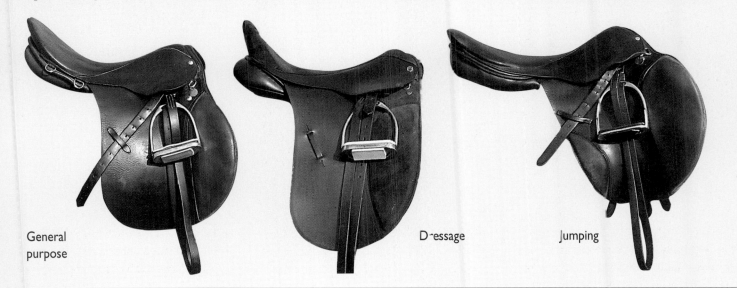

General
purpose

Dressage

Jumping

Basic tack

Putting on a saddle

Before saddling up, attach the girth on the off side and fold it over the saddle, with the stirrups run up, not dangling, and if a numnah or saddle pad is used under the saddle it can be attached to the girth straps before saddling up. When a martingale or breastplate is worn, it must be in place before the girth is done up, so it can be looped through the girth.

Above top: Folded leather girth shaped for comfort. Middle: Practical nylon girth absorbs sweat and is strong and easy to maintain.

Bottom: Dressage girth with buckles clear of the saddle to maximize contact between the rider and the horse.

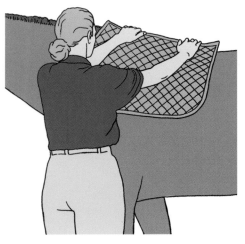

1. If you are using a saddle cloth or numnah under the saddle, place it on the horse's back first, slightly forward, toward the withers. Make sure it lies flat and level under the saddle, safely secured so it can not slip.

2. Place the saddle on top of the numnah and pull the numnah into the saddle arch. Slip the saddle down and back – never forward – into the correct position, laying the hair flat. Secure the pad to the saddle, if not already done.

3. Drop the girth, which is attached on the off side, into position, and check it for comfort and position. Walk around in front of the horse to fasten the girth on the near side, to the first two, or first and third, girth straps.

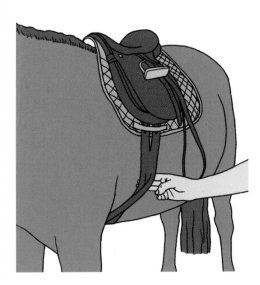

4. Tighten the girth gradually until it cannot slip around but does not pinch the skin either. The buckles should be level. There should be at least three girth holes above the buckle on each side. You should just be able to slide the flat of your fingers underneath the girth.

5. For some horses, it is necessary to smooth the skin under the girth after tacking up. To do this, feel the horse's shoulder and leg down as far as the knee and pull the foreleg out from the knee as far as it will go. Slide the stirrups down before mounting.

6. To remove the saddle, run the stirrups back up as far as the stirrup bar. Undo the girth on one side and place it over the saddle. Holding the saddle and the numnah together, lift the saddle off the horse, moving them slightly backward as you do so.

The stirrup must be wide enough for the foot to slide in or out easily. Stirrup leathers are sometimes made of rawhide for extra strength. Stirrup irons are sometimes curved, and safety stirrups, for children, are designed so that if the rider falls, they will not trap a foot.

BREASTPLATES AND GIRTHS
Breastplates and breast girths are used to prevent the saddle from slipping back. Both must fit tightly enough to be effective, yet must not be restrictive in any way.

✦ The breastplate is a neck strap that attaches to the D-rings under the skirt on the saddle, and to the girth between the forelegs.

✦ A breast girth, which can be elasticated or made of leather or webbing, fits across the chest and is attached to the girth straps on either side of the saddle.

MARTINGALES
Martingales are designed to prevent the horse from raising its head too high, making it easier to control. They are held in place by a neck strap and are an effective device, although they are no substitute for training.

Running martingale
A running martingale has a strap that runs through a loop in the neckstrap, from the girth, and divides into two branches that have rings on the end.

Right: Safety stirrups are designed so that the outside rubber attachment comes off, allowing the foot to be released, if the rider falls.

To check the correct length, the rings should reach up to the withers, or into the horse's gullet. The reins pass through these rings on either side of the neck. "Stops" on the reins are important since they will prevent a ring from catching on the buckle at the bit, which can be dangerous.

Standing martingale
A standing martingale can be more restrictive and should not be too short, although it is used to prevent a horse's head being raised too high. The strap is attached at the girth, runs between the forelegs and through the neckstrap, secured by a rubber stop, and loops around the cavesson noseband.

Irish martingale
An Irish martingale is a simple gadget used mainly on racehorses. It has two rings separated by a short piece of leather that holds the reins in place on either side of the horse's neck.

BOOTS AND BANDAGES
Boots and bandages are designed to protect a horse's legs from the knee and hock joints down to the hoof. Bandages are more difficult to apply correctly, but can give better all-round support than protective boots, which come in a huge variety, made from

DEVELOPMENT OF TACK
◆

Padded saddles and bridles made of skin exist which date from *c.*3000 BC, while older European cave paintings show horses wearing head collars. The Scythians, one of the first horse peoples, were using bridles on onagers in 2500 BC. Previously made of wood, bone or horn, bronze bits appeared between 1200 and 1300 BC. Stirrups were a later invention. They were first used in Europe by the Franks at the Battle of Poitiers in AD 732 against the Moors.

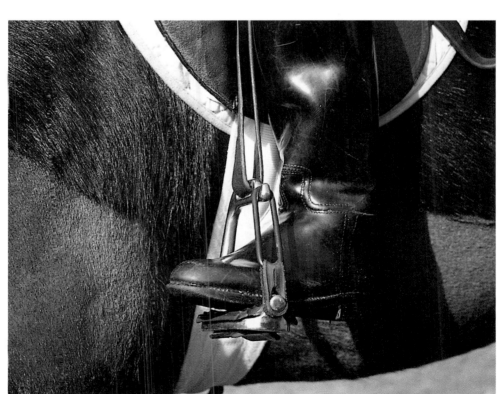

Basic tack

plastic, rubber, felt or leather materials, and are quick and easy to put on. All boots and bandages should be fastened on the outside of the leg. Extra adhesive tape may be necessary to surround some boots if there is any risk of them becoming loose or detached, which could be dangerous.

✦ Overreach boots protect the heels of the fore legs from being stepped on.

✦ Fetlock boots are worn to protect this protruding joint against knocks from the opposite leg, when the horse has faulty action or the going is rough.

✦ Brushing boots can protect most of the lower limb from friction or blows. They should be strong but light, and must be put on firmly and evenly, but never too tight, when they may damage the delicate tendons.

✦ Tendon boots are applied to the front legs, to prevent injury if a hind foot should strike the tendons. These can be open-fronted, especially for showjumping, and are well padded for extra protection. They are secured with evenly spaced straps.

Exercise bandages

Exercise bandages, for protection and support, must be put on very carefully, to achieve this. Uneven pressure can

Above: On the front feet, this horse wears rubber overreach boots, which are pulled on, and tendon boots, which protect the front tendons against knocks. Fetlock boots are worn on the hind joints to prevent injury from "brushing."

Left: The breastplate will stop the saddle from slipping back too far or from slipping round, if the girth is too loose. It must never restrict shoulder movement at fast paces or when jumping.

Below: Brushing boots are worn as a precaution against knocks if a horse does not move straight or is likely to jump about and hit itself if it is being lunged, working on circles and lateral movements.

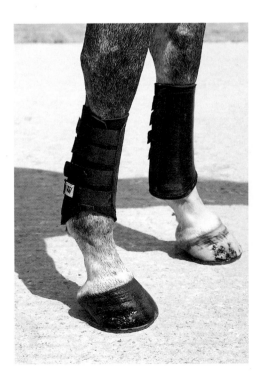

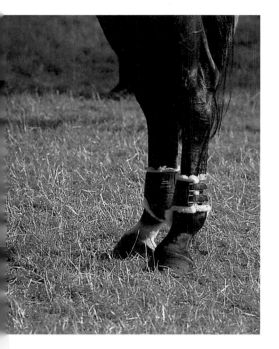

It is helpful to know the length of a bandage, so as to judge the depth of the turns. Starting on the outside of the limb, near the top, and bandaging counterclockwise, work down and up again, for equal pressure, and fasten safely with the same amount of pressure, neither tighter nor looser, and never on the back or front of the leg.

REMOVING TACK

There is more than one way of "untacking," but the saddle is usually removed first (see page 72).
✦ Run up the stirrups and undo the girth on the near side.
✦ If a martingale or breastplate is worn, detach it from the girth.

✦ Hold the saddle at the front and back, and lift it off sideways on to a bent left arm. Fold the girth over the saddle. Place it carefully out of range.
✦ Pick up a head collar and hang it over a shoulder.
✦ Keeping the reins over the neck for control, unbuckle the throatlash and noseband, and the curb chain if worn. Now place the left hand on the front of the horse's head, above the nostrils, before slipping the headpiece off the ears and on to the arm, while slowly easing the bit out of the mouth.
✦ Keep hold of the reins until the head collar is in place, before taking them over the head. Tie up the horse, if required.

provoke serious damage. The bandages must first be rolled up firmly and evenly. All leg bandages are applied the same way, although the area that they cover, and the tension, vary according to their purpose. An exercise bandage starts just below the knee and ends on the fetlock joint, but must not interfere with its movement. If padding or foam is used under bandages, it must fit smoothly without any lumps or creases.

Below: Bandaging is a skill. Well-applied exercise bandages, like this one, will support and protect a leg when ground is hard or extra safeguards are needed, for example, when galloping or jumping.

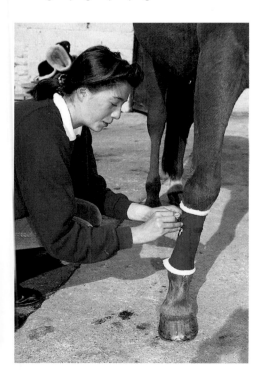

CLEANING AND STORING TACK

Tack needs cleaning to prolong its life, and its condition must be safe, particularly the stitching and folds in the leather, and the reins, stirrup leathers and girths. Broken tack can be dangerous and dirty tack can spread infection (see p.107). You need: saddle soap; neatsfoot oil; 2 sponges; an old toothbrush (for the difficult bits); and a bucket of warm, not hot, water.
✦ All tack should be sponged off and checked after you use it. It should also be taken apart at frequent intervals for thorough dressing.
✦ Begin with a damp cloth or sponge, to clean off sweat and dirt, then work in the saddle soap, and apply a preservative oil to very dry or hard leather.
✦ Wash the bit, and any other metalwork, with warm water and dry it. Girths made of webbing or nylon, and saddle pads, can be brushed off and hung up, or washed if very sweaty and dirty. Chafing from dried sweat or mud must be avoided. Leather girths must be kept soft and supple.
✦ Store the tack in a dry place, to avoid mildew, and away from heat, which dries out the leather and may cause it to become brittle.

Exercising

Which type of exercise? ✦ *Exercise from the ground* ✦ *Riding on roads*

Stabled horses need regular exercise, particularly if they are not turned out at all. Most horses should have at least one hour of exercise each day, depending on the level of fitness and the work required of them. For example, a horse that is being prepared for riding club activities every weekend, should have a work program, to build up and maintain muscle, to establish fitness, and to prepare it both physically and mentally for the tasks ahead. Intensive schooling in an arena, or under instruction, is very different from

People may talk of first love — it is a very agreeable event, I dare say — but give me the flush, and triumph, and glorious sweat of a first ride.
GEORGE BORROW, LAVENGRO, 1851

casual hacking, which expends much less energy, while jumping practice and fast work, including galloping, require more energy. To maintain fitness and condition, the horse's diet should match the work it does. A balanced program will space out strenuous work, to avoid fatigue or risk of strain, and the week should include a rest day, normally following a busy one. Working horses should have complete rest, ideally turned out at grass, for about a month every year.

LUNGING

Lunging is the controlled exercise of a riderless horse on a circle, using a long rein. It is also used to train both horses and riders and should be carried out in an enclosed area on a good, safe, even surface. The person lunging the horse should wear gloves and a hard hat. Lunging is a skill, and it can go very wrong in inexperienced hands. Beginners should practice on an old, reliable horse.

When and how to lunge

A very fresh or exuberant horse may be lunged before it is ridden, and a horse with a sore back, for instance, can still be kept fit by being lunged.

Lunging requires a strong, close-fitting padded cavesson, which has a reinforced noseband and rings on the front that swivel. It can be fitted over the bridle. The lunge rein, made of canvas webbing or rope, is at least 23ft (7m) long. The lunge whip must be long enough to influence the horse on a large circle. If side reins are used, for easier control, they are attached to a roller or saddle. The horse should wear protective boots.

Horses are controlled on the lunge by the voice, the rein, and the whip. The tone is more important than the words, but a clear intention must be conveyed to gain a horse's respect, understanding, and trust. When it is obedient, lunging can improve a horse's balance, paces, and fitness.

Above: The handler stands still in the center of the circle and controls the pace, rhythm, and size of the circle, changing direction about midway through the exercise. Spoken instructions must be given clearly and kept to a minimum.

Below: Driving a horse in long reins is a skill best left to experienced hands. It is very useful for encouraging a horse to move forwards willingly and straight and to teach it to stop, turn, and respond to driving aids,

Above: The pleasure and excitement of galloping horses over good ground has enormous appeal for most riders, while horses also enjoy it, especially in a group.

LONG-REINING

Like lunging, long-reining, driving the horse in a pair of long reins from the ground, is a skill and, if not done properly, it can damage the horse. But in experienced hands, it will teach a horse to learn obedience, accept the bit, and to go forward and turn well.

Before being long-reined, the horse must go well on a single lunge rein. The equipment used can be the same as for lunging. A second rein can then be introduced, on the circle, until the horse is used to feeling it against its hindquarters or hocks. The handler may then try turning and going straight, before leaving the enclosed environment, to educate the horse on hills or roads, for example.

ALTERNATIVE EXERCISE

Alternative ways of exercising horses without riding them are to lead one while riding another – although the two horses must be compatible – or to use a mechanical horse walker. Up to eight horses can be exercised using a horse walker, and most horses happily accept it. It is useful for a large yard of horses and when stable staff are scarce or lack riding experience.

The horse walker can be used for several purposes: for exercise; to settle an excitable horse; to dry off and relax a horse after exercise; or to warm it up gradually before riding. The walker must be supervised, and the speed controlled. A brisk walk is best.

ROAD RULES AND ETIQUETTE

Riding in traffic is dangerous, even when a horse is "traffic proof," since many drivers do not understand how horses behave and often pass too close or too fast. New riders should be escorted by at least one reliable person.
✦ All riders must be aware of the road regulations that apply to them, and show courtesy to other road users.
✦ Riders must be aware of potential hazards and keep the horse attentive to the aids, never allowing it to slop along on a loose rein.
✦ Bright clothes should be worn.
✦ Drivers must be given plenty of warning before riders cross a road, or require them to slow down or stop. NEVER assume that drivers will stop.
✦ When possible, riders should try to get off the road to allow traffic to pass.
✦ A large group should divide to let cars pass, with experienced lead and end riders to warn others.
✦ Avoid riding in poor visibility. Otherwise, be sure you are SEEN. Wear stirrup lights and reflective clothing.

Below: After a ride, tack can be removed outside. It is usual to take off the saddle before the bridle and the boots. After exercise, the horse will need to be rubbed down.

PLANNING A RIDE

◆

Before setting out on a ride, decide on the length of the ride and the route. If riding alone, someone else should be informed of this plan. If jumping is to be included, or if the horse is unreliable, it is wise not to ride alone. Places to canter or gallop may be planned, but it is important to know the ground well. You should be sure that no new hazards, such as rabbit holes or litter, have appeared, or an electric fence has not been unexpectedly erected just around a corner. If in doubt, walk the route the first time to make sure it is safe and the ground is suitable for jumping and fast work.

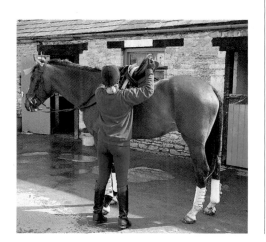

Horse Travel

The horse trailer ✦ Preparing your horse for travel ✦ Loading and unloading

Most horses travel willingly, provided that the horse trailer is suitable, is driven well, and they have been sensibly introduced to it. Once a horse has had a bad journey, it will remember it, and could become a nervous traveler and be reluctant to load.

THE HORSE TRAILER
A horse trailer must have a strong, safe non-slip floor and ramps, with rubber or other matting, or be well bedded down. Ample headroom is required and the stall must be long enough and wide enough to allow the horse to spread its hind legs wide, for balance, and to adjust its weight on changes of direction. If facing forward, horses need a chest bar for support and to prevent injury if the vehicle stops suddenly. The trailer should be checked regularly for safety.

Below: Bandages protect the horse's legs against impact while traveling, reduce the effects of jarring and keep the legs clean. They must be applied evenly but not too tightly.

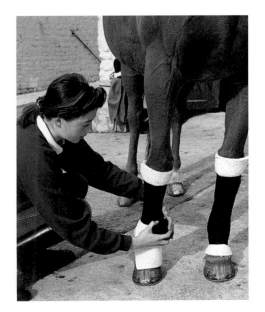

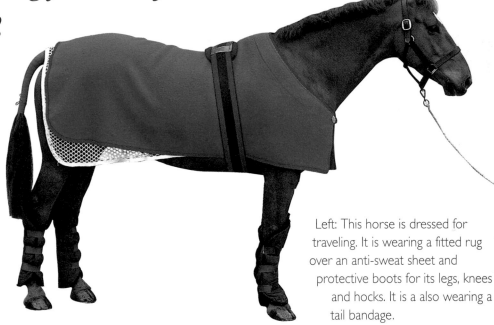

Left: This horse is dressed for traveling. It is wearing a fitted rug over an anti-sweat sheet and protective boots for its legs, knees and hocks. It is a also wearing a tail bandage.

PREPARATIONS
Some horses travel simply with a headcollar and rope, or even loose in a horse trailer without partitions, but most owners prefer to provide some forms of protection as a precaution.
✦ A tail bandage keeps the tail clean and prevents rubbing.
✦ Leg bandages, or wraps, protect against knocks. Some boots, or leg wraps, cover the knees and hocks as well as the lower leg. Bandages, over cotton wraps or other padding for even pressure, take longer to put on than velcroed wraps, but they are more secure and offer better support.
✦ Separate knee pads and hock boots can be worn; a tail guard is optional.

Clothing and feeding
The horse's clothing depends on the weather and on the individual. A cold horse will have cold ears and its coat may stand on end. A hot, sweating horse may become restless, and could suffer a chill. Good judgement must be used, therefore, as to what your horse should wear, and checks should be made during the journey. A spare rug is often useful.

In winter, a clipped horse will need a traveling rug, held in place by a surcingle. It may need a sweat sheet beneath the rug, or a thermal rug, which will allow moisture through, while keeping the horse warm and dry. A thin-skinned horse will probably need a thicker rug or extra blanket.

An unclipped horse requires only a light sheet or toweling rug to keep the coat flat and clean, or a thermal rug. On a mild day, it may not need anything. All rugs must be secured, yet not be uncomfortably tight. In summer, a sheet should suffice, or a light traveling rug in cool temperatures.

Over short distances, a horse may travel tacked up. If the bridle is worn, the reins should be over the neck, and the slack secured inside the throat lash or inside the headcollar, which is worn over the bridle. The stirrup irons must be up, and a rug or sheet secured over the saddle.

Horses may be fed normally before travel, but leave at least one hour for digestion, as before exercise. On a long journey, or to keep the horse occupied, supply a haynet, but do not

- ✦ Hay and haynet
- ✦ Water in a large container
- ✦ A shovel and broom for droppings
- ✦ A lunge rope, if needed, for loading, and whip, if needed, for lungeing
- ✦ Grooming kit, including hoof oil and brush
- ✦ Two buckets
- ✦ Two sponges
- ✦ Sweat scraper
- ✦ Tack as required, with spare reins, bit, saddle pad, or gadgets that could be useful
- ✦ Travel rugs and surcingle, leg protectors, two tail bandages and guard, knee pads, etc.
- ✦ First aid equipment including bandages, antiseptic, wound powder, etc.

Above left and left: When leading a horse into a horse trailer, it is advisable to make sure that its legs are protected. A confident, straight approach is best; allow the horse time to see exactly where to place its feet. Unloading should be handled with care, too, and the horse's movements controlled, to make sure that it does not rush down the ramp.

feed hard food while in motion. Offer water periodically. Reward the horse once it is safely inside and secured.

LOADING

For the best control, a horse usually wears a bridle or lunge rein (see page 76) when being loaded. The ramp must be stable, easily accessible, and lie with a minimal slope.

- ✦ Approach the ramp purposefully and straight to give confidence. Any hesitation is soon communicated. Do not drag the horse if it is reluctant.
- ✦ Once inside, attach the breaching strap or close the door, before tying up the horse. Then praise or reward it.
- ✦ If a horse tries to turn around or look behind, its head may be tied on either side. Make sure it is tied short

enough to stop it biting or annoying another horse, but so that it can still reach a haynet and move its weight. Use a quick release knot (see page 59).

- ✦ When transporting a single horse, place it on the right-hand side of the box, as it will travel more smoothly toward the center of the road.

Handy tips for loading

- ✦ To acclimatize young horses to a horse trailer, lead them in and out, and/or, feed them in it occasionally.
- ✦ To give encouragement, load a steady companion first.
- ✦ Place straw bales to form a passage.
- ✦ To persuade an unwilling horse, put straw on the ramp to make it more inviting, or widen a partition in the trailer so it looks easier to enter.

- ✦ Use food as a lure.
- ✦ Pick up and place a foot on the ramp.
- ✦ If a horse refuses to load, attach two lunge lines or ropes on either side of the entrance, held at the free end by two assistants who will cross them behind the horse's hindquarters as it nears the ramp, holding them taut. The horse should respond to the pressure, and load without damage or fear.

UNLOADING

It is always safer to unload a horse forwards down a ramp, if possible. Untie the horse before removing any front bars or opening the door, but make the horse wait until you are ready to lead it steadily and straight down the ramp. Unload the horse nearest to the ramp first.

Conception, Pregnancy & Birth

Things to consider ◆ Timing ◆ Covering ◆ Pregnancy and birth

*I*t is far easier to buy the horse you want than to breed it. Although the science of breeding is now so advanced and well documented that there is an excellent chance of breeding the type of horse desired, luck remains a vital ingredient. It should never be the main ingredient, however, since this will usually result in an unwanted horse, without a job in life. Mares with any hereditary unsoundness or defective conformation should not be used, while a bad temperament is also risky.

Having decided to breed from a mare, owners must plan ahead. They must make sure there is somewhere suitable to keep the mare, under knowledgeable supervision, before and after she foals, and also somewhere to keep both horses after weaning. Costs are a major consideration, allowing for extra veterinary expenses, and it will be at least three years before the offspring can be broken in and ridden. It could be four or five years before the breeder knows if the horse is what they wanted.

CHOOSING A MATE

The owner of the mare must first decide what their aim is, and assess the mare before choosing a stallion. What type of horse do they want to breed? Should it be smaller than the mare, or bigger? Finer boned, or more

Right: Trying a mare with a stallion to establish that she is ready for mating is known as "teasing." The horses should be separated by a solid fence to prevent either of them being injured.

Left: The stallion, as well as the mare, should be checked regularly by a vet for signs of ill health and transmittable diseases. He must be free of parasites and be wormed regularly.

substantial? Wider or narrower? Should it have a flatter or more rounded action? A better shoulder? A shorter back? Stronger bone and feet? A better quality head with larger eyes? Temperament is also important, to achieve a balance of boldness and calm, spirit with kindness. Color may be a consideration, for instance, if dark genes are preferred to pale chestnut or cream. Finally, the pedigrees should be assessed for family history, soundness, and performance. Does the breeder want a jumping horse, a racehorse, a light pulling or carriage driving horse, a dressage horse, a pure-bred show animal or a small child's pony?

WHEN TO BREED

Normally, a filly first comes into season, or "on heat," at two years old, but should be left at least another year before breeding. This period of heat last around six days, and will occur at regular intervals of 18 to 21 days, from early spring until the autumn. The mare will only accept a stallion during her heat. The gestation time is

---

ARTIFICIAL INSEMINATION

◆

Semen can be collected from a stallion with the aid of a suitable mare or by artificial means. It is then stored at a very low temperature. The main benefits of artificial insemination (AI) include disease control, reduced risk of injury to the stallion and the timing, which can be calculated exactly to ensure pregnancy. But strict rules must be enforced to ensure the blood lines are not falsified when AI is used.

about 11 months, and, in the northern hemisphere, most foals are planned to be born after March, when the weather is warming up and nutritious spring grass has arrived. For competition purposes, it is best to foal a mare as early in the spring as possible (see page 40).

When a mare is in season, she is often irritable, swishing her tail and keen to be with other horses. She passes small amounts of urine frequently and the clitoris becomes prominent with signs of mucus. The mare's temperature is a guide to her heat cycle, and an internal examination by a vet will make sure. However, the best way to tell if she is ready to be covered is to try her reactions to a stallion. This is known as "teasing." The mare is introduced to the stallion, with a padded partition between them for safety, and she makes it obvious if she wants to accept him by holding her tail to one side. If not ready, she will repel his advances, and try to kick or bite him.

VISITING A STALLION

Before visiting a stallion, the mare's hind shoes must be removed. She will also need a veterinary examination

Above: Covering a mare, although a natural act, should be supervised by experienced handlers to minimize the risks of injury and, if necessary, to reassure both mare and stallion.

and a "swab" test to establish that she has no infections and is in a healthy condition to be covered and to conceive. Preferably, she should be reasonably fit and not too fat.

The stallion fee must be agreed beforehand, and if the mare is to remain at the stud there will be boarding charges too.

Mating

The mare is likely to be covered by the stallion on more than one day during her heat, to increase the chances of success. She might then remain at the stud until her next heat is due, about 21 days, in case the mating needs to be repeated. If she does not come into season, she is probably in foal. She can be scanned from 45 days after covering, or tested manually after about five months, to make certain. Although her shape should change by this time, it is not always an accurate guide. A foal can be lost without the owner noticing. It can be absorbed in the womb, aborted at an early stage,

Conception, pregnancy & birth

or "slipped" prematurely. If the mare goes full term, preparations must be made for foaling.

Mating is usually supervised by the stallion handler and at least one assistant. The mare is held, and sometimes hobbled, to prevent her from kicking. The stallion mounts the mare, with his forelegs straddling her shoulders, to "cover" her. On average, the process lasts about five minutes. Most stallions need little assistance, but some are shy, or intimidated by aggressive mares, and may need encouragement.

CARE IN PREGNANCY

A mare in foal can be ridden as normal for a few months, without risk, provided that she is fairly fit. Riding should ease off after about 16 weeks.

During the winter, or when grass is scarce, a mare in foal needs extra food if she is to nourish her foal. Hardy

Left: Ultrasound scanning for pregnancy can be carried out any time after day 20. It is then used to monitor the pregnancy. A manual check, possible after six weeks, would be used in unusual cases, such as twins.

breeds, such as mountain and moorland ponies or desert horses, may survive on little sustenance, but more delicate breeds, such as the Thoroughbred, require more feeding and attention. A healthy foal is dependent on a healthy mare. If she looks poor, she may need stabling at night and supplementary feeding, using a special brood mare mixture and perhaps milk powder, as recommended by a vet or nutritionist. Most ponies and self-sufficient breeds can foal outside, unattended, and probably prefer "natural" conditions. However, highly bred mares should have a foaling box prepared for them, and be watched constantly as their foaling time approaches.

The foaling box should be at least 14ft x 14ft (4.3m x 4.3m), and larger for a big mare. A surveillance window will allow someone to watch the mare without disturbing her. Foaling often takes place early in the morning, when all is quiet. The bedding should be deep and clean, on a non-slip floor, and the sides well banked up to minimize the risk of injury during labor, and when the foal first tries to stand.

When she is almost ready to foal, the mare's belly will drop, her udder will swell, and a waxy substance will appear on the teats. She should still be turned out, even for a short while, and can be brought in if signs of labor begin.

BIRTH

During the mare's pregnancy, the embryo foal is curled up in the womb, growing rapidly in the last four months. In the final, tenth, month, the foal turns in the uterus, so that its forefeet and nose will emerge first.

✦ The first contractions occur as the foal moves into position to be born, and the mare's body adapts to allow it to be propelled outward. The mare will become restless, and will probably lie down and get up a few times.

✦ Contractions intensify, recurring at frequent intervals, as the foal passes through the pelvic arch and then the cervix. Some mares foal easily, while others suffer painful contractions, usually caused by an awkwardly positioned foal. If the birth looks like being other than straightforward – a normal foaling should be over in about 20 minutes – the vet should be called.

✦ Just before the foal appears, the water bag will rupture, dispersing fluid from the womb. The mare will then lie down, straining to give birth. She may groan and sweat with the effort.

✦ The forefeet should emerge first, probably wrapped in membrane, which will gradually disperse. If the feet and head are not to the fore, the vet's assistance may be needed.

✦ The nose and head, flattened against the outstretched forelegs, then appear, followed by the shoulder. The rest of the body should follow more easily.

✦ As the membrane breaks over its nose, the foal begins to breathe.

✦ The umbilical cord is usually severed as the foal struggles clear and the mare gets to her feet. It seals itself

Below: The membrane around the foal has broken and its front feet appear, one after the other, followed by its nose. The foal emerges,

its hind legs coming out last. It starts to breathe by itself when the membrane around the nose breaks away, which usually occurs naturally.

The foal finally struggles free – the umbilical cord attaching it to its mother breaks off by itself. The mare whinnies to her new foal.

Once the foal is suckling regularly and bonding with its mother, its prospects for good health are high.

The afterbirth from the womb comes away from the mare within four hours of foaling, and should be removed in a bucket and kept, in case the vet needs to examine it for abnormalities. If the mare retains any of the afterbirth, she may become infected, and the vet must be called. He or she will be needed anyway, since the foal should be injected against tetanus and joint-ill, soon after birth (see pages 95 and 105). Any remains of the membrane around the foal's nostrils should be sponged away. Help will be necessary to hold the mare, which may not want her foal to be touched, and to hold the foal still. To hold the new foal, pass one arm under the neck, round the chest, and the other arm round the hindquarters.

Typical early problems include scouring, when droppings are liquid and the digestion is faulty (see page 93); difficulty with urinating; infection of the navel; or possible rejection by the mother. The foal must be watched carefully for early signs of trouble so that help can be sought as soon as possible if necessary.

Below: The foal tries to stand about 30 minutes after birth. Its long legs are weak and it takes several minutes before is steady enough to stand and suckle its mother.

Above: Bonding between mare and foal is essential and they should be allowed to do this without distraction. After a rest, the mare can be washed with warm water to remove dry fluid and the foal can be checked.

naturally, retaining blood from the placenta for a good start to life.
✦ The mare licks her foal, to dry it and warm it.

THE FIRST HOURS OF LIFE
The foal should stumble to its feet after about 30 minutes, and will be nuzzled by the mare, eventually taking its first drink, the colostrum, which gives it vital nutrients from the mare, as well as providing important natural properties of immunity.

Caring for a Foal

Acclimatization ✦ Leading ✦ Feed ✦ Company ✦ Weaning

A foal handled soon after birth learns to accept contact with humans, and to trust them. This is easier when the foal is born in a stable. A foal born outdoors may be more wary, and its mother, following her instincts, will be protective, making communication difficult.

HANDLING YOUR FOAL

To handle your foal, bring the mare into a large stable, with the foal following. Only start handling once both of them are settled. Bring them in every day, taking care not to frighten the foal, since any setback may take time to overcome. Allow the foal the reassurance of standing close to, or touching, its mother. Once the foal can be caught and held, use a foal "slip," or halter, to bring it in. This must be soft and close fitting.

The foal should be handled consistently every day, until it is used to being touched all over, starting from the shoulder and neck area. It should not be groomed, however, if living out, since grease in the coat is necessary to keep it warm and insulated. Never tie up a young foal, since it may fight to get away, injuring and frightening itself. However rough its behavior – and foals can be extremely strong when wanting to escape – never give way to sharpness and impatience. Foals respond best to quiet, reassuring handling, which gives them confidence. If you leave handling the foal until it is older, the task will be harder, and the foal stronger.

Once it is wearing a halter, and handling quietly, the foal should learn to stand still while held, and to move over when asked. It should be taught, from an early age, to lift up each foot in turn, in preparation for having the feet picked out, and later, when the farrier starts to trim its feet.

LEADING YOUR FOAL

To teach a foal to lead, a slip rein looped through the halter is safer than a fixed lead rope. Strong arms, one held around the front, the other

Right: This foal is being taught to lead by the handler enveloping its length between the her arms for maximum control while persuading the youngster to move forward.

Below: A stable rubber or similar material is looped around the neck – not the throat – so that no damage is done if the foal struggles to escape.

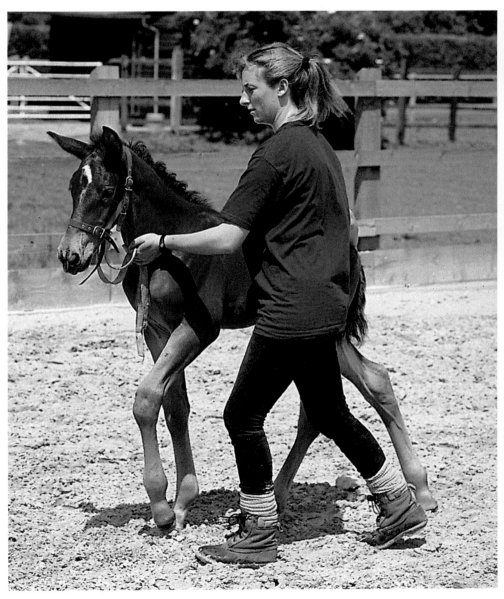

passing behind, or stable rubbers, similarly positioned, can be more effective and safer than a halter and rein. When first teaching the foal to lead, choose an enclosed space so that if the foal escapes it is easily caught. Lead it beside its mother, until it is confident and does not pull back or rush forwards. When it seems ready, progress to leading it, with an experienced assistant, if possible, behind the mare, and then in front. This prepares it to be led on its own later on.

To lead the foal securely, when using a foal slip and rein, the rein should be held close behind its chin, with the slack folded in the other hand. Do not wrap it around your hand as this may trap your fingers if the foal takes off. Stay level with the foal's shoulder, to keep better control.

If the mare and foal have a routine for feeding, handling, including picking out the feet, and being turned out, the handling will become habitual, and the farrier should have no trouble when he starts to trim the foal's feet at about 12 weeks of age.

FEEDING

Initially, the mother will suckle the foal, but it will eat grass as soon as it can chew it. Usually all both need is good grazing into autumn, and the foal will continue to suckle until it is weaned. Tough, resilient breeds do not need hard food, unless the weather is cold and wet and either mare or foal is losing condition. As soon as the

---

Ken ... went down the path twenty yards or so — an easy halt turn — and back again, with Flicka following so close the lead rope was slack.

MARY O'HARA, MY FRIEND FLICKA, 1941

---

grazing is no longer nutritious, feed soft, easy-to-digest hay and hard food where necessary. Both mare and foal need to go into winter in good condition, in order to keep warm and healthy. For finer types, if the mare is being fed concentrates, the foal will start sharing her feed from about two months old. This must be introduced gradually and carefully, with an easily digestible diet. Signs of constipation or scouring (see page 93) must be noticed, and the food adjusted; take expert advice if in doubt. Additives that aid development, such as bone meal and cod-liver oil, may be of benefit. Foals and their dams must be wormed regularly.

WEANING

Weaning can be traumatic, for the mare, its foal, and the owner. Weaning several foals together is less stressful for all concerned because the foals enjoy each other's company.

To wean your foal, separate it from its mother at six to eight months, when it is fairly independent and can feed itself (you can delay if it is more

convenient). They must be separated for at least a month, without being able to see or hear each other. It is usually best to take the mares away, rather than the foals, as they can be led into a horse trailer more easily, and are less likely to damage themselves. You can keep two foals in a large, deeply bedded stable and several foals in a cattle pen or similar, safe area. Sensible foals can remain in their field, which is less stressful and often safer. In a herd, a mare will wean a foal herself a year after its birth.

An alternative method of weaning foals in a field together is to remove one mare every few days, so that the foals gradually form new friendships. It is better for both mare and foal if they have food and companionship.

After weaning, foals often lose condition and need careful feeding. Continue handling with firmness and kindness, to ensure that it is easy to educate young stock later on.

Colt foals may be gelded before weaning so that they are quieter to handle, or may be left until they are more mature, depending on circumstances. The operation cannot be performed until both testicles have dropped into view. If it is decided to keep a colt foal "entire," make arrangements to keep him separate from sexually mature females after weaning As colts develop and mature, they require experienced handling.

Below: The foal soon learns to be led if well handled and allowed to walk close to its mother so that it feels secure and relaxed.

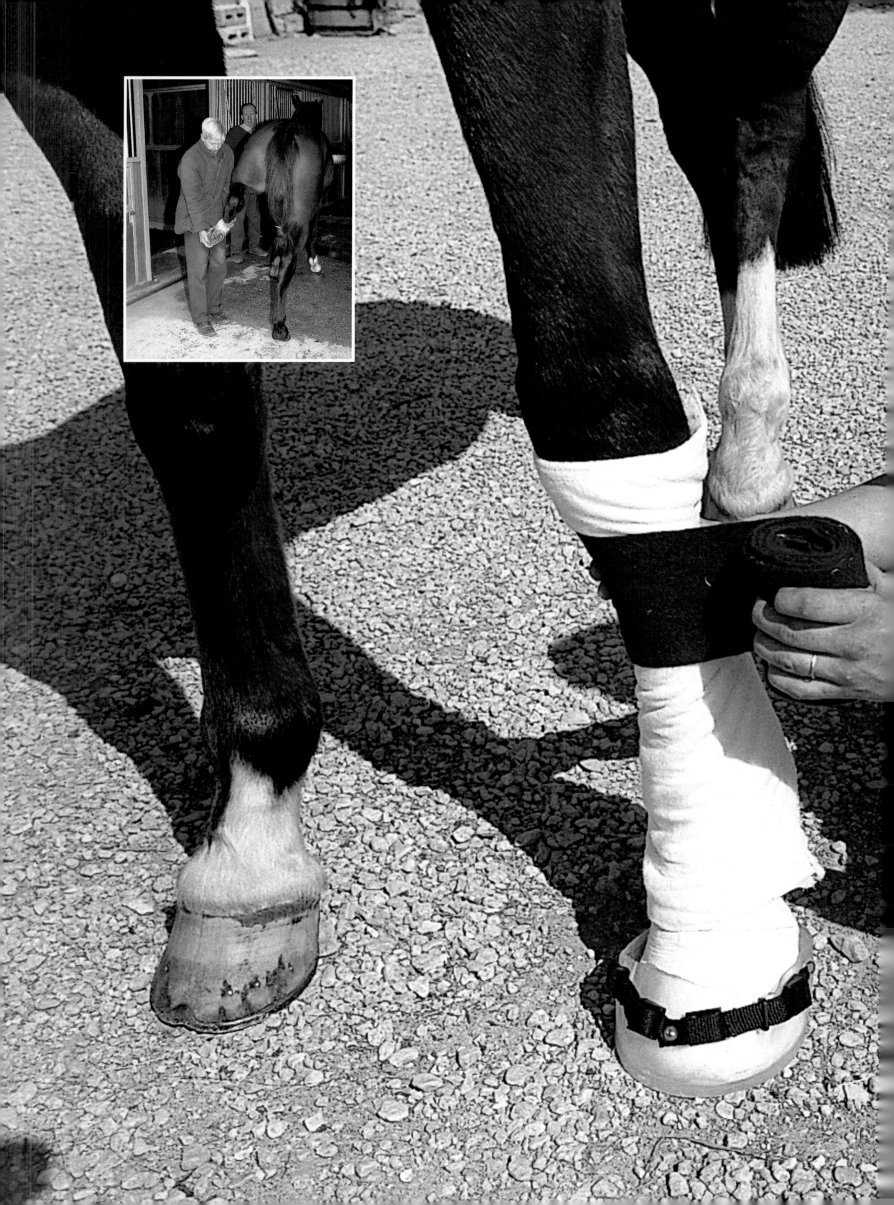

PART 3

YOUR HORSE'S HEALTH

Most horse and pony owners wish that they could spend more time with their animals. The more time that is spent together the more valuable it is for them both, and it will mean that the owner gets to know their horse really well. Time spent leaning over a gate or stable door simply looking is never misspent. No two animals are the same. The response to pain, fear, temperature, and other stimuli are all different, and subtle changes can be missed by an unobservant owner. Some horses tolerate pain more easily than others; some are naturally phlegmatic and quiet. If such an animal becomes frightened or seems to be in pain or upset, then more importance may be attached to the symptoms than if the patient is a flighty Thoroughbred. If in doubt, call your vet.

Health & Disease

Mismanagement ✦ Preventing problems ✦ When to call the vet

Many of the diseases and ailments that afflict horses and ponies are the result of domestication. Naturally designed to live in herds, eat small amounts of grass, and to keep moving, the domesticated life is a not a natural one and human error or ignorance can cause many health and behavioral problems.

For example, as sociable, roaming, herd creatures, horses do not respond well to long, lonely hours in a stable or loose box. Many problems such as crib biting, wind sucking, weaving, (see page 111), or even constipation and colic (see pages 90–2), which are often a result of a horse eating its bedding, can be a direct result of boredom, loneliness, and frustration.

Mismanagement can also cause laminitis, a painful foot disorder (see page 103), if owners allow an animal to become too fat and fail to give it enough exercise. This is a particularly common problem in the spring among ponies if owners allow them to eat too much succulent grass. Laminitis causes severe pain and distress and, if the suffering cannot be alleviated by treatment, will all too often signal the end of a useful working life and sometimes even death.

Chronic Obstructive Pulmonary Disease (COPD, see pages 95–6), an allergic condition similar to asthma in people, is often brought on by poorly ventilated stables and loose boxes – a problem found even in many of the most modern design. Contrary to common belief, a half-open stable door will not supply a horse with sufficient fresh air. In recent years there has been a huge increase in COPD caused by sensitivity to hay spores. Dust and pollen can also be implicated. Dusty, poorly ventilated stables make the condition much worse and are probably the cause of the condition in the first place. Horses and ponies in the wild

Above: Horses and ponies are herd animals and are much happier when they are kept together in a group.

Below: The most common cause of laminitis in ponies is obesity brought about by overfeeding and lack of exercise.

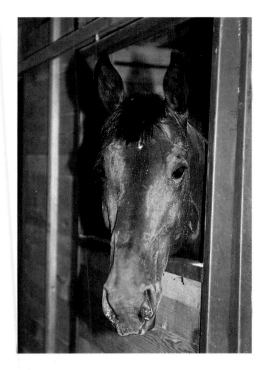

never get this condition and the best and cheapest preventative treatment for animals with COPD is fresh air.

PREVENTING PROBLEMS

Many of the uses to which we put our horses place heavy strains and stresses on their joints, tendon, and ligaments. As a result, lameness is very common and, indeed, many vets spend their entire working lives diagnosing and treating its causes. Unfortunately, there is no vaccine against lameness, so all that can be done is to make sure that we breed from genetically sound animals and never put a horse or pony to a use to which it is not suited.

However, there are very good vaccines against many diseases, although the equine-owning public does not yet make full use of them. Only about 20 to 30 per cent of horses and ponies in the UK are vaccinated against equine influenza (see page 94) and it is positively criminal not to vaccinate against tetanus (see page 95). Clostridial spores are thick on the ground wherever horses graze and tetanus still has a very poor survival rate once clinical symptoms appear, despite the modern drugs available. Vaccinating an animal after it has

Right: A healthy horse will usually run when turned loose and will instinctively flee from any perceived danger.

Left: This horse's respiratory condition is not helped by poor ventilation – a half-open door will not ventilate a stable properly.

been injured is not sufficient. In many cases, tetanus occurs when there is no visible wound. Horses and ponies have given the human race so much that they deserve the best possible care and attention.

KNOW YOUR HORSE

The most important skill a person must develop when looking after any animal is the art of observation. Many good horse people seem to have this skill from an early age, but, even if you are not one of them, there is still no reason why, with application and determination, you should not learn. A vet attending a sick horse needs as accurate a history as an owner or attendant can give. Poor or unhelpful information can delay diagnosis and, on occasion, may lead to fatal results.

Get to know your horse and learn how to recognize what is normal behavior and what is not. Time spent quietly watching is not wasted, for, until you know what is normal, you will never reliably be able to see the abnormal. Be systematic in your learning and write down your observations. Do not simply rely on instinct. Start at the head and work your way along, making a point of noting any little detail that you think might be wrong. Buy a veterinary thermometer and learn how to use it.

SYMPTOM CHECKLIST
◆

This checklist will give an idea of what to consider when assessing the health of your horse. For normal temperature, respiration, and heart rates, see page 57. If you are in any doubt, call the vet.

Discharge: Where from? Eyes? Ears? Nose? Anal? Vaginal? Is it purulent, clear or bloody?

Ears: Are the ears swollen? Drooping? Is there a discharge?

Mouth: Is your horse salivating? Does it drop its food?

Eating and drinking: Is your horse eating and drinking? How much? Too little or too much?

Coughing: Is the cough dry, harsh or soft? Is it productive?

Breathing: Is it fast or slow?

Diarrhea: Is it watery or bloody? Is there mucus?

Constipation: How long has your horse been constipated?

Urine retention: Is the urine dark, bloody or purulent?

Skin hair loss: Does the skin itch? Are there any sores? Where?

Lameness: Which leg?

Temperature Is it high or low?

Weight: Is your horse over or underweight?

Swellings: Any unexplained lumps or bumps? Where?

Digestive Disorders

Mouth care ✦ *Choke* ✦ *Abdominal pain* ✦ *Grass sickness* ✦ *Diarrhea*

The digestive tract of the horse has evolved over millions of years, enabling it to eat, grow, and thrive on a completely vegetation-based diet. With a mouth and teeth designed to grasp food and grind it to a pulp that is easy to swallow, any oral abnormalities can upset this vital process and cause digestive upsets.

MOUTH PROBLEMS

Congenital abnormalities, such as overshot jaws or the absence of cheek teeth, can make grasping food difficult. This may result in the horse bolting partially chewed food or having difficulties in taking food in, both of which will cause loss of condition. Sharp points and hooks can also develop in the molar teeth and cause discomfort. To try to avoid these problems it is important that horses and ponies should have their teeth checked at least once a year and the sharp edges rasped flat as necessary. Problems with the wolf teeth (vestigial premolar teeth on the side of the jaw, see page 25), can also cause digestive disorders, but more usually result in the horse mouthing the bit while it is being ridden. Wolf teeth can be removed if necessary.

Dental disease is not very common in horses but tooth abscesses can occur. In these instances, the offending molar will have to be removed.

Signs of mouth problems include salivation, difficulty in chewing and swallowing, and food being dropped from the corner of the mouth. A vet must be called if any such difficulties are observed.

CHOKE

Choke is the impaction of the gullet or esophagus – the tube that conveys food to the stomach. Although it is quite common and can be treated, it is very alarming to see food and saliva pouring out of your horse's nostrils as it stands with its head and neck extended. Choke is almost always caused by food material, such as beet pulp, that has not been soaked properly (see page 61). The condition always looks worse than it is but a vet must be called. It is usually treated with sedatives and muscle-relaxant drugs. Occasionally, this does not work and the food blocking the esophagus may have to be siphoned off with a stomach tube, which can be a slow and laborious process.

ABDOMINAL PAIN (COLIC)

Colic, the condition most feared by horse owners, is not a diagnosis but a symptom and is simply another term

Left: Parrot mouth, or an overshot jaw, is a congenital defect. Animals with such a defect will require extra care and attention, since they are less likely to process their fodder well, which, in turn, may make them prone to suffer from digestive disorders.

for abdominal pain. There are several types of colic and symptoms will vary depending on the degree of pain. Mild to moderate sweating and general unease may progress into great distress, with the animal kicking at its belly or constantly getting up and down and rolling in pain. As well as the types listed below, colic may also occur if there is a blockage in the urinary tract due to urinary calculi. However, this is not a common condition and is more likely to affect stallions and geldings than mares.

Spasmodic colic

Spasmodic colic is the result of the muscle wall of the intestine going into spasm, a condition that may be caused by migrating worm larvae (see page 98). It is usually treated with muscle-relaxant drugs and larvicidal doses of anthelmintic.

Impactive colic

Impactive colic is caused by constipation, usually brought on by eating unsuitable feed, such as straw bedding. The pain may not be as severe as for spasmodic colic but it can be more protracted. Large doses of liquid paraffin and salt water are usually given by stomach tube, as well as an intravenous pain-killing injection. Constipation can be prevented by feeding a suitable diet (see pages 60–1).

Above: Tooth rasping is often required once or twice a year to ensure good digestion. Dropping food or excessive salivation are evidence of dental problems. While rasping, the vet will use a mouth gag, shown above, to prevent the horse from biting down.

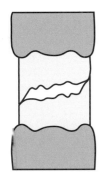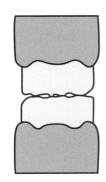

Above: These pictures show a horse's teeth before (left) and after rasping (right). The rasp removes the sharp edges on the outer edges of the top molars and on the inner edge of the lower molars. These are caused by grinding food unevenly with the teeth.

Right: A common symptom of abdominal pain, or colic, is the horse falling to the floor and rolling. A vet must always be called.

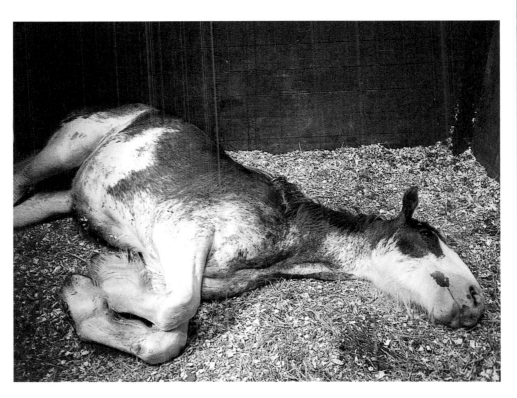

Digestive disorders

Gaseous colic

Gaseous colic, caused by excess gas in the intestine, is usually the result of eating feed such as lawn cuttings or fruit that can ferment in the bowel. If fermentation does occur, it produces a gas that distends the stomach and the intestines, causing great pain. Gaseous colic is treated with pain-killing injections and by passing a tube down the esophagus to allow the gas to escape from the stomach.

Intestinal catastrophe

Intestinal catastrophe is the most severe type of colic and may follow on from one of the others. The most common cause is a twisted gut, which causes very great pain and without surgical intervention will prove fatal. Some cases can be saved if they are referred quickly enough to a vet with an equine operating facility. But sadly, many horses, once diagnosed, have to be put down.

What to do

All colic is potentially very serious and requires veterinary attention as soon as possible. Until the vet arrives, try to keep the horse on its feet. If the symptoms seem to disappear with gentle walking exercise, do not allow the horse to eat before the vet arrives.

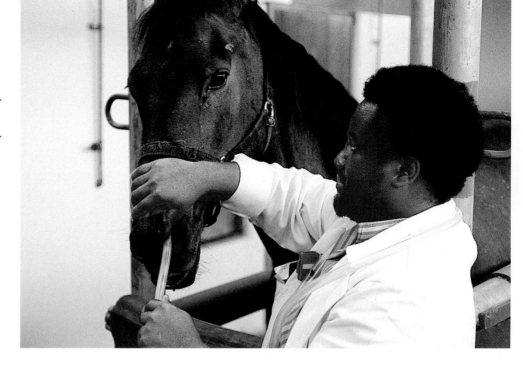

GRASS SICKNESS

Grass sickness is usually a summer condition that affects animals over two out at pasture in certain climatic conditions. It is found most notably in Scotland, northern England and Sweden. Its cause is not proven, but experts consider it to be a neurotoxic agent that damages the nerves controlling the intestines and the stomach, resulting in the cessation of all normal bowel and stomach activity.

The clinical signs of grass sickness vary enormously, which can make reaching a diagnosis very difficult. There are four different forms and symptoms will vary depending on

Above: When a horse has colic, the vet often passes a tube through its nose into its stomach, either to remove gas or as an effective way of giving medication.

whether the illness is in the peracute, acute, subacute or chronic form. A horse can get any form of the disease.

In the peracute form, the animal is usually dead within 24 hours. In the acute form, death may occur within two days due to the stomach filling up with fluid to the point of rupture. Green stomach contents will come down the nostrils and saliva will pour from the mouth. Colic may be severe.

Subacute cases usually die within a few of weeks of the first symptoms, while chronic cases can linger for months. Clinical signs are not specific and can include weight loss, patchy sweating, intermittent colic, and a tendency to be dull or wander restlessly. Attempts to eat and drink are often followed by regurgitation and colic. Constipation may occur. The horse will soon look very emaciated and die through debility and exhaustion. There is no specific treatment, but improved nursing techniques mean that the survival rate for chronic cases can be as high as about 40 per cent.

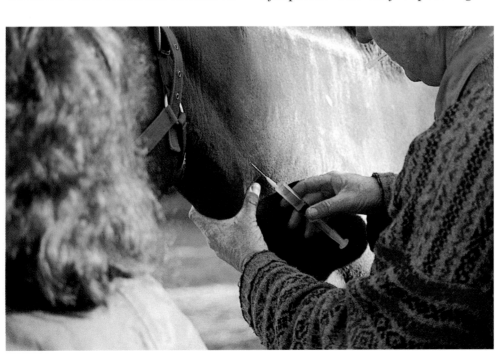

Left: An intravenous injection of a pain-killing drug, usually given in the neck, is often used to treat colic.

DIARRHEA

Diarrhea is not a disease but a symptom of various diseases. It can be the result of diet – lush spring grass, for example – which is normal; or more problematically the result of bacterial, viral or parasitic infection, singly or in combination. All three cause enteritis, or inflammation of the intestine, resulting in diarrhea.

Bacterial infections

Salmonella bacteria, of which there are many types, cause the severest infections and can result in septicemia, dehydration, and death, especially in young horses. Take great care if your horse is infected, since it can also affect humans.

Escheria coli cause severe diarrhea in young animals. It is treated with antibiotics, fluid therapy, intestinal absorbents, and good nursing and aftercare are needed.

Clostridial infection, although less common than salmonella, is as severe and may cause death through shock

and dehydration. Chronic cases may relate to inflammation of the lining of the colon.

Viral infections

Young animals are especially prone to viral infections and a secondary bacterial infection may make the initial enteritis more severe. Vitamins and fluids, by mouth or injection, may be all that is required but antibiotics may be used for secondary infection.

Parasitic infection

Parasitic infection (see pages 98–101) is a very common cause of diarrhea. In adult horses, *Trichonema* or *Cyathostiminae* larvae coming through the bowel wall, sometimes complicated by migrating *Strongylus vulgaris* larvae, can cause severe diarrhea. If not successfully treated, this can become a long-term condition. A vet will administer doses of larvicidal anthelmintic.

In foals, *Strongyloides westeri* causes diarrhea and can be confused with a foal heat

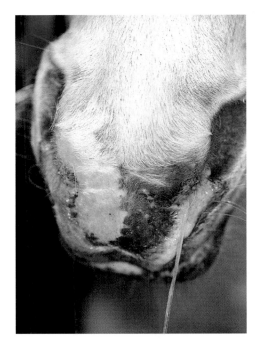

Above: If green matter pours from your horse's nostrils when it is out at grass, you should call the vet immediately. It may be a symptom of choke, but may also be an early indication that your horse is suffering from grass sickness, which can be very serious.

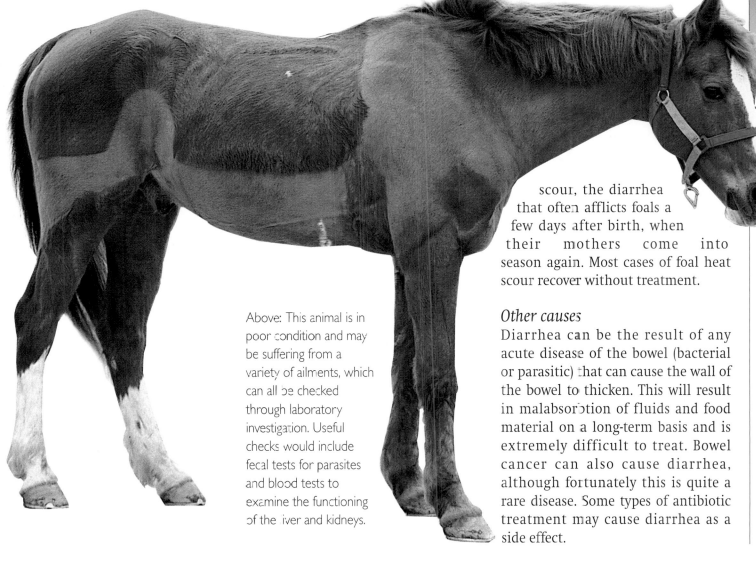

Above: This animal is in poor condition and may be suffering from a variety of ailments, which can all be checked through laboratory investigation. Useful checks would include fecal tests for parasites and blood tests to examine the functioning of the liver and kidneys.

scour, the diarrhea that often afflicts foals a few days after birth, when their mothers come into season again. Most cases of foal heat scour recover without treatment.

Other causes

Diarrhea can be the result of any acute disease of the bowel (bacterial or parasitic) that can cause the wall of the bowel to thicken. This will result in malabsorption of fluids and food material on a long-term basis and is extremely difficult to treat. Bowel cancer can also cause diarrhea, although fortunately this is quite a rare disease. Some types of antibiotic treatment may cause diarrhea as a side effect.

Coughs, Colds & Breathing Difficulties

Bacterial disease ✦ *Viral infection* ✦ *COPD* ✦ *Endoparasites* ✦ *Other causes*

Many coughs and colds are the result of infection, either bacterial or viral, or sometimes both. Occasionally, endoparasites, such as lung worm, can be a causal agent, but this is more rare. The most common cause of a cough or respiratory distress in horses is Chronic Obstructive Pulmonary Disease (COPD), the equine form of asthma.

BACTERIAL INFECTION

The most common form of bacterial infection of the upper respiratory tract is strangles, a disease caused by *Streptococcus equi*. Strangles usually affects younger animals, especially those up to five years old, and is still much feared by the horse-owning public. Clinical indications of infection are a moderate-to-high temperature, a lack of interest in food, and severe depression. A purulent nasal discharge becomes apparent as the disease progresses, and the neck glands become swollen and sore. The horse will have a soft, persistent cough and may have difficulty in swallowing.

The next stage is for the glands in the neck to become abscessed – but once these have burst or been lanced the horse will feel better.

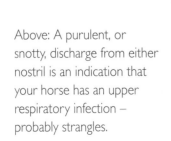

Above: A purulent, or snotty, discharge from either nostril is an indication that your horse has an upper respiratory infection – probably strangles.

Penicillin is still the best antibiotic to treat the infection, although many vets will not prescribe it until the abscesses have ruptured.

Secondary complications can occur, such as internal abscesses, *purpura haemorrhagica* or laryngeal paralysis. This will cause "roaring," a noise that horses make when the airways are partially obstructed. Severe obstruction will cause respiratory difficulties and the animal will need an operation in order to breathe properly.

Strangles is a highly infectious disease for which no vaccine is currently available. Control is based on strict isolation and good disinfection of stables, tack and other equipment.

Streptococcus zooepidemicus is a similar but less vicious infection.

VIRAL INFECTIONS

Equine influenza (flu) is the most common viral infection to affect the respiratory tract. Caused by a myxovirus and highly contagious, it has many strains and, like strangles, usually affects the younger horse. Equine flu comes on suddenly, with a high temperature, a harsh, unproductive cough and, usually, a clear nasal discharge. The horse will be depressed and may suffer from muscle stiffness.

There is no specific treatment for equine flu, but antibiotics are often given to avoid secondary bacterial infection. Non-steroidal, anti-inflammatory drugs may help to reduce a high temperature and mucolytic and bronchodilator drugs

will help to alleviate a severe cough.
Good nursing and the cessation of all
work is important to aid a rapid recovery. Isolation may limit the spread of
the disease.

Vaccination against equine flu is
very effective and highly recommended. Two initial injections are given six
weeks apart followed by another one
six months later. Yearly boosters are
then all that is required. These injections are combined in the same
syringe with the tetanus vaccine (see
page 110).

Equine herpes infection

The equine herpes virus (EHV) exists
in different strains worldwide. EHV1,
EHV2, and EHV4 occur in the UK.
EHV4 is the least dangerous and
causes only a respiratory infection.
The symptoms are not usually as
severe as for flu – the horse will have
a temperature and be dull and off its
food, but the cough will be productive
and not as harsh. There may be a
nasal discharge – clear at first, but
thick and discolored, or muco-
purulent, later.

EHV1 is the most dangerous strain
and can cause abortion, respiratory
infection and, on occasion, hind leg
paralysis and recumbency, which is
often fatal. Treatment is non-specific
and is similar to that for flu. However,
there is now an effective vaccine. Two
injections given four to six weeks
apart are then followed by six-
monthly boosters. It is especially
important to vaccinate brood mares.

Above: This horse has been placed in an
isolation box because it has equine influenza,
which is a highly infectious respiratory
disease. The patient must be isolated for
seven to ten days until it is no longer
infectious to other horses.

Below: Edema is an excessive accumulation
of fluid. This condition is usually the result of
an infection that has damaged either the
lymphatic drainage system or the blood
vessels. This damage allows fluid to escape
and accumulate in the tissues.

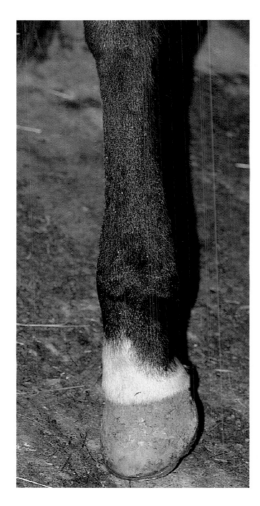

Equine viral arteritis

Equine viral arteritis is an infection
that is relatively unknown in the UK
and is the result of infection by a
virus from the arterivirus group. It
can be spread both by the respiratory
tract (coughs and sneezes) and by
venereal contact. The horse will be
depressed, off its food, and have a
high temperature. There will also be a
discharge from the eyes and nostrils
and breathing will be more rapid
than usual. Fluid swellings will be
present in the legs and along the ventral abdomen and, if pregnant, a
mare will abort within a few days.
There is no specific treatment. Antibiotics will be given to control
secondary infection and diuretic
drugs to reduce edema, or swelling, in
the legs. Control of the disease is
based on isolation and hygiene and
blood tests to identify carriers. A vaccine is now available.

CHRONIC OBSTRUCTIVE PULMONARY DISEASE

Chronic Obstructive Pulmonary Disease (COPD) is the equine equivalent
of asthma and is caused by an allergic
reaction to fungal spores in hay and
straw. The condition is made worse by
dusty, poorly ventilated stables. In a
mild form, the warning signals are an
occasional, dry, hacking cough, which
will usually be heard after light exercise or when the animal is feeding,
and in some cases, a persistent, thin,
gray, nasal discharge. The animal
could at any time develop severe

Coughs, colds & breathing difficulties

respiratory distress, a condition that used to be known as "heaves.".

Diagnosis is usually straightforward but is occasionally made more difficult by secondary bacterial infection. The use of a flexible endoscope is useful to confirm diagnosis.

Treatment of COPD in its more mild, chronic form usually takes the form of bronchodilatory drugs to open the airways and mucolytic drugs to aid the passage of the thick mucus that may be blocking the smaller bronchi. A horse with acute breathing distress will need intravenous injections of the bronchodilatory drug or a steroid anti-inflammatory injection. Any secondary bacterial infection will also require antibiotic treatment.

Prevention of the disease is all-important. Fresh air is essential. For the most severely affected horses, the only remedy in the winter months is to turn them out covered with a New Zealand rug and allow them access to a field shelter only. This will protect them from the most severe weather but will still allow a free passage of air. If this is not possible and the animal has to be stabled, you should keep it on a shavings, peat or paper bed in order to ensure a dust-free environment. All animals within the same air space must be treated in the same manner. All dust and cobwebs must be removed from the stable, either by power washing or an industrial hoover. The ventilation within the stable must also be looked at critically and improvements made. This can often be done quite easily.

Hay, if used, must be completely immersed in water for 30 minutes and then drained before feeding. Keep an eye on the timing because if hay is soaked too long it will lose much of its nutritional value and be unpalatable. An alternative to using hay is to feed commercially available fiber diets, such as haylage or alfafa.

Once the acute symptoms of COPD have been relieved, sodium cromoglycate is administered to many horses using a nebulizer and face mask. This drug can be very useful in preventing a reoccurrence of symptoms if the animal is again exposed to dust and hay spores.

Summer pasture COPD

This disease is very similar to normal COPD but is caused by an allergic reaction to pollen of certain crop plants, such as oil seed rape and lin-

Left: This haynet is ready to be completely immersed in a tub of water for 30 minutes. After immersion, it should drip dry before it is fed to the horse. Water should be always be fresh and clean for every net of hay.

Below: If a haynet is suspended at or above head-height, dust and pollen often falls directly into your horse's nostrils. Feeding from the floor helps to avoid this problem.

seed. It often affects animals that are already sensitive to fungal spores. It may be necessary to house the animal in a clean environment to keep it away from the source of the pollen. Treatment is along similar lines to that for COPD, but antihistamines and steroid anti-inflammatory drugs may be more useful in some cases.

PARASITE INFESTATION

Internal parasites can affect the respiratory apparatus of horses and ponies. Treatment is usually straightforward, but it is much better to worm your horse regularly and avoid infection in the first place (see page 99). A regular dose of wormer is a small price to pay to keep your horse cough-free.

lungs become filled with fluid. This is a serious condition and can be life threatening.

Glanders disease, a severe respiratory infection caused by *Actinobacillus mallei*, was once the scourge of the equine world. It stills exists and is universally distributed. In its most acute form, it can kill an animal very quickly. Antibiotics may be effective if given early.

African horse sickness is caused by an arbovirus and is spread by biting insects. It is quite widespread in southern and western Africa, Pakistan, and India and has been seen in Morocco and Portugal – a result of transporting animals by air. African horse sickness can cause death with extreme respiratory distress within four to six hours of the onset of the first symptoms.

Below: A Cromovet inhaler can be used in treatment of COPD for animals that cannot be turned out because they are too old and frail or are suffering from other infections.

Lung worm

Lung worm, *Dictyocaulis arnfieldi*, affects both horses and donkeys. In donkeys it is very common and causes little trouble. However, it gives horses and ponies a persistent dry cough, sometimes with an increased respiratory rate. Treatment is simple. Fenbendazole at twice the normal dose is effective, as is Ivermectin at the standard dose.

Round worm

In foals, large round worm (*Parascaris equorum*) can cause a mild cough and nasal discharge if it migrates from the stomach into the windpipe. However, most modern anthelmintic drugs are an effective treatment. To prevent infection, the foaling stable must be disinfected before use and regularly cleaned thereafter, and the mare should be dewormed before entering the stall. After foaling, the mare and foal should be turned out to clean pasture, which has not been grazed by youngsters the previous year. Thereafter, the foal must be dewormed every six to eight weeks starting at three to four weeks of age.

OTHER DISORDERS

Bronchopneumonia can affect any equine as a secondary disease after initial primary infection by a virus, bacteria or parasite, or after food has been sucked into the air passages.

Chronic heart failure may also cause coughing and respiratory distress in the older animal because its

Internal Parasites

Nematodes ✦ *Cestodes* ✦ *Trematodes* ✦ *Worming regime* ✦ *Other worms*

Left: This is a typical wormy animal. It looks thin, is in poor condition and has a pot belly and a staring coat.

Below: Helminths, the largest group of parasitic worms, include nematodes, cestodes, and trematodes. Nematodes have a simple life cycle; cestodes have an indirect cycle that needs two hosts; trematodes have the most complex cycle, with an intermediary snail host.

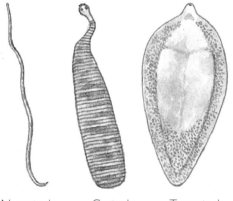

Nematode Cestode Trematode

All grazing animals will harbor parasites of one sort or another. In the horse, parasitic worms probably evolved at the same time and at the same rate as the animal itself did. There are many different types of endoparasite, or worm. Some are very similar but others vary radically in terms of appearance and life cycle. Most endoparasites belong in one of three different categories: roundworms (nematodes); tapeworms (cestodes); and flukes (trematodes).

SYMPTOMS OF INFESTATION

Clinical signs of worm infestation vary according to the type of parasite and its location in the body. Poor condition is the most common sign of a horse being overburdened with parasites. It will lose weight, may lose its appetite, and will generally look unhealthy, with a dull coat. Youngsters – which are particularly prone to suffer from large roundworm – will be anemic and may have a pot belly and staring coat, a condition in which the hair stands on end rather than lying flat (see page 99).

NEMATODES

Nematodes are large, round, unsegmented worms found in the intestines. Animals are infected when they graze on contaminated pasture. Nematodes take several weeks to develop, burrow into the intestinal wall and then migrate to other areas of the body, where they cause varying degrees of damage. Egg counts done on fecal samples in summer may show alarming numbers of nematode eggs even in recently dewormed animals. In the winter, however, counts will be low even in heavily parasitized animals. Blood tests for immunoglobulins give a better assessment of potential problems when taken in the winter.

Redworm

In the horse, the largest and most important group of nematode is *Strongyles*, or redworms. These vary in size from the large *Strongylus vulgaris* to the small *Trichonema* spp. From the intestinal wall, the larvae travel toward the large intestine, where they continue to develop. As adults, they feed on the lining of the large gut, where they damage areas of tissue and blood vessels. Spasmodic colic may be the result of immature strongyle larvae in the blood vessels of the gut blocking the free flow of blood to the bowel and causing it to go into spasm (see page 91). Diarrhea, particularly if it develops rapidly, can also be associated with the sudden emergence of small strongyle larvae through the lining of the large intestine (see page 93). This can cause severe weight loss and the legs to swell with fluid, a condition

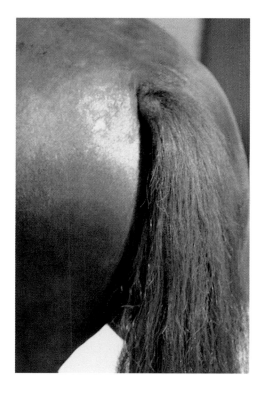

Left: Pinworm can cause large areas of irritation around the horse's hindquarters. If these areas are left untreated, the animal is likely to rub itself against hard surfaces in order to relieve the itching, thus causing painful sores to develop.

called edema (see page 95). Without rapid and effective treatment, the prognosis for redworm can be poor.

Pinworm

Pinworm (*Oxyuris equi*) are roundworms that occur in the large intestine of the horse. They are most commonly found in younger animals. The female worm crawls out of the anus of the horse and lays sticky worm eggs on the skin under the tail. This causes intense irritation around the base of the tail, and not only will the animal lose hair from its tail, it may also develop sores around the anal area. The worm is killed by most modern worming preparations and the prevention program for strongyles should be effective in controlling the parasite.

Large roundworm

The large roundworm (*Parascaris equorum*) is white and can be up to 19½in (50cm) long. Taken in from pasture, its eggs hatch in the horse's intestine, pass through the intestinal wall into the liver and then migrate into the lungs from which they are coughed up and then swallowed again. This worm usually affects only foals, causing mild symptoms (see page 97). However, on very rare occasions, worms have been known to block the intestine completely, resulting in peritonitis and death.

Threadworm

Threadworm (*Strongyloides westeri*) is a very small fine worm that is mostly found in foals and causes diarrhea. It is transmitted as larvae via the mare's milk, usually in the first few days of life. If stable conditions are wet, dirty, and warm, the foal will often become reinfected within ten days of the original infection. This usually occurs through the skin. Threadworm infection is sometimes confused with foal heat scour (see page 93). If severe, the diarrhea may be very watery and contain blood.

Threadworm is treated with standard doses of modern deworming drugs, which may have to be administered when the foal is only a few days old. Bedding in the foaling box should be as clean and dry as possible to stop reinfection, and mares should be dewormed with Ivermectin before they foal to reduce the number of larvae passed in the milk.

DE-WORMING PROGRAM

◆

De-worming is an essential part of horse care. The program below is an example of one approach to administering treatment. In this program, de-wormers are rotated over a three-year cycle, between April and August. The drugs are admistered every six to eight weeks.

September: Double dose of Pyrantel embonate, the only drug effective against tapeworm.

October–late November: Larvicidal doses of Fenbendazole (ie double normal dose, usually in the form of Panacur Guard), the only effective drug for immature and encysted strongyle larvae.

December: Panomec or Eqvalan, Diclorvos (Astrobot) or Haloxan (Equilox), against stomach bots.

February: As for October/November

March: As for September

Year 1: Use Benzimidazole drug (eg Panacur, Telmin or Systamex) between April and August.

Year 2: Use Pyrantel embonate at normal drug rates between April and August.

Year 3: Use Panomec or Eqvalan between April and August.

Internal parasites

Lungworm

Lungworm (*Dictyocaulis arnfieldi*) is a common parasite in donkeys where it does little harm. Although relatively rare in horses and ponies, it causes a chronic cough and, on occasion, an enhanced respiratory rate. The parasite lives in the lungs and diagnosis is difficult even with endoscopic examination. Diagnosis is often made after treating the affected animal with Fenbendazole (Panacur) or Ivermectin (Panomec or Eqvalan). If the cough resolves with treatment, then the problem was almost certainly parasitic. Treat all the animals in the paddock regardless of whether they are coughing or not, since this will limit transmission of the parasite. Do not graze horses and ponies with donkeys, or even in an adjacent field, since lungworm can transfer over quite a distance and survive for several months in moist conditions.

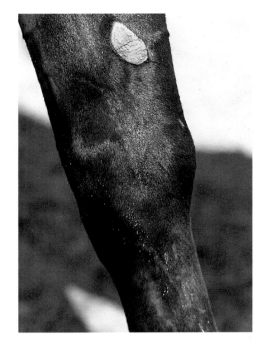

Above: Botfly eggs are laid in late summer and autumn in temperate climates. When the larvae hatch, they migrate through the tissues and can spend up to nine months inside the horse.

Below: Horses and sheep graze together to the benefit of both species. Mixed grazing helps to reduce parasite burdens.

Filarial worms

This worm (*Onchocera cervicalis*) infects the skin especially in the neck and very occasionally in the tendons on the front legs. The larvae can cause skin lesions and swellings in the leg but this is rare. Ivermectin will destroy the microfilaria in the skin.

CESTODES

Cestode, or tapeworm, infection is common. Opinion differs as to whether it is a major health hazard. There is a suggestion that it might lead to an increased risk of colic since tapeworms are commonly found at the junction in the bowel between the small and large intestine when horses have emergency colic surgery (see page 90).

The tapeworm cyst, the infective part of the worm that develops in the egg, is passed out in the animal's droppings, infects the pasture and is consumed by the harvest mite, which survives on spring and summer pastures. In winter, this mite lives in hay and bedding, and so horses can be

Right: Removing dung from a pasture is not only imperative for parasite control but also helps to keep more grazing available for the horse. Motorized field vacuums are also available for removing dung if the pasture is too extensive for it to be collected manually.

exposed to tapeworm infection all year round. Deworming horses every six months (September and March) is, therefore, essential. The only effective drug against tapeworm is Pyrantel embonate (Strongid P or Pyratape P), which must be given at double the normal worming dose.

TREMATODES

Trematodes are parasitic, unsegmented flatworms with adhesive suckers. Commonly called liver flukes (*Fasciola hepatica*), they are carried by snails. Animals are affected by drinking contaminated water or grazing on wet, contaminated pasture. Liver flukes are usually found in cattle and sheep and it is rare for horses to become infected. However, when they do, the parasite, which passes into the liver, can cause anemia, diarrhea and jaundice and will normally be diagnosed by the discovery of fluke eggs in fecal samples. There is no drug licensed against the infection but oxclozanide has been reported to be effective. The best control is to stop animals from drinking water inhabited by the snails by supplying clean water in troughs and fencing off contaminated streams and ponds.

BOTFLY LARVAE

The larvae of the botfly (*Gastrophilus intestinalis* and *G. nasalis*) are found in the stomach of the horse where, according to most veterinary opinion, they do little harm. Adult botflies usually lay their eggs on horses in mid-to-late summer on the hairs of the neck, shoulder and legs. The horse licks and bites the eggs which stimulates them to hatch into larvae. These then penetrate the mouth and migrate to the stomach, where they make craterlike depressions in the mucosa as they attach themselves firmly to the stomach wall. This is liable to upset normal digestive

processes. Botflies greatly irritate the horse and the eggs can be difficult to remove. Ivermectin (Panomec or Eqvalan) given orally in winter will kill the adult worm in the stomach.

CONTROL AND TREATMENT

All horses and ponies should be dewormed every six to eight weeks all through the year. Remove all dung from the field at least twice a week in summer and once a week in winter. Avoid overcrowding and try not to graze older and younger horses together. Grazing horses with sheep and cattle is useful, since they can eat horse worms without harm and in the process reduce the number that can infect the horse. New horses should be dewormed at least 24 hours

before going onto common grazing. Try to deworm all horses in the same field at the same time. Ideally, use reseeded pasture or fields that have not been grazed by horses the previous year.

Whatever worm control system is used, whether for prevention or treatment, it is important to monitor its effectiveness from time to time. This can be done by checking worm-egg counts in fecal samples twice a year – usually in the spring and autumn. Blood samples can also be helpful in monitoring levels of globulin, which rise in the presence of worms. Resistance of worms to drugs, particularly to Benzimidazole anthelmintics can be a problem and has been detected in horses all over the world.

Lameness

Injury ✦ *Infection* ✦ *Inflammation* ✦ *Muscle damage* ✦ *Disease*

Lameness can involve one or more legs at the same time and may come on suddenly or gradually. It is most noticeable when the horse is walking or trotting.

Almost all lameness is a result of pain, although occasionally it may be the result of a "mechanical impediment," such as contracted tendons. Some lameness is the result of injury, some the result of infection, such as a foot abscess, others types may be the result of a specific disease process, such as arthritis (see page 105).

Predisposing factors in a horse include bad conformation, age, the degree of fitness, and poor attention to foot care and shoeing (see page 67).

Diagnosing lameness can be very difficult, and a veterinary surgeon may use nerve blocks, X-rays or ultrasound imaging. Nuclear scintigraphy, a new, advanced imaging technique, is now being used by specialist diagnostic centers.

FOOT LAMENESS

More lameness occurs as a result of foot disorders than for any other reason. The most common cause is an abscess, which can be extremely painful and may be a consequence of poor foot care resulting in brittle feet,

cracks in the hoof wall or a nail being badly positioned when the horse is shod. The abscess must be drained and the foot poulticed to get rid of all infection (see page 113).

Thrush is a foul-smelling infection in the frog, the result of poor hygiene and failure to clean the feet regularly. It is treated by keeping the foot clean and dry and by applying either antiseptic or antibiotic preparations to the foot.

Bruised soles and corns are more common in flat-footed and thin-soled horses. Poorly fitting shoes and working on hard, stony ground will cause the necessary trauma and result in the horse becoming lame.

Navicular syndrome

Navicular syndrome causes lameness as a result of pain in the navicular area of the foot. The navicular bone can degenerate for various reasons. The disorder affects the front feet and occurs very gradually. The first sign of a problem is a tendency to stumble; lameness will follow and become increasingly obvious with time.

Diagnosis is based on nerve blocks and X-rays. Treatments vary between remedial shoeing, surgery, and drug therapy, all of which may achieve

Above: Trotting up is a standard procedure used to begin examining a horse for lameness. This should be done on hard, level ground (concrete or tarmac) if possible. The head should be allowed free movement to aid in the detection of the condition.

Below: Pointing is a characteristic pose that a horse will tend to adopt if it has a severe pain in the foot. The most common reason for this type of pain is an abscess, but other possible causes will have to be investigated if an abscess is not found.

The shank bones ought to be stout, for they are the supporters of the body;
but they should not be thickly coated with flesh and veins: if they are, in riding
over hard ground the veins would fill with blood and become varicose, the legs
would swell, and the flesh recede. With the slackening of the flesh, the back
sinew often gives way, and makes the horse lame.

XENOPHON (C. 430–355 BC)

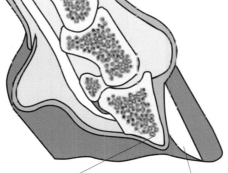

Tip of rotated
pedal bone
pressing on sole

Space left where
laminae tear away
from hoof wall

Above: Laminitis is the result of a disruption in the blood flow to the foot. This can permanently damage the laminae and result in the tilting or sinking of the pedal bone. Without enough healthy laminae, swift action must be taken to support the pedal bone within the hoof. This is usually done with heart-bar shoes, but in an emergency a roll of bandage taped to the frog will help.

CHECKING FOR
LAMENESS

If your horse seems to have a hoof problem, check for lameness by following the procedure below.
◆ Hold your hand over the suspect hoof and check for heat. Compare with the opposite hoof.
◆ Trot up the horse on level ground, keeping its head free. If it is lame in a foreleg, the head will rise as the affected foot hits the ground. If it is lame in a hind foot, it will drop as the affected foot hits the ground.
◆ If you suspect laminitis, *do not* hose the feet to relieve pain. Allow the animal to stand on a thick, soft surface and *do not* force it to walk. Call the vet as soon as possible.

some success. The chronic form of the syndrome may mean the end of the horse's working career.

Laminitis

Laminitis, a common complaint, occurs when the laminae of the foot become inflamed and the normal blood supply to the foot is disrupted.

The two main causes are either that the animal is overweight, a problem common among ponies who often gorge on spring grass, or that

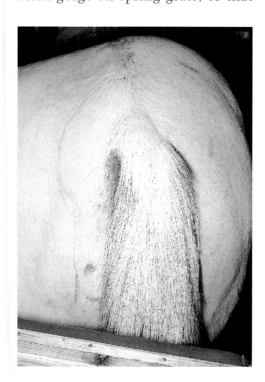

toxins have been liberated, either from the bowel, as a result of feeding errors, or from the uterus following infection. In some horses, laminitis can be caused by long, tiring journeys, by cancer of the pituitary gland or by Cushing's Disease, when high levels of hormones are secreted (see page 106).

In severe cases, the horse can hardly move and, if not lying down, will adopt a "rocking horse" posture to take as much weight as possible off the affected feet. The feet will be warm to the touch and the digital arteries can be easily palpated.

Acute laminitis is treated with analgesics and by confining the horse to a "starvation paddock" or a loose box with deep bedding, to cushion the feet, or by treating the cause of the toxemia. Heart-bar shoes, increasingly made of plastic and glued on to

Left: Muscle wastage over the pelvis is a very obvious sign of lameness in that leg but may not mean that the source of the lameness is high up in the leg. Once the lameness is cured, the muscles may take some time to return to their former size.

Right: Hoof testers are very useful to pinpoint the source of pain within the foot. They are especially useful for detecting abscesses.

avoid more trauma, support the pedal bone and give some relief. Sometimes, the pedal bone rotates, sinks, and perforates the sole, in which case the horse has to be destroyed.

Pedal osteitis

Pedal osteitis is inflammation of the bone within the foot and its cause is not yet fully understood. Lameness comes on gradually and a diagnosis is reached only by eliminating other possible causes and X-raying the bone. The treatment is rest, remedial shoeing and, if the pain is severe, analgesics. Unfortunately, the prognosis is always guarded.

MUSCLE LAMENESS

Muscle lameness is common in all athletic animals and the horse is no exception. It is a result of muscle

Lameness

damage – anything from muscle strains, when the fibers are over-stretched, to tears, which heal more slowly. In most cases the outcome is favorable. Rest and localized therapy and physiotherapy speed recovery.

Azoturia is a generalized muscle condition that can cause severe dysfunction. Many horses suffer from the disorder after a period of rest if their diet has not been restricted, but it can also happen if a horse has been overexercised, especially if mistakes have been made in its management and diet. In its mild form, azoturia causes the horse to be stiff and reluctant to turn. In its severe form, the

Right: After picking out a horse's foot, allow the foot to lie easily in the hand with the sole upward for visual inspection. Obvious defects can be seen and the foot balance assessed. Smell can also help in the detection of thrush.

Below: X-rays are most commonly done in clinics or centers, although mobile units can also be taken to the patient. The supervising vet has to take great care to ensure that this procedure is carried out safely to avoid overexposure of potentially harmful X-rays to the handlers of horse and equipment.

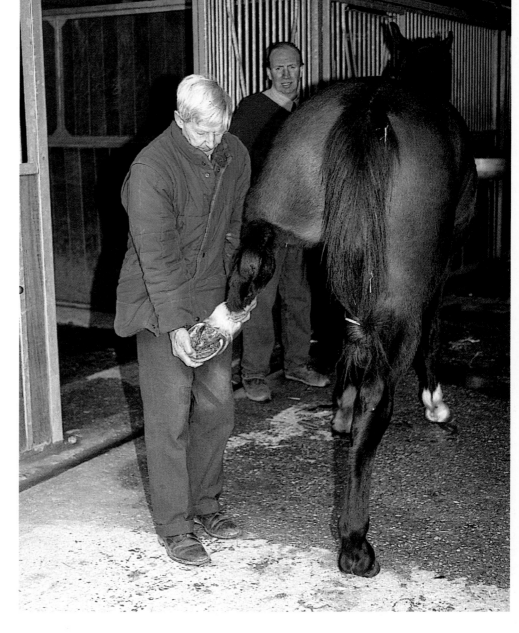

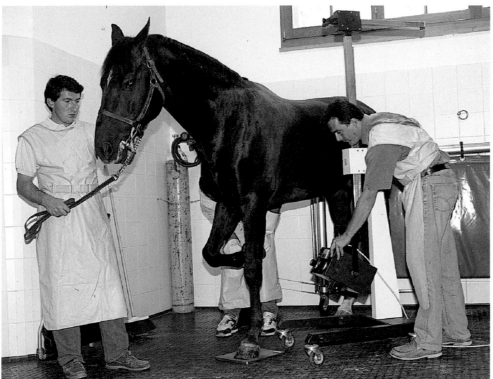

animal will have painful muscles and a high temperature and will sweat profusely. The urine will be very dark.

Azoturia is treated with non-steroidal, anti-inflammatory drugs to give pain relief. Intravenous fluids are given in severe cases. Exercise and feed must be carefully controlled.

BONE DISORDERS

Fractures are the most common bone disorders and vary in type and severity. The complete fracture of a long bone will require the horse's destruction, since no current techniques allow these to heal. Incomplete fractures and those below the fetlock may heal after surgery.

Young animals may have nutritional deficiencies, such as rickets, which may result in lameness and leg

Above: Heart-bar shoes are applied to the foot to support the pedal bone in cases such as laminitis. These should never be fitted without first taking X-rays of the foot to determine the exact position of the bone.

deformities. This can be prevented and rectified with a balanced diet and an adequate supply of vitamin D.

Bone infection, or osteomyelitis, may be the result of an infection via the blood stream or by direct entry through a wound. This can be very difficult to cure and may require surgical drainage as well as heavy doses of antibiotic.

Splints and sore shins are localized areas of periostitis. This causes pain initially through inflammation and tearing of the periosteum of the shin bone. These settle with time and rest but may leave hard bony swellings. Although they may be unsightly, they are not significant.

Bone cancer is rare in equines.

Joint lameness

Joint lameness can be the result of trauma or a symptom of disease. Severe lameness arising from an accident will require X-ray examination to determine whether the bones within the joint are fractured. Dislocation of a joint is not common but is serious when it does occur. Joint sprains are the result of the joint being over-flexed or overextended and will be resolved with rest.

Even a minor injury to a joint will almost always involve the joint becoming swollen with excess joint fluid – a condition that is called edema (see page 95). This may become a chronic complaint, and even when the animal is sound again, the swelling may still be present.

Windgalls in the fetlocks and bog spavins in the hocks are chronic, disfiguring swellings, but do not usually seriously impair a horse's function.

Osteoarthritis is one of the most common joint diseases and can end the useful life of an athletic animal. Erosion of the surface of the bones in the joints causes pain and swelling. It is treated with non-steroidal anti-inflammatory drugs, and other drugs have been developed to help lubricate badly damaged joints. Bone spavin in the hock and ringbone below the fetlock are the most common forms of arthritis in the horse.

Septic arthritis in the joint is very serious and is most commonly found in foals when it is known as "joint ill." Aggressive antibiotic treatment is required for several weeks and an incision may need to be made the joint flushed out with saline to remove infected debris

Ligaments and tendons

Ligaments and tendons are similar elastic structures – ligaments attach one bone to another and tendons attach muscle to bone. They are both slow to heal when damaged.

Superficial flexor tendon sprain is the most common sprain and an animal may need several months rest before it is sound again. Tendon

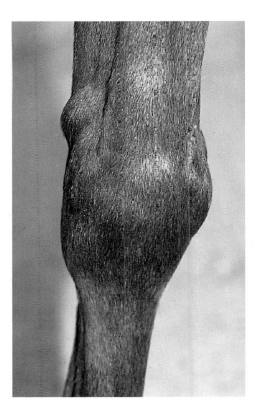

YOUR HORSE'S
HEALTH
Lameness

105

injuries are best diagnosed using ultrasound imaging, which shows the extent of the damage very clearly.

An acute sprain will require complete rest, cold compresses, support bandages, and analgesics. Many different treatments have been tried to improve the quality of healing of chronic tendon and ligament sprains, including tendon splitting, carbon-fibre implants, and ultrasound and laser therapy. New drug treatments are being trialed in the USA and UK. Complete rupture of a tendon usually carries a very poor prognosis.

Left: Chronic arthritis is common in older horses. The animal will have a stiff, swollen joint and a varying degree of lameness.

Below: Septic arthritis, usually the result of infections, is most common in younger animals. The joint is painful and swollen and the patient will have a temperature. If it is not treated quickly, the joint may be badly damaged. Lameness may persist through life.

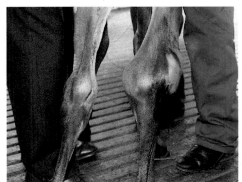

Skin Disease

Bacterial disease ✦ Parasites ✦ Fungal infection ✦ Allergies

*T*he skin is the largest of the body organs and a harsh and staring coat can be indicative of a horse's general poor health. A curly coat is a symptom of Cushing's Disease (above), caused by a benign tumor of the pituitary gland. A few general illnesses, such as *Purpura haemorrhagica,* can be diagnosed from symptoms appearing on the skin. This disease often follows strangles (see page 94) but is probably an immunological reaction and not restricted to strangles. The symptoms are fluid swellings along the legs and stomach and the skin seeming to exude a serum. Initially fluid-like, it dries rapidly, becoming crusty. The horse can be very ill but often responds well to steroid and antibiotic treatment.

However, most symptoms appearing on the the skin relate specifically to skin problems and are the result of

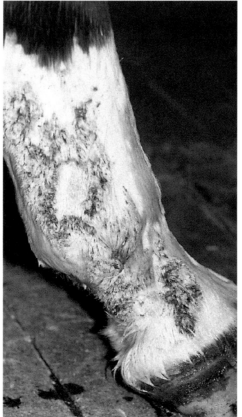

bacterial, parasitic or fungal infection. These may be the primary cause of discomfort or secondary to a trauma, such as rubbing. Allergic skin disorders are also common.

BACTERIAL SKIN DISEASE

Rain scald, mud fever, and greasy heel are related conditions caused by the organism *Dermatophilus congolensis,* which proliferates in wet, dirty conditions. The skin becomes matted and tufted and comes away, revealing a grayish purulent material on the surface of the skin. The skin on the lower legs and heels can become cracked. The affected area must be kept clean and dry, and antiseptic skin washes

Left: Cushing's disease most commonly affects older ponies. Symptoms include having a long, shaggy, curly coat, a distended abdomen and a tendency to laminitis (see p.103).

Left: Mud fever, a bacterial infection affecting a horse's legs, is most prevalent in muddy, wet conditions and can be resistant to treatment. It can often be avoided by washing your horse's legs down after exercise and drying them thoroughly.

Below: Saddle sores are painful and can become infected. They should be cleaned with a mild antiseptic solution or with soap and water, and antibiotic cream supplied by a vet should be gently applied.

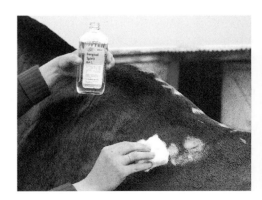

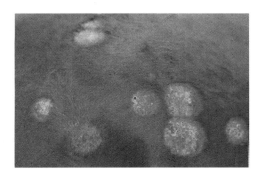

Above: Ringworm, circular, tufted areas with scaly deposits, is commonly found around the girth, head, and neck areas of horses. Highly contagious to other horses and to humans, it is caused by the fungal infections *Trychophyton* and, less often, *Microsporum* species.

Above: Sweet itch is caused by an allergy to the midge *Culicoides*. It manifests itself as intensely irritated areas of dermatitis, especially around the mane, poll, and root of the tail. It can also affect the neck, shoulders, and hindquarters.

that have been subject to mild rubbing, such as saddle and girth areas. Lesions ½–¾in (1–2cm) in diameter appear, which have hairs raised and tufted above the skin. When the scab falls off, it can leave an area with a dry, scaly appearance.

Skin or hair samples must be examined in a laboratory to confirm the diagnosis It is treated by spraying topical antifungal preparation on the affected area and using it to disinfect equipment and surfaces. Oral antimycotic agent mixed daily in the feed for seven days is another way to treat the infection. Griseofulvin is the

are useful, but the most severe cases require either topical or systemic antibiotic treatment. These conditions should be treated at once, since they can become severe if left.

Acne in horses is the result of the skin becoming infected with the bacteria *Staphylococcus epidermis*. Small pustules can appear anywhere on the skin but are most common in the saddle and girth areas. Acne is treated with antiseptic skin washes and topical or systemic antibiotics.

Skin sores, such as saddle sores and galls, are the result of pressure and can become infected. They can be prevented by ensuring that tack is clean and fits properly (see pages 70–2). Skin sores are treated in the same way as other bacterial skin infections.

FUNGAL SKIN DISEASE

Ringworm is caused by the fungi, *Trichophyton* and *Microsporum*. It is very common, is highly contagious and can affect humans. The spores can survive for years and spread very quickly if communal tack or grooming equipment is infected.

Ringworm can be seen anywhere on the horse but is especially obvious on surfaces.

Right: Sunburn (see p.109) is common on non-pigmented areas such as the muzzle. It can cause severe swelling and discomfort, and if it is not possible to keep the animal indoors, a sunblock, such as calamine, will give some protection.

Skin disease

active ingredient, which is very effective. However, it must not be used on pregnant animals and pregnant women must not handle the product.

PARASITIC SKIN DISEASE

Two species of lice commonly infect the horse – the biting louse, *Haematopinus asini*, and the sucking louse, *Damalinia equi*. Both can be seen with the naked eye but are easy to miss.

Infection is most common in the winter or early spring. The main symptom is irritation, with the horse biting and rubbing the affected areas, commonly the neck, mane, flank and base of the tail. In severe cases, the coat will look very moth-eaten and some horses become anemic. Lice are treated with synthetic *pyrethroids*, which are available as sprays or washes.

Harvest mites can also cause great irritation to the animal in the late summer and autumn (see page 100).

Chorioptic mange is quite common among heavy horses with a lot of "feather". It is the result of infection by a burrowing mite, *Chorioptes equi*, which is not visible to the

human eye. The legs become very sore, inflamed and thickened, and the horse will usually become extremely restless. The affected areas should be clipped, cleaned and treated with a suitable parasiticide.

Another form of mange is Demodectic mange, but this is rare and can only be diagnosed by taking a skin scraping from the animal for laboratory examination.

Worm infestation

Nematodes, or roundworms (see page 98), the primary parasites in horses, may also cause skin disease, although this is not common everywhere.

Parafilaria multipapillosis is a common infestation of horses in Eastern and Central Europe and may be seen in the UK on imported horses. Adult worms live just under the skin of the neck and withers. In the spring months, small fluid swellings may appear in those areas. Close inspection of these swellings will show small central holes from which eggs and micro larvae exit. These are then spread to other horses by biting flies.

Heavy infestatons of *Strongylus edentatus* has been known to cause bile duct obstruction, sufficient to cause jaundice. When this happens, bile

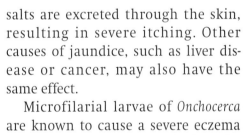

Skin complaints are painful for your horse and measures can be taken to avoid them.

✦ To prevent your horse standing in mud for too long, put down shale wherever horses congregate, such as by gates and water troughs.

✦ Always remove mud from your horse's legs, brushing dry mud gently to prevent scratches that will allow bacteria to enter the skin.

✦ To reduce midge and fly bites, keep your horse stabled between dawn and 10 AM and 4 PM and dark.

✦ Cover your horse with a summer sheet, a linen hood, and tail guard.

✦ Feed your horse garlic, which, when sweated through the skin, acts as a fly repellent.

✦ Avoid grazing near stagnant water.

✦ Apply midge repellent to your horse regularly.

✦ To prevent saddle sores, make sure your horse's tack is correctly fitted.

✦ Keep tack clean and supple.

✦ Always check your horse's tack once it has been put on.

salts are excreted through the skin, resulting in severe itching. Other causes of jaundice, such as liver disease or cancer, may also have the same effect.

Microfilarial larvae of *Onchocerca* are known to cause a severe eczema on the lower abdomen during the summer months. This results in hair loss, the skin thickening with crusts forming on the surface and a severe itch, which adds to the problem as the horse attempts to rub the skin on every available edge and corner. Treatment can be difficult and prolonged. Affected animals may require steroid therapy, antibiotics and severe cases will be kept in their stable.

Left: This horse has slipped and rolled into a bed of nettles and come out in urticarial plaques. Biting insects can cause a similar reaction in sensitive horses.

ALLERGIC SKIN DISEASE

Sweet itch is an allergic reaction or "hypersensitivity" to the biting midge, *Culicoides*. It can occur in any animal over the age of one but is most common in ponies. In some places, it is seasonal and usually occurs between April and October when there are more midges. The major symptom is irritation of the skin, which causes the pony to bite at the base of its tail and to rub its mane. Hair loss will result and the skin will have a dry, crusty appearance. In chronic cases, the skin will become dry, thickened and ridged. Sweet itch is treated with synthetic *Pyrethrin* repellents, which are applied along the animal's back every six days. Steroids and antibiotic cream may be necessary to heal skin lesions.

Urticaria, is the skin's natural response to an allergen, resulting in the sudden development of nodules of various sizes, which may, or may not, be itchy. Fly bites are often the cause. Horses on high-protein diets

Below: Nodular sarcoids are wart-like structures. They are usually removed surgically, but this is difficult around the eye. Other treatments include autogenous vaccination and implantation of radioactive material.

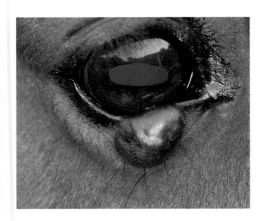

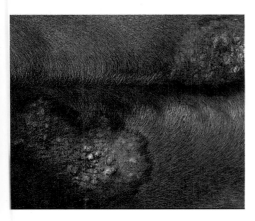

may be more prone to the condition. If treated intravenously with steroids, the condition will disappear rapidly.

Midges and flies

Midges bite mostly at dawn, dusk or when the weather is hot and humid. To limit exposure, keep susceptible animals indoors between dawn and 10am and between 4pm and dusk. If a horse cannot be stabled, it should be kept away from trees, hedges and ponds where midges are prevalent.

During the summer, a number of biting flies, stable flies, horse flies and even household flies cause severe annoyance to the horse. If there are any open wounds, blow flies may lay eggs, which, if neglected, can result in maggots developing. This can have severe consequences. However, flies usually cause only a local nodular reaction that eventually disappears. Fly repellents are usually very effective and it helps to keep manure piles on grazing to a minimum.

Photosensitization is seen in grazing animals in the summer. It affects white areas of the coat and is commonly seen on the muzzle as sunburn. Severe cases may be caused by eating photosensitizing plants such as St. John's Wort. If it is a bad case, the horse should be kept out of direct sunlight. Human sun-block can be applied in less severe cases. Sunburn must not be neglected, since skin can become badly damaged and antibiotics may then be required.

SKIN GROWTHS

Warts are often seen in young horses. They are generally small and appear in clusters around the muzzle. Unless they become infected, there is usually no need for treatment, since the disease, caused by a papilloma virus, generally cures itself in a few months.

Sarcoids are very common skin tumors that can be caused by viral infection. They can occur anywhere

Left: Verrucose sarcoids are commonly seen along the belly, chest and groin of horses. These are commonly removed by thermocautery or cryosurgery, but it is not unusual for them to reappear.

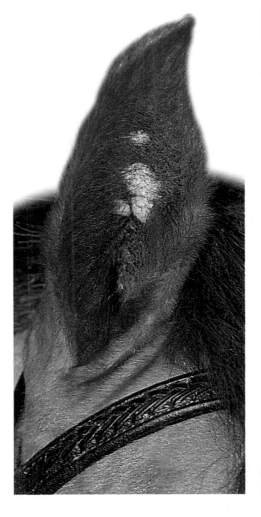

Above: Ear plaques are white raised areas on the inner surface of the ear. The cause of the condition is obscure and the plaques are best left undisturbed, since they do the horse no harm.

on the body but are common on the head or legs. Although they can be locally invasive, they do not spread elsewhere, but can be unsightly and may become infected. They are usually treated by excision or by cryosurgery. Unfortunately, many tumors regrow, even after surgery.

Melanomas usually develop in old grey horses and are found most often around the back passage, vulva and sheath. There is no medical treatment but surgical excision may be possible.

Excess granulation tissue, or proud flesh, is quite common on legs where wounds have occurred. Simple cases may only require medical treatment; advanced cases may require surgery.

Ear plaques – raised, white, thickened plaques sometimes more than an inch in size – can appear in a horse's ears. The cause is unknown and no treatment is required.

Neurological Disorders & Behavioral Problems

Poisoning ◆ Dummy foals ◆ Fits ◆ Behavioral problems

The horse feels pain, fear, anger, hot, cold, and a wide range of other sensations. It can respond rapidly to internal and external stimuli, since it has a highly developed nervous system, composed of the brain, spinal cord, and a large network of peripheral nerves. Any injury to nerve cells and fibers due to trauma, infection or poison will have an immediate, and potentially very serious, effect.

TETANUS

Tetanus is the most important neurological disorder in the horse and is almost always fatal. It is caused by a neurotoxin produced by *Clostridium tetani*, bacteria that proliferate in dung and rust.

The animal becomes infected when bacteria penetrate a puncture wound, although it can also invade via the umbilical cord in foals and via the vagina after foaling (see page 112). The incubation period is at least three weeks. The first symptoms are general muscle stiffness and anxiety. The animal will have progressive difficulty in swallowing and may hold its tail out stiffly behind. The third eye lid comes across the medial side of the eye, the ears will be pricked and the nostrils dilated. Soon the animal will fall over in spasm, with the head held back and the legs extended. Mild cases sometimes recover, but if the horse is down and the spasms severe, it is kinder to practice euthanasia.

An animal with tetanus should be kept quietly in the dark and treated with high doses of penicillin and antitoxin to reduce the muscle spasms.

Tetanus can be prevented by vaccination. Initial doses are given six weeks apart, with a booster a year later. Boosters are then given every two to three years. Animals at risk that have not been fully vaccinated should be given protective doses of the antitoxin.

RAGWORT POISONING

On the whole, horses do not eat things that are unpalatable, and this is true of the adult ragwort plant (see page 55). However, when dry in hay, it is less bitter and is readily eaten. It will also be consumed in a bare-earth paddock when there is no other greenery. The symptoms may take a

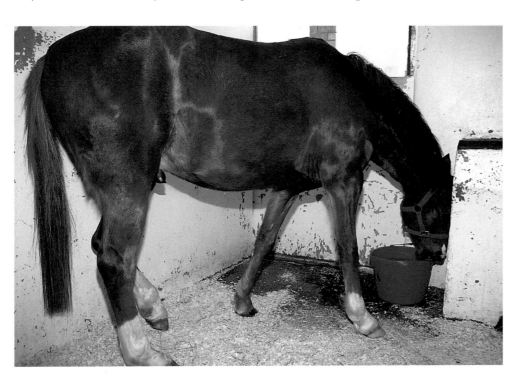

Below: Head pressing is a symptom of a neurological disorder often secondary to liver failure. A common cause is ragwort poisoning and at this stage the animal should be put down to alleviate any further suffering.

Above: An anti-weaving grid prevents a horse from moving the head and neck from side to side excessively when it becomes upset – often when other horses leave the yard.

while to develop and are the result of liver failure. The animal becomes blind and completely unaware of its surroundings. It will often blunder through any obstacle or wander in circles. Others will press their heads against a wall and become aggressive.

Once nervous signs are apparent, there is no cure and the animal will have to be destroyed. If the horse is not showing signs of neurological disease, then high doses of vitamins and a high carbohydrate diet may help to combat the liver failure.

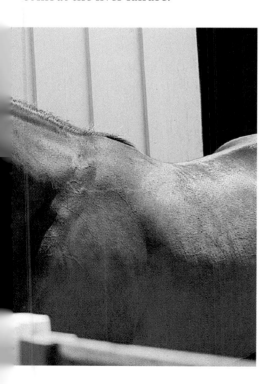

Left: A horse that crib-bites will fix its teeth on a horizontal surface and bite down. At the same time, it flexes its neck and takes in air, often accompanied by an audible "grunt."

NEONATAL MALADJUSTMENT SYNDROME

This syndrome has many different names, including "dummy foals", "barker foals," and "wanderers." It is mostly seen in Thoroughbred foals within 24 hours of birth. Symptoms include the foal wandering aimlessly, apparently blind, and not feeding. This may alternate with periods of coma, interspersed with convulsions.

There is no specific treatment and a high level of intensive nursing is needed. Its cause is not properly understood although equine herpes virus type 1 (see page 95), which can cause neurological disease in the young foal, may be implicated. The prognosis is usually very poor.

EPILEPSY AND NARCOLEPSY

Epilepsy, fits, and narcolepsy (falling asleep momentarily and sometimes falling over) are not uncommon in horses. Although treatment for epilepsy may control convulsions, it is never safe to ride the horse again. Most have to be put down, since they often injure themselves during a seizure.

BEHAVIORIAL PROBLEMS

Common "stable vices" include weaving, head-nodding, box-walking, cribbiting, wind-sucking, wood-chewing, and self-mutilation. These have long been considered genuine impairments to the effectiveness, value, and possibly the performance of the horse.

Such monotonous behaviors or "stereotypies" are generally defined as invariant, repetitive behavior pattens with no obvious goal or function. As they develop over a period of time, it is critical when managing young horses to learn to recognize the early signs of such undesirable behavior.

Stereotypies are frequently stress responses to certain domestic management measures. Once established, they are virtually impossible to eradicate because the brain and nervous system still act to maintain the

Goats make excellent companions for horses that do not like being kept alone. Showjumpers, in particular, seem to need this type of company. Sheep can also be used, but they are more difficult to manage, since they will require clipping and dipping at certain times of the year. Goats are easier, but they do have their own nutritional requirements that have to be satisfied.

"abnormal" behavior, even when the horse has been removed from the situation that prompted its development.

Lack of contact with other horses, inadequate time spent feeding or turned out at grass, certain types of stabling, abrupt weaning, insufficient exercise and stressful training regimes are all potential causes of stereotypic behavior.

There is no conclusive evidence that horses can learn stereotypic behavior by imitating others directly. But it is clear that it is very stressful for a horse to be kept close to others that are behaving in these ways. This may explain why those stabled close to individuals with behavioral problems often develop similar symptoms themselves. Preventing animals from carrying out abnormal behavior by using gadgets (such as cribbing collars and weaving grids), electric shock treatment, drugs, and surgery may provide solace for desperate owners, but at the end of the day these can only provide a means of arresting the symptoms of the problem and do not treat the root cause.

First Aid & Nursing

Accidents ✦ Bleeding ✦ Wound care ✦ Strains ✦
Nursing environment and routine

First Aid knowledge is essential for all animal owners – you never know when such knowledge may prove invaluable, if not life-saving, for your own or a friend's horse. Good first aid and nursing skills and will ensure the most complete recovery for your horse after an accident or illness.

ACCIDENTS

In the event of an accident, stay calm. Warn traffic if necessary, and if the animal is still on its feet, restrain it with a halter or head collar. If possible, get it off the road and seek help. If the horse is on the ground, place something soft under its head to minimize further injury. It will be trembling and may be sweating. Cover the horse with a blanket or something to keep it warm. Stay with the horse until professional help arrives.

FIRST AID SKILLS

If a wound is bleeding, apply a pressure bandage. If blood seeps through, add another layer using cotton wool or any other clean padding. Flush a bleeding wound with cold water only if the horse is amenable and the wound is grossly contami-nated with soil or other debris. Otherwise, do not wash a bleeding wound – it does not stop the flow of blood. Nose bleeds can look very serious but will be self-limiting. Do not attempt to plug a nostril, it does not work and will only upset the patient.

Wounds and strains

There are four types of wound – contused wounds, or bruising; puncture wounds; lacerated wounds; and incised wounds.

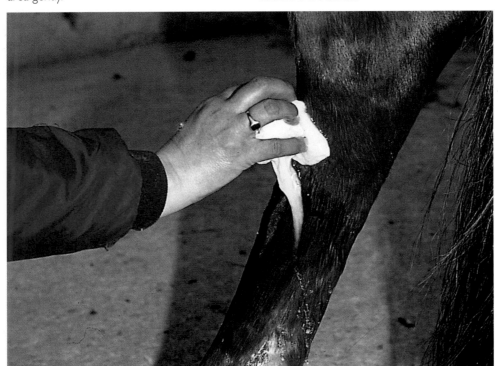

Every stable should have a first aid kit that is kept handy and up to date. A kit should always be available when you are travelling or competing. It should contain:
Antiseptics: liquid, aerosol
Bandages: crepe bandage, zip-up lycra bandage, self-adhesive bandage ventilated elastic adhesive bandages
Dressings: scissors, cotton wool, gauze, all-purpose dressing, perforated plastic film, dressing powder
Cold treatments: freeze pack, cold pack, hosing boot
Temperature: Thermometer
A Poulticer

✦ A bruised leg that is starting to swell can be hosed or bathed with cold water to stop the blood flowing to the injured area. This will reduce inflammation.
✦ Puncture wounds may bleed initially but can be controlled by a pressure bandage (see above). Chronic wounds (especially in the feet) may be contaminated and will become infected. Poultice the wound to 'draw out' debris and purulent material.
✦ Incised wounds are usually clean cuts. They may bleed readily and will usually require suturing. Do not bathe (see above) but do apply a pressure bandage until the vet arrives.
✦ Lacerated wounds are usually caused by contact with a hard surface, such as a road. They can be very dirty but do not bleed a lot. These may be washed with salt water or flushed with a cold hose. A vet should check for possible infection.
✦ If your horse has a tendon strain, treat it very seriously. Symptoms are moderate to severe lameness with

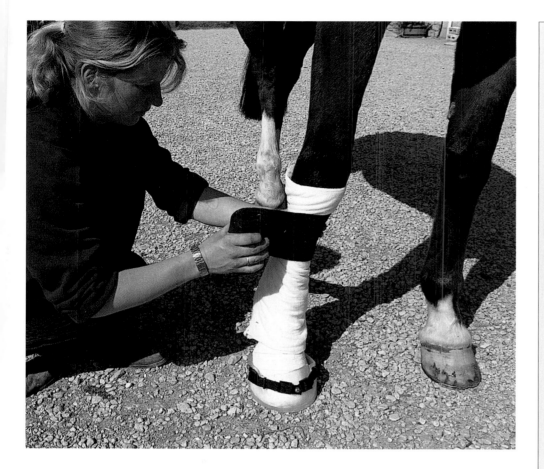

Above: A support bandage consists of a ventilated elastic bandage over a layer of cotton wool. It should be changed at least once a day unless your vet tells you otherwise.

swelling around the tendon of the affected leg. Apply a support bandage to the leg and prevent further movement until the vet arrives. This is to limit any additional damage that could be done to the tendon.

Bathing eyes

If your horse has discharge from its eyes, it will usually have conjunctivitis. Treatment is best left to the vet since the cause may be a seed or husk in the eye, which will require removal under local anaesthetic. But until the vet arrives, there is no harm in bathing the eye in a saline solution made from a teaspoon of salt in 1 pint (0.57 litres) of tepid boiled water.

NURSING CARE

A sick horse should be housed in a large, clean, light and airy loose box, which should be cleaned out regularly. Good ventilation is very important, especially if the horse has a respiratory complaint. A dusty, cobwebby stable will not speed recovery.

Visit your horse frequently, checking its general behavior. Is its dung normal and passed regularly? Is it breathing normally or getting worse? Is it drinking? Is it cold and in need of a rug? Is it sweating a lot and needs to be rubbed down and dried off? Does the water need changing? Does the stable need cleaning?

A sick animal may need to have its nostrils cleaned and eyes bathed to stop secretions building up. This can be done with a saline solution (see above). The dock area may need regular cleaning, especially if the animal has diarrhea. A mild soapy solution is best for this. Light grooming will help tone skin and improve the animal's well-being. All these tasks must be approached with patience and care in order not to excite the horse and add to its distress.

Leg swellings and foot abcesses

Any animal that has to be confined without exercise will require less food than usual. If quantities remain the same, it may develop laminitis or azoturia (see pages 103–4) or the legs may fill with fluid (lymphangitis). The legs may fill anyway, and if they do it is good practice to apply stable

MAKING UP
PREPARATIONS

◆ Keeping a foot poultice in place can be difficult. Poultices can be made from various materials including kaolin, bran or even bread but most people now use commercial products. The material is heated, cooled to about 38°C (100.4°F) and then applied to the affected area. It can be kept in place on the foot with a special poultice boot, or something simple like hessian can be strapped on. Poultices should be changed once or twice every 24 hours.
◆ A high-fiber diet is useful if your horse is prone to constipation. However, bran should not be a daily part of the diet, especially for young horses because it can cause mineral imbalances.
◆ Always follow instructions carefully when making up antiseptic solutions. Solutions that are too strong may be harmful.

bandages. Any bandage with a dressing must be changed daily unless your vet instructs otherwise.

Constipation is another hazard for stabled animals. If your horse is not working, feed it a high-fiber diet.

Chronic swellings are reduced by applying hot and cold water alternately, using a sponge. This works by causing blood vessels in the skin to expand and then contract, which may improve fluid drainage from an affected area.

Foot abcesses should be flushed with an antiseptic solution and then poulticed with kaolin or a commercially prepared poultice. Instructions can be followed from the packet. You should change a poultice twice a day unless told otherwise. If an animal will not keep a poultice in place, the foot can be tubbed in warm salt water, which will have a similar effect. This must be done for up to 20 minutes five or six times a day.

PART 4

EQUESTRIAN SPORTS

O f the 60 million horses that exist today, the overwhelming majority have a relationship with the human race. Most of these are involved in the business of leisure and pleasure that we call sport. Interest in equestrian activities is greater now than it has been in the past, and riding horses, driving them, or just being with them, is a pastime that crosses national, ethnic, and social boundaries; people all over the world, old and young, expert and novice, enjoy their horses through sport. The sporting horse ranges from the humblest backyard pony to the blue-blooded, purpose-bred racehorse, from the beloved old hunter to the Olympic showjumper. The competitive nature of the human race, and the delight still found in the power, speed, grace, and nobility of the equine species, has ensured that the horse has survived and thrived since mechanization, thankfully, overtook its role in battle, working the land, and as a beast of burden.

The Right Horse

Finding the perfect horse ✦ Conformation ✦ The purpose-bred Thoroughbred

To find the right horse – that special horse with that extra something – is the quest of every equestrian. In the racing world, billions – in any currency – have been spent in search of perfection. Nature decrees that in every era some horses excel – Eclipse, Ormonde, Sceptre, Hyperion, Sea-Bird, Secretariat, Shergar, Nashwan, Peintre Celebre – but no foolproof formula has yet been found. "Put the best to the best – and hope for the best" still seems, after 300 years, to be as good advice as any.

In the modern era, the horse is no longer a beast of burden, but one of leisure and pleasure and the cachet of the sporting horse, from an elite Derby winner to a local 4H Club pony,

Above: Peintre Celebre, a son of Nureyev and the Alydar mare Peintre Bleue, lived up to his top pedigree as European champion of 1997.

Right: George Bowman has bred his own strain of strong, handy, driving horses by using Hackneys and Welsh Cobs (see pp.161–2).

has never been higher. Apart from racing, nearly any horse, if properly trained, can take part in any sport at the lower levels. A hobby rider can do a little showjumping, a little dressage, enjoy a day's hunting or a long-distance ride, take part in a hunter trial, or go to a local show.

But once the climb toward the elite begins, so does the specialization. Of course, there will always be horses that succeed against the odds, but certain types do tend to do well in certain sports. The clichés are broadly true: warmblood horses, with their strength, muscle power, flexible limbs and lightness of foot for their size, are ideal for power sports such as showjumping and dressage, whereas full or near Thoroughbreds, which are lean, wiry, and athletic, built and bred for speed, do well as eventers or polo ponies. The racing sports are outside the "type" equation, since only Thoroughbreds (see page 160), compete in ridden races and only Trotters and Standardbreds (see pages 167, 180 and 191) in harness races.

THE SPORTING HORSE

Nonetheless, in every sport there will be common factors shared by the best horses, which the experienced rider will actively seek. Balance is the key to success in most sport (equestrian or not) and a horse that carries itself well in the walk is more likely to be well coordinated in its faster paces. The shoulder is one of the main hinges for locomotion, acting as a

Right: Willie Melliger's showjumper Calvaro V, is a superb example of a Holstein warmblood, a German breed (see p.173).

Below: Grand National winner Earth Summit by Celtic Cone out of Win Green Hill by National Trust has a stamina-fillled pedigree.

The right horse

pendulum for the front legs, and must be correctly angled. Too straight, and the horse will not be able to gallop downhill with any freedom.

Looking at the front legs head on, the center of the knee should be over the center of the hoof, giving an impression of strength. From the side, any concavity at the knee could put excessive strain on the tendons on the back of the leg. If the pastern below the fetlock is too straight, there is the risk of jarring, but if it is at an angle that slopes too much there may again be the risk of tendon strain.

Depth through the body means that there is plenty of room for heart and lungs. The horse is a rear-engined animal, and good length from the point of the hip to the point of the hock, combined with a straight, strong hind leg, indicates superior powers of propulsion. Feet, as first point of contact with the ground, should be regular in shape and made of hard, dense horn. The head will portray character. Inspection of successful sporting horses should show such similarities among the different types and sports.

THE THOROUGHBRED

The ultimate sporting horse must be the Thoroughbred, bred primarily for speed but talented in many different spheres. It has been said, with some truth, that there is nothing a common horse can do that a Thoroughbred cannot do better. Indeed, it has, through judicious crossing, brought quality to breeds formerly less refined.

The men who created the Thoroughbred developed a breed with distinct characteristics, unlike any seen before, evident in changes in bone structure, musculature, heart, lungs, and glands, whichmade it ideal for superior athletic performance.

The finer bones of the Thoroughbred incorporate strength with relative lightness, allowing a high degree of flexion and extension that contribute to the length of stride, and the greater bone mass in the upper limbs (as opposed to the lower) means that the center of gravity is near the

Left: Mary King's powerful mount King William, a top-class cross-country horse, is by the Thoroughbred Nickel King out of an Irish Draught-cross mare.

Below: A typical Thoroughbred cross polo pony – quick, balanced and responsive.

Above: A Standardbred – a breed influenced by the Thoroughbred Naragansett Pacer and the Morgan – shows off its lateral pacing gait.

Below: The Canadian endurance horse Garnet Gallant is an Arab – a breed that excels where stamina and soundness are at a premium.

major pivoting points, the hips and shoulder. This produces a high, efficient stride frequency, which is abetted by powerful and frequent contractions of the major propulsive muscles in the hindquarters.

The Thoroughbred shows a rapid response to circulating adrenaline, which initiates physiological and metabolic reactions during exercise, a large heart-to-weight ratio and a larger than usual reserve of red blood cells in the spleen, which ensures a good oxygen supply to the heart and muscles during strenuous exercise.

These qualities, given by the Thoroughbred to other breeds and types, have been essential to the development of the sporting horse worldwide. But even when a horse excels, it is impossible to be dogmatic about the reason why. The physiological rate of stimulus and response from the brain to nerve and muscle is certainly a crucial element. Temperament and courage are also important and good conformation is desirable. Blended in one individual, they can create that unusual phenomenon, a champion.

Above: A group of racehorses takes an early-morning exercise on the gallops. As for any athlete, regular training is essential for the development of speed, stamina, and balance.

Flat Racing

History ✦ *Structure* ✦ *Calendar* ✦ *Courses*

ECLIPSE

———— ✦ ————

Eclipse, born in 1764, was sired by Marske, grandson of the Darley Arabian, one of the Thoroughbred's three founding sires. A chestnut, with a white blaze and one white leg, Eclipse ran and won his first race, a 4-mile (6.4-km) heat, at Epsom Downs aged five. Thereafter, he won every race that he ran in his 17-month racing career. He stood at stud for 19 years, sired 335 winners, and founded one of the three principle male Thoroughbred bloodlines, with 90 per cent of today's Thoroughbred racehorses thought to be his direct descendants.

Flat racing is many things to many people. Primarily, it is a high-profile international industry involving large sums of money and massive employment. What goes on in front of the public on the racecourse is merely the shop window; the bloodstock and training businesses behind the two are financially interdependent. The racecourse can also simply provide fun for spectators and participants; horse owners range from the mega-rich to ordinary folk who perhaps have a small share in a racehorse just as a hobby.

Synonymous with the Thoroughbred horse (see page 160), flat racing is the Formula 1 end equestrian sporting industry, and not just because speed is the essence. Huge sums are invested in what might broadly be called research and development - equipment, veterinary care, breeding techniques, transport - and, just as the driver of a standard car will ultimately benefit from the research and development carried out by Grand Prix motor racing teams, money spent at the highest level in racing results in improvement that will trickle down to the ordinary weekend rider. The evolution of the crash helmet, which was first used by jockeys, is an example; another is the development of transport for horses. The first horsebox used to transport a racehorse in 1816 and, because of the cosmopolitan nature of the bloodstock industry, equine air travel is now common.

The oldest surviving racecourse in England is Chester, where racing was first recorded in 1540. Queen Elizabeth was known to attend races on Salisbury Plain in the 1580s, and before the turn of the century a racecourse had appeared on a map of Doncaster. There was racing at Epsom by the 1640s and Newmarket's position as the sport's headquarters was established by 1700, thanks to the royal patronage that was an essential part of its popularity. James I was the first monarch to visit the town, in 1605, and Charles II virtually made it his home from the 1660s.

Racing, and with it the Thoroughbred industry, spread to every country where there was British influence. North America's first formal racecourse was laid out on Long Island, New York, in 1665, but horseracing took

Above: Over five furlongs (1,000m), the minimum distance at which they compete, racehorses can top 40mph (64k/ph). Speed records are still broken regularly, although times tend not to be cut as dramatically in the modern era as in the days of the Thoroughbred's early development.

place in other colonies as well. In heavily wooded Virginia, for example, horses would be raced in short dashes down the main streets of the village. In the late 1700s, America's racing enthusiasts imported horses too old to race but still valuable at stud; the legendary Diomed sired 600 foals, 236 of them winners.

France's first official meeting was held near Paris in 1776, Germany's in Mecklenberg in 1822, and Italy's in Florence and Naples in 1837. In the Southern Hemisphere, the first recorded meeting in Australia was in Sydney in 1810 and in New Zealand, in Auckland in 1842.

The Racing Calendar, an account of race meetings and results, was first published in 1727. In 1740, Parliament had to outlaw nearly all races worth less than £50 to check the rapid growth of the sport. The Derby, the race on which all others of the name are modeled, was first run in 1780 and won by Diomed.

STRUCTURE OF THE SPORT

The structure of the sport is something that often puzzles outsiders, but essentially it is simple and the same all over the world. The starting point is the owner, on whom everyone else depends. The owner (who may be an individual, a partnership, a syndicate, a club or a business) employs a professional trainer to look after and condition his or her horse

Above: Air travel is a common occurence for top racehorses, which are flown all over the world for export and for race meetings. Inside the airplane, the horses are placed in secure stalls and kept under constant supervision.

for racing, and a jockey to ride it. He or she can be someone of the status and wealth of Sheikh Mohammed Al Maktoum, a member of the family of the oil-rich Arab emirate, Dubai, with thousands of horses to run in his colors all over the world, or a small syndicate or racing club with just one horse to its name.

Owners may keep horses purely for fun, with no thought of financial return; purely as a business venture (the horse can carry a commercial name or advertising on the jockey's silks); or a combination of both. An owner can breed his or her horse, or buy from a commercial producer of

Flat racing

bloodstock. Major owners in Europe are Sheikh Mohammed and members of the Maktoum family, Khaled Abdullah, the Aga Khan, Cheveley Park Stud, and in the United States, the Hancock family of the legendary Claiborne Farm.

The front-line professionals in the racing business are trainers and jockeys. The best trainers generally have the patronage of the leading owners and may have more than 200 horses under their care and, consequently, a large labor force of stable lad and work riders, jockeys (who can be of either sex, though men are overwhelmingly dominant) may have a retainer with a particular owner or trainer or operate on a freelance basis, earning per ride. Amateur riders are catered for with a small number of their own races.

Behind the scenes are those involved with the production of racehorses in the bloodstock business, supplying the needs of owners who wish to purchase. At the top of the market commercial breeders supply young horses – generally yearlings - by the hundred, sometimes for huge sums (the most expensive yearling ever sold cost $13.1 million in 1985); others operate on a small, almost hobby, scale, with only one or two sent to the sales each year. The vast majority of commercially bred horses are sold at auction, the world's biggest sales uses being Tattersalls in Newmarket and Keeneland in Kentucky.

THE CALENDAR

Horses race on the flat from the age of two and over distances from 5 furlongs (1,000m) to 2¾ miles (4,400m). The most prestigious races tend to be the Classics for three-year-olds and middle-distance all-aged contests (between 1¼ and 1½ miles – 2,000 and 2,400m), from which winners can acquire high value for breeding. Most countries have a set of Classics that test various aptitudes; the originals are the British 1,000 Guineas (first run in 1814, for fillies) and 2,000 Guineas (1809, for colts and fillies), both over a 1 mile (1,600m) at Newmarket; the Derby (1780, for colts and fillies) and the Oaks (1779, for fillies), both over 1½ miles (2,400m) at Epsom; and the St. Leger (1776, for colts and fillies) over 1¾ miles (2,800m). In the USA, racing on dirt is preferred to turf; the most famous race is the 10-

Above: The racing saddle is smaller and lighter than a normal saddle with an exaggerated forward-cut panel to accomodate the jockey's shorter riding length. The smallest, made of plastic, weigh a few ounces and are little more than a pad from which to hang stirrups.

Below: The Derby is run over a switchback 1½ mile (2,400m) course at Epsom, UK, which tests the horse in all departments – the winner will need balance and agility as well as the obvious speed and stamina. The track is the most difficult in the world to ride and the jockey needs a good tactical brain in order remain ahead of the field.

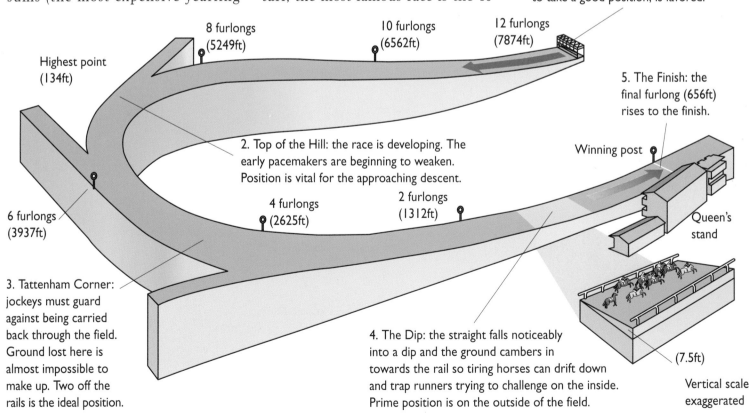

1. The Start: from the off, a middle draw, which gives the jockeys freedom to take a good position, is favored.

8 furlongs (5249ft)

10 furlongs (6562ft)

12 furlongs (7874ft)

Highest point (134ft)

5. The Finish: the final furlong (656ft) rises to the finish.

Winning post

2. Top of the Hill: the race is developing. The early pacemakers are beginning to weaken. Position is vital for the approaching descent.

6 furlongs (3937ft)

4 furlongs (2625ft)

2 furlongs (1312ft)

Queen's stand

3. Tattenham Corner: jockeys must guard against being carried back through the field. Ground lost here is almost impossible to make up. Two off the rails is the ideal position.

4. The Dip: the straight falls noticeably into a dip and the ground cambers in towards the rail so tiring horses can drift down and trap runners trying to challenge on the inside. Prime position is on the outside of the field.

(7.5ft)

Vertical scale exaggerated

Above: All the color and excitement of flat racing as horse and riders fight out a close finish. Some of the world's most famous owners are represented here, including Hamdan Al Maktoum (striped cap, right), Robert Sangster (spots, second right) and Khaled Abdullah (pink cap, center).

SECRETARIAT

—— ◆ ——

Secretariat, foaled in Virginia in 1970, had perfect conformation and an awesome 25-ft (7.6-m) stride, and was the *beau idéal* among race horses. He won 16 of his 25 starts, including the first American Triple Crown for 25 years, and achieved lasting fame in the Belmont stakes, the second half of which he turned into a glorious exhibition of power and speed. At the finish he was 31 lengths ahead, took 2.6 seconds off the record for 12 furlongs (2,400m) and, as his rider, Ron Turcotte, tried to pull him up, set a world record for a mile and five (2,600m) to boot.

furlong (2,000m) Kentucky Derby at Churchill Downs, first run in 1875, which together with the Preakness Stakes and the American Oaks makes up the prestigious Triple Crown.

In Europe, the most important all-aged races are the King George and Queen Elizabeth Diamond Stakes at Ascot and the Prix de l'Arc de Triomphe at Longchamp, Paris. Their monetary value is now exceeded, by newer races such as the Japan Cup, the Dubai Cup, and the Breeders Cup series in North America.

RACE COURSES

One of the beauties of British racing is the variety of its racetracks. There are the wide-open spaces of Newmarket, the tight circle at Chester, the undulating downland of Goodwood, the tricky downhill sweep of Epsom and the fair, sweeping turns of York. Flat racing in Europe is primarily a spring, summer and autumn sport, but all-weather tracks (there are three in England) allow it to continue on a bread-and-butter scale during the winter. It is a year-round sport in the US as well.

All US racecourses are left-handed ovals, but they are not all identical, and experienced jockeys can take advantage of their individual peculiarities. The most obvious difference is their length, which can be as short as five furlongs (⅝ mile). Belmont Park, at 1½ miles, is the longest. Most

major tracks are a mile. In a country that has preferred dirt racing since 1821, more than half of the racecourses have only dirt tracks; where there is a turf course, it is usually on the inside.

The turns at either end of the oval connect the straightaways – the backstretch and the homestretch (closest to the grandstand). At opposite ends of the stretches are short spurs, called chutes, that allow the horses a straight start whatever the race distance is in relation to the track length. And while the finish line is always on the homestretch, its placement can affect the race outcome. Short stretches favor speed horses; longer stretches favor come-from-behind runners.

IMPORTANT RACING DATES

Kentucky Derby, first Saturday in May, Churchill Downs, U.S.A; Preakness Stakes, two weeks later, Pimlico, U.S.A; Belmont Stakes, three weeks later, Belmont Park, U.S.A; 1,000 and 2,000 Guineas, May, Newmarket, U.K.; Derby, June, Epsom, U.K.; Oaks, June, Epsom, U.K.; King George VI and Queen Elizabeth Diamond Stakes, July, Ascot, U.K.; St. Leger, September, Doncaster, U.K.; Prix de l'Arc de Triomphe, October Longchamp, Paris, France; Melbourne Cup, November, Flemington, Australia; Breeders' Cup, November, North America; Japan Cup, November, Tokyo.

Steeplechasing

History ✦ *Racing today* ✦ *Aintree* ✦ *Point-to-point*

Steeplechasing is often called the poor relation of flat racing and, in terms of the finances involved, it is. Prize money is lower and there is no residual stud value involved, since most of the horses that take part are geldings. But if flat racing is largely an industry, steeplechasing is largely a sport. It takes place in one form or another worldwide, but its heart is in Britain and Ireland.

HISTORY

In 1752, when two Irish hunting men named Blake and O'Callaghan agreed to match their horses over the country between the churches of Buttevant and St. Leger in County Cork, they had no idea of the far-reaching effects of their 4½-mile (7,200-m) race. With the spire of St. Leger as their visible target, they gave a name to what they were doing: steeplechasing.

The earliest recorded steeplechases in Britain were in Leicestershire in 1792. In the sport's formative years, the racing was across natural country and competitors took their own line. It was, in fact, closely related to run out hunting, with a prize at the end instead of the death of the quarry. It was not until 1811 that the first steeplechase over an artificial course was held, at Bedford.

Above left: A worm's eyes view as a field of steeplechasers streams over an obstacle. Spectators standing close to a fence get a real sense of the speed and noise of the sport denied to those in the grandstand.

Left: Runners parade at Cheltenham, with the superb panorama of Cleeve Hill as a backdrop to the bustle of the tented village that mushrooms on big race days. The Gloucestershire course has an unrivalled setting in a natural amphitheater.

Steeplechasing reached the US after the Civil War. In 1869, a steeplechase took place at Jerome Park, New York and was a great success. Thereafter steeplechases were arranged on race tracks across the country. However, hunting over open country became increasingly popular and threatened to eclipse steeplechasing on tracks. In 1895, the National Steeplechase and

> *There is something*
> *about jumping a horse*
> *over a fence, something*
> *that makes you feel good.*
> *Perhaps it's the risk,*
> *the gamble.*
> *In any event*
> *it's a thing I need.*
>
> WILLIAM FAULKNER, NATIONAL OBSERVER,
> FEBRUARY 3, 1964

Hunt Association was formed to regulate both these sports and together with persistent and enthusiastic owners, has kept the sport alive.

THE MODERN SPORT

Steeplechasing nowadays refers to racing over fences, as opposed to hurdles. In Britain and Ireland chase fences are constructed of close-packed birch, 4ft 6in (1.37m) high, faced by a sloping apron and a guard rail at the base. On each course there will also be two or three fences with a shallow ditch in front, called open ditches, and an optional water jump – a low brush fence in front of an oblong of shallow water. Hurdles are smaller, 3ft 6in (1.6m) high, and constructed in sections that can be knocked flat if they are hit hard enough.

Aintree, home of England's Grand National is the exception among British courses. The course for the world's most famous steeplechase, first run in 1839, is unique: 30 spruce-covered obstacles more than 5ft (1.5m) high, including Becher's Brook, the

Above: Desert Orchid, one of steeplechasing's modern icons shows his style over a fence, shadowed by his less talented lookalike Charcoal Willy. In ten seasons Desert Orchid won 34 of his 72 races, including the King George VI Chase an unmatched four times.

Chair and the Canal Turn, in a 4½-mile (7,200-m) race. The American Grand National, created to rival the UK race, is run at Belmont Park.

In the US, races are held at major race tracks, such as Belmont Park or Saratoga, over brush and hurdle fences. Some courses also contain water obstacles, known as "Liverpools", which have a water ditch on the take-off side.

In Britain and Ireland the obstacles on most courses are similar; the variety comes in the configuration of the tracks. Cheltenham, where the world's premier steeplechase is staged every March, with the Gold Cup and Champion Hurdle its centerpieces, is an undulating course with a stiff uphill finish and a premium on stamina; Kempton is flat and suits a handier, sharper kind of a horse; and Sandown provides some extra-tricky distances between obstacles.

In continental Europe, however, there is a variety of fences on any one course. The most important track in France is Auteuil, Paris, France, where obstacles include a bullfinch, an in-and-out water, a ditch and rail and a rubber-topped wall. Hurdles in France are miniature editions of English steeplechase fences. In Britain and Ireland steeplechasing – also called National Hunt racing – gives much

Steeplechasing

more opportunity to the amateur rider, but is still largely a professional spectator sport, providing opportunities for gambling.

Steeplechasing's premier prize is the Cheltenham Gold Cup, first run in 1924. Red Splash was the first winner, the incomparable Arkle (1964–66) the best, and five-times hero Golden Miller (1932–36) the most prolific. Golden Miller is the only horse to double up with the Grand National in the same year, a feat that he achieved, with only 17 days between the races in 1934. Seargeant Murphy was the first American horse to win the Grand National in 1923 and Battleship, a son of Man O'War, won the both the US and UK Grand Nationals in the 1930s.

POINT-TO-POINT

Steeplechasing's links with hunting and the countryside are much stronger than those of flat racing, with the amateur version, point-to-pointing (the name has a similar derivation to steeplechasing) providing the bridge. Point-to-points are end-of-season fund-raisers organized by hunts, and are confined to horses that have been "regularly and fairly

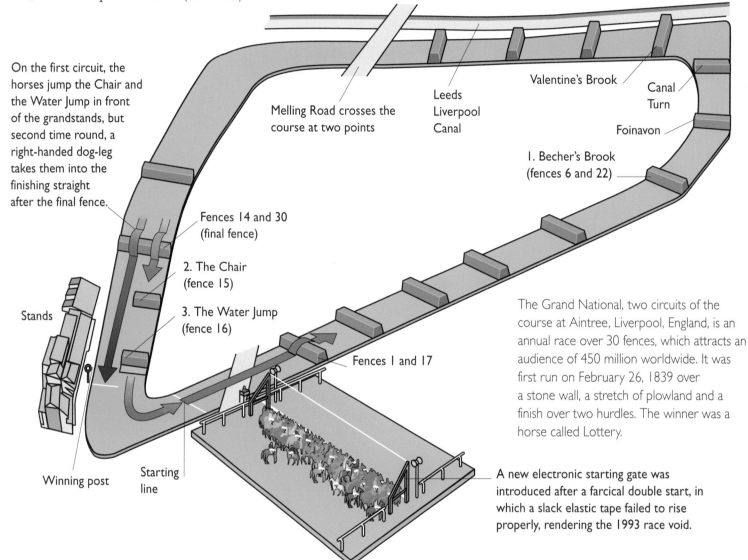

On the first circuit, the horses jump the Chair and the Water Jump in front of the grandstands, but second time round, a right-handed dog-leg takes them into the finishing straight after the final fence.

Melling Road crosses the course at two points

Leeds Liverpool Canal

Valentine's Brook

Canal Turn

Foinavon

1. Becher's Brook (fences 6 and 22)

Fences 14 and 30 (final fence)

2. The Chair (fence 15)

3. The Water Jump (fence 16)

Stands

Fences 1 and 17

Winning post

Starting line

The Grand National, two circuits of the course at Aintree, Liverpool, England, is an annual race over 30 fences, which attracts an audience of 450 million worldwide. It was first run on February 26, 1839 over a stone wall, a stretch of plowland and a finish over two hurdles. The winner was a horse called Lottery.

A new electronic starting gate was introduced after a farcical double start, in which a slack elastic tape failed to rise properly, rendering the 1993 race void.

1. Becher's Brook (fences 6 and 22): the infamous drop landing lost its trappiness when the backward slope towards the now-tiny stream was levelled for safety in 1990.

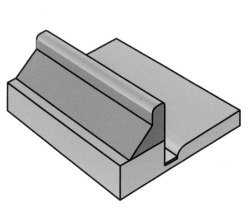

2. The Chair (fence 15): the biggest fence at 5ft 2in (1.57m), and also the narrowest, it is preceded by a 6-ft (2-m) ditch. An accurate approach is needed to jump it smoothly.

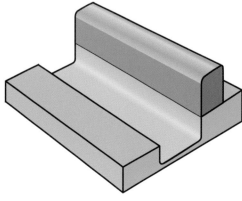

3. The Water Jump (fence 16): the widest of its type, it rarely causes problems and even provides a short respite before the runners turn to face the second circuit of the course.

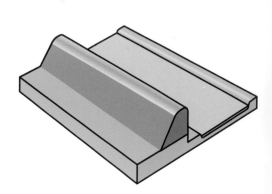

Above: Delightful Auteuil, the premier jump racecourse in France, lies in the Bois de Boulogne in Paris, within sight of the Eiffel Tower. The course includes a twisting figure of eight and a wide variety of obstacles.

LONESOME GLORY

◆

At age 11, Lonesome Glory, a Kentucky-bred chestnut gelding, had eighteen US and UK victories. He was one of only two horses to win four steeplechase Eclipse Awards (1992, 1993, 1995, and 1997). Trained by Bruce Miller, he is the first US steeplechaser to have earned over $1 million. A three-time winner of the Colonial Cup, he has won notable victories in the 1993 Breeders' Cup Steeplechase, the 1998 Hard Scuffle Steeplechase at Kentucky's Churchill Downs, the 1992 hurdles and the 1995 fences at Cheltenham. His 1999 season began with an auspicious victory in the Grade I Carolina Cup.

hunted" with any recognized pack of hounds. Typically, the races staged at such a meeting would include a members', a maiden, and men's and ladies' open races. Pointing can provide a valuable nursery both for riders and horses.

MAJOR RACES

The Grand National is the world's most famous steeplechase. It is a handicap race – one in which horses carry different weights so that, theoretically, each has an equal chance and a lightly-weighted animal with no pretentions to greatness could win.

Britain's steeplechasing crown is the Cheltenham Gold Cup. The 3¼-mile (5,200-m) contest over 22 fences is run at level weights and is rarely won by a moderate horse. In France, the equivalent race is the Grand Steeplechase de Paris, 3⅔ miles (5,800m) at Auteuil in June. Only two horses have won both races, Mandarin in 1962 and The Fellow, which won at Paris in 1991 and Cheltenham in 1994.

In provincial France and the rest of Europe, courses are closer to the sport's cross-country roots. The most gruelling is the 4¼-mile (6,800-m) Velka Pardubika in the Czech Republic, some of which is run over plow like the early Nationals.

In the United States, the steeplechase Triple Crown comprises the Grand National, run in Charlottesville, Virginia; the Temple Gwathmey at Belmont Park, and the Colonial Cup at Camden, South Carolina, the climax of the steeplechase season late in the year. Among hunt race meetings, the most historic and prestigious is the Maryland Hunt Cup, Maryland. A prominent 1930s rider said the UK Grand National was the hardest race to win, and the Maryland Hunt Club the most difficult to ride.

Below: Amateur riders in action at a point-to-point.

Showjumping

Early competitions ✦ *Rules and organization* ✦ *Hickstead* ✦ *Course design*

Showjumping is the newest of the competitive horse sports, arguably the most artificial, and certainly the most instantly identifiable. The concept is simple; the horse is asked to jump a course of brightly-colored knock-down obstacles in an enclosed arena, a dramatic and appealing spectacle in which power and accuracy are essential.

HISTORY

An embryonic version was held at a Dublin horse show in 1865, when high and wide "leaping" contests were held. In 1866, in Paris, a *concours hippique* took place, in which competitors were judged on their appearance before disappearing to jump a series of natural obstacles in the countryside. The obvious next stage was to bring the jumps into the arena for the benefit of those watching, but in its early years "leaping," over dull, flimsy poles and mock hedges, was little more than a diversion for spectators between more important events, such as driving.

In 1883, high- and long-jumping competitions were staged at a New York show, and by 1900 the sport was beginning to resemble today's format. The sport was given significant impetus in 1908 by the establishment of an annual International Horse Show at Olympia, London.

Showjumping was an international sport from its earliest days. The first Nations Cup – still the most important annual international team

Left: Britain's Geoff Billington and his superb bay gelding It's Otto show the power and accuracy that have taken them to the top level internationally. A horse like It's Otto, with flashy looks and flamboyant style, is always a favorite with the public.

Above: Showjumping is a sport that lends itself extremely well to the indoor environment, under bright lights and with the audience in close proximity to the action, as shown here at the Horse of the Year Show at Wembley, London.

Right: The fences on the course of the 1996 Atlanta Olympic Games, with each fence representing an aspect of the United States of America, were most imaginatively designed. Here, a member of the unplaced British team, Michael Whitaker on Two Step, clears the Mount Rushmore vertical.

GEM TWIST

◆

The most popular show jumper in decades, Gem Twist was trained by Olympian Frank Chapot, the only horse ever to win three American Grand Prix Association Horse of the Year awards in 1987, 1989, and 1992. When he was retired in 1997, his saddle was replaced with a blanket of roses by Greg Best, whose partnership with the Thoroughbred gelding made stars of them both. Together they won the 1985 USET Talent Derby, helped the USET to win a Silver Medal at the 1987 Pan American Games, and won two Silver Medals for the USET in Individual and Team Jumping at the 1988 Seoul Olympics.

competition – was held in 1910; an American team appeared at Olympia in 1911; and a year later team medals (won by Sweden) and individual medals (won by Jean Cariou of France on Mignon) were on offer at the Stockholm Olympics.

In the early days, penalties were given for dislodging light slats laid on top of the fence, and differentiation was made between a strike with the front or hind legs. A competitor – nearly all were from the military – was allowed to show his horse the fence before jumping it. Marks could be gained or lost for style, and for the difficulty of the obstacle. Rules varied between countries and even between shows in the same country.

The turning point

The turning point came after World War II. The rise in the sport's popularity stemmed from one show, the Victory Championship held at White City, London, in the late summer of 1945. It was planned by Colonel Mike Ansell and the newly reorganized British Showjumping Society. Ansell introduced color, variety and imagination to the jumps, using painted poles and fillers, shrubs and flowers. A

decade later television brought a sport – which, because of its compactness, immediacy and easily understood reformulated rules, proved perfectly suited to the medium – before a new, wider audience. Pat Smythe (the first woman showjumper to compete at the Olympics, in 1956) and Flanagan, David Broome and Sunsalve became household names.

In North America and continental Europe the sport is hugely successful and the big indoor shows, in particular, attract large, partisan audiences, although its popularity has waned slightly in Britain since the 1970s.

RULES AND FORMATS

Showjumping can be staged indoors or out. Courses are built from scratch for each competition, the exceptions being the so-called "Derby" contests – the most famous of which are at Hickstead and Hamburg – which are jumped over the same, permanent track each year. The Derby Bank and the Devil's Dyke at Hickstead are the most famous showjumping obstacles in the world.

The basic format for a showjumping competition is a preliminary round, from which the clear rounds

Above: Aachen in Germany is one of the most important equestrian centers in the world. The huge complex, with its permanent arenas and housing for equine and human competitors, regularly hosts championships at all national and international levels.

Showjumping

go forward to a timed jump-off over a raised, shortened course. But there are many variations on this theme: a speed class goes straight against the clock; a puissance involves fences raised ever-higher – notably the "big red wall" – until a winner is found; a six-bar is six fences in a straight line; a take-your-own-line invites the rider to jump the fences in the order that he or she thinks will be the quickest. Penalties are now universal: four faults for a knockdown, three faults for the first disobedience (a refusal or run-out), six for the second and elimination for the third.

Fences

The fences can be built in various basic shapes: upright or vertical, staircase (a spread sloping upwards from front to back), parallel or oxer (a spread with the front and back bars the same height), and hog's back (a spread with the center at the highest point). A water jump, with or without a low fence in front, tests the ability to jump width, or distance; water can also be included in the form of a ditch, called a Liverpool, in front of an obstacle. Imaginatively designed fences can be visually stunning, notable examples being the themed courses at recent Olympic Games.

The course

The course builder's objective is to provide entertainment for the audience, with a high standard of jumping for the level of competition, and a thrilling finish. A good course designer tests the horse-and-rider team with the need for tactical and practical solutions to difficult jumps. These might be combination double or triple fences with only a stride or two between them, or upright fences, which generally require the most

Below: The upright, or vertical, type of fence requires the most accurate riding; it can comprise poles or planks in one vertical plane or take the form of a wall or gate.

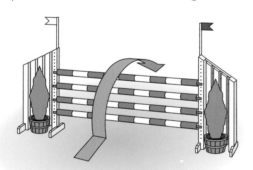

Below: The triple bar, the most common form of staircase fence, slopes up from front to back and is the easiest to jump. The rails can also fan from a single wing on one side.

Below: The square shape of the oxer is achieved by adding a back rail to the front element. In the slightly easier version, an ascending oxer, the back rail is slightly higher.

Below: The hog's back is one of the least common configurations, but is an essential shape in competition, where the fence may be jumped from either direction.

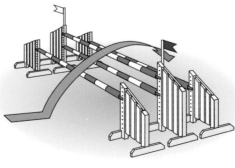

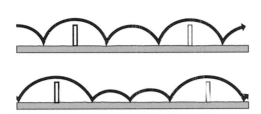

technical approach, placed immediately after wide spreads, which might have encouraged the horse to become outward bound. Distances between all fences in the arena are carefully measured to allow riders to complete the course within the time limitations.

Riders are allowed to walk the course on foot before the class and will plan his route from fence to fence with such considerations in mind. He or she will be aware of the jump-off course, too, looking for places where time can be saved. If there would normally be a comfortable six strides between two fences, for example, it may be possible to press on and cover the distance in only five, thus "taking a stride out".

HICKSTEAD DERBY

Derbies are the Grand Nationals of showjumping. They are arduous competitions in that the courses are long and demanding and only rarely produce more than one clear round. Even so, they are favorites with the public.

The original, the Jumping Derby at Hickstead, Sussex, UK, is probably the most famous annual showjumping contest in the world. It is run over the same 6-furlong (1,200-m) track every year with 16 fences involving 23 jumping efforts in a huge, undulating arena; stamina in horse and rider is at a premium.

The famous permanent obstacles include the Derby Bank, involving 10-ft (3-m) vertical drop with a 5ft 3-in (1.6-m) set of white rails just two strides away; the Devil's Dyke, a one-stride triple of flimsy 4ft 9-in (1.45-m) rustics set in a hollow; the 15-ft (4.5-m) open water; the opening Cornishman, a 4ft 8-in (1.42-m) wall topped by a rustic rail; and the final Silver Birch Oxer, 4ft 10-in (1.47-m) high, with a huge 6ft 6-in (2-m) spread.

Above: The spread fence into a double encourages a bold leap, which should bring the horse to a close, accurate take-off at the vertical second element. Double combinations can be one stride (left, above) or two-stride (left, below).

COURSE DESIGN

◆

A showjumping course is a test of the partnership between horse and rider, with different challenges presented by the size, construction, sequence, and relationship of the single and combination obstacles. The course for the team competion at the 1996 Olympic Games in Atlanta, designed by Linda Allen, is a superb example, made up of a 13-fence track (with 16 jumping efforts), with the accent on technicality rather than size.

A six- or seven-stride option was offered between the 11th, a vertical, and the 12th, a double with an triple bar in and an oxer out.

After opening up to extend over the 14ft (4.3m) water, the test was to shorten stride enough to jump a vertical, a choice of the ranch-stye gate or wall in one obstacle.

This five-fence line was the first test: a Liverpool facing a vertical; four strides to a one-stride, two-stride treble of two verticals and a wide spread; then five or six strides to the oxer.

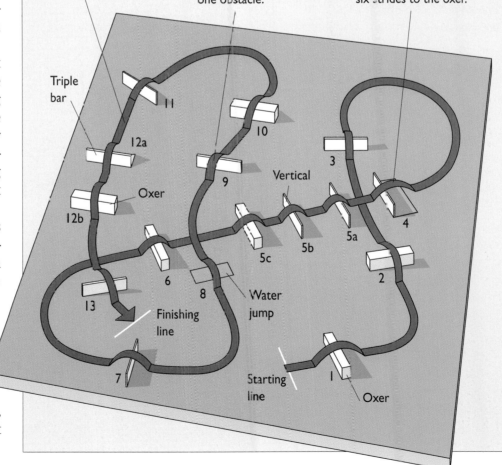

Dressage

Origins ✦ Competitive sport ✦ Tests and arena ✦ Freestyle to music

*D*ressage is a French word that can be translated as training and its objective is to produce a correctly developed, supple horse, obedient to the rider and comfortable to ride. Thus, any riding horse will – or should – have learned the basics of dressage during its early education.

The first evidence of a progressive training system is in the writings of the Greek general Xenophon (435–355 BC), who was the first to regard riding as a science and an art. His words became an inspiration during the Renaissance, at which period horsemen in Europe began to develop "classical" riding, which forms the basis of modern horsemanship. Classical precepts were then largely the preserve of the military – usually the best-mounted and best-disciplined equestrians – and an early form of

Above: Germany's Isabell Werth and Gigolo show the style in extended trot that made them 1996 Olympic champions.

competitive dressage was 19th century competitions for the best-trained officer's charger.

MODERN DRESSAGE

As a competitive sport, modern dressage involves the execution of a series of laid-down movements at different paces (walk, trot, and canter) at certain points in a rectangular arena. There are dressage tests suitable for horses and riders at all stages of training, from the simplest at Preliminary level to the Grand Prix of international and Olympic competition.

At whatever level, dressage is judged against a set standard. The grades in Britain are Preliminary, Novice, Elementary, Medium and Advanced. Similarly, the American Horse Shows Association has standardized US levels of gradually increasing difficulty, beginning with the Training Level and advancing through the First, Second, Third, Fourth, and Fifth Levels. The four tests at the Fifth Level correspond to tests standardized by the FEI (International Equestrian Federation). The final grade, FEI Levels, includes the Prix St. Georges, Intermediare I, Intermediare II and Grand Prix. Within the Grand Prix are the Grand Prix Special and the Grand Prix Freestyle, which is a musical ride choreographed by the rider.

The simplest tests involve very basic movements. In Preliminary Test 10, for example, the rider's first movement is "at A, enter at working trot and proceed down center line. At C, track right" and the second is "M-B-F working trot, F-D half-circle 10 meters diameter, returning to the track at B."

As the horse and rider progress, the movements required become more difficult. The horse must be able to move sideways as well as forward and to extend and shorten his strides in all three paces. At the highest levels, some of the most difficult movements include the pirouette, where the horse pivots on a hind leg and turns a complete circle; the passage, an elevated, springy trot; the piaffe, a passage with little if any forward movement (the horse is in effect marking time); and flying changes, where the horse changes from one canter lead to another without a trot step in between. In a series of one-time changes the horse seems to skip.

Dressage imposes great physical and mental strain at the top levels and the best type of horse will need good conformation, with particular strength in the back and hindquarters, and an equable temperament.

At any level, the horse will be judged on the regularity and freedom of its paces, its calmness and obedience, its balance and cadence and its attentiveness and willingness to accept the rider's requests. The rider is judged on his or her ability to achieve these qualities in the horse, and on the accuracy with which they describe the movements. Just one judge – watching from a point outside the arena at the C mark (riders always enter at A) – is involved at the lower levels, but five judges will deal with international competitors, to ensure an even spread of marks.

The four highest-grade tests are, in order of difficulty, the Prix St. George, the Intermediate I and II, and the Grand Prix, each slightly revised every four years to avoid staleness in competition. The dressage test used as the first phase of a three-day-event is Medium standard.

FREESTYLE DRESSAGE

A rapidly growing branch of the sport is freestyle dressage to music, which, like ice-skating, has marks for artistic impression. This development emphasises the classical origin and content of dressage, sometimes lost in the search for technical accuracy. This is drawing a new generation of enthusiasts.

Below: To remember the sequence of the test in a full-size (20m x 60m) dressage arena requires a high level of mental concentration from the rider. The origin of the letters, seemingly unrelated, is unknown.

Below: Barbara Perkins and Wotan perform a half-pass to the right. The sideways steps taken by the horse demonstrate its elasticity and balance, essential qualities required for dressage.

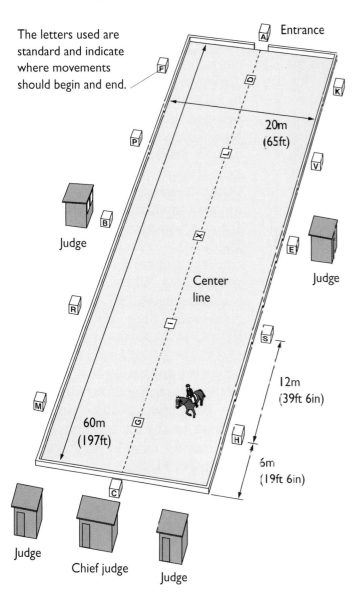

The letters used are standard and indicate where movements should begin and end.

Entrance

20m (65ft)

Center line

12m (39ft 6in)

6m (19ft 6in)

60m (197ft)

Judge

Judge

Judge

Chief judge

Judge

Above: Welton Boogie prepares for take-off. This type of obstacle – a bank, ditch, and fence – looks more imposing to the rider and spectators than to the horse, but a bold, controlled approach is vital nonetheless. Any hesitancy or inaccuracy could result in a refusal or, worse, a fall.

Below: An upright fence requires respect, despite its simple appearance. The trick is not to approach it too fast, but on a comparatively short, attentive stride.

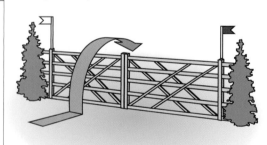

Below: Impulsion and balance are vital for a jump onto or off a bank, especially over a ditch like this. The rider must be prepared for a hesitation on top as the horse sees the drop.

Eventing

Phase D, the cross-country, is the most popular section with spectators and, generally, with riders too. At international level it is a truly daunting and demanding test, featuring a course of upwards of 30 obstacles of every conceivable variety, set in different types of natural terrain. The distance is in the region of 4½ miles (7km) and will take around ten minutes to complete. It is a high-risk sport; falls are frequent, and deaths of horse or rider do occur.

Cross-country riding appears as a separate entity at local level in competitions such as hunter trials (for individual riders) and team chasing (for teams of four together), but it reaches its pinnacle in the three-day event. Before riding the course, the rider will walk it to study the obstacles, the approaches to them, the state of the ground on take-off and landing, and distances in between.

Below: A spread is fairly straightforward and can take an onward-bound, though controlled, approach. Absolute accuracy is not as important as with an upright.

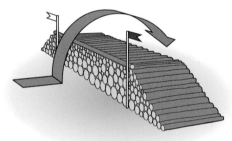

Below: This rustic seat is basically an inviting spread fence that can be approached confidently. The trellis frame should not be a distraction for an experienced horse.

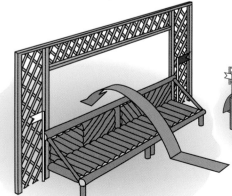

CROSS-COUNTRY FENCES

The fences, unlike those in show-jumping, are fixed, solid obstacles that are not knocked down if hit, although they can be dismantled if a horse becomes entangled. A good course designer will make the obstacles look more difficult than they actually are, and thus keep the rider thinking and alert all the way. In the early days of eventing, the fences were the sort of thing that might have been met in the natural course of a non-competitive ride in actual country – a fallen tree, a gate, a stream, a hedge, a ditch – but now obstacles are highly sophisticated, technically designed versions of the originals.

Horses can find themselves jumping over an upturned boat into a lake; through a representation of a Western cattle ranch; over a couple of pick-up trucks back to back; up or down a series of steps; over or into water splashes; facing fences styled as palisades, rails, shark's teeth, banks, walls, tables, timber wagons; jumping into sunlight from the shade of a

Below: The quickest, but riskiest, way through this combination is to jump over the corner. The middle route is safer but slower and requires three jumping efforts instead of one.

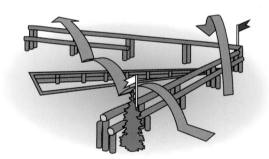

Below: Moving through water reduces speed. This jump can be approached in two ways – straight into the water or, more easily, by going left on to hard ground and then on.

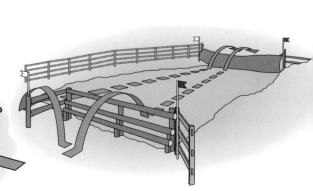

wood or vice versa; or even through a circular hole cut in a hedge. The modern course is wonderful to look at from the spectator's point of view.

The cross-country phase of an event requires absolute mutual trust between horse and rider. Cross-country obstacles are often awkwardly placed and sometimes the horse cannot see his route through one, or his landing point, and so must have the confidence to believe that his rider is not asking the impossible.

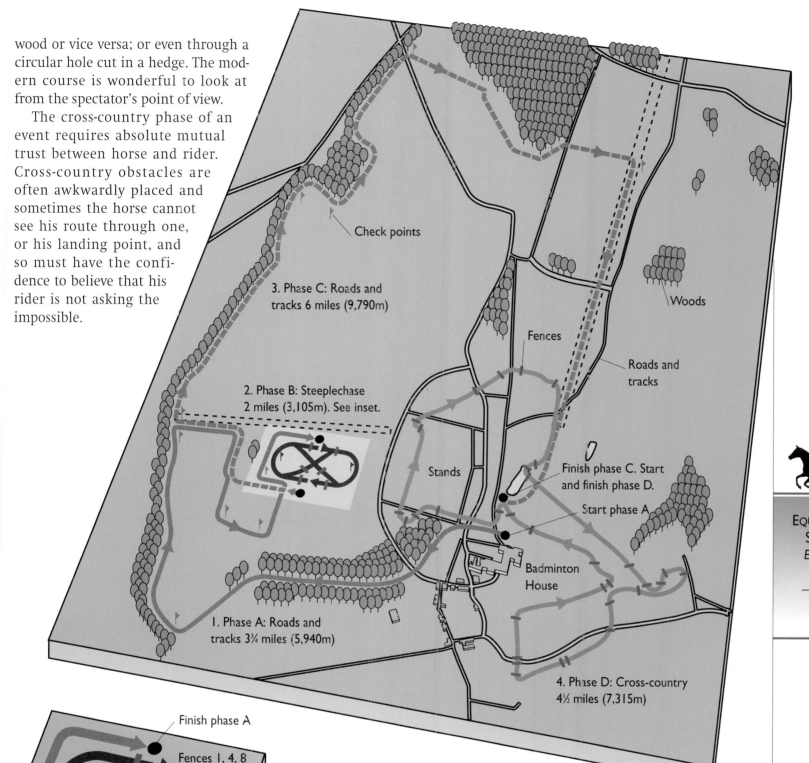

Check points

3. Phase C: Roads and tracks 6 miles (9,790m)

2. Phase B: Steeplechase 2 miles (3,105m). See inset.

Woods

Fences

Roads and tracks

Stands

Finish phase C. Start and finish phase D.

Start phase A

Badminton House

1. Phase A: Roads and tracks 3¾ miles (5,940m)

4. Phase D: Cross-country 4½ miles (7,315m)

Finish phase A

Fences 1, 4, 8

Phase B

7

3

2

6

5, 9

Start phase C

Above: Badminton Horse Trials has come far since John Sheddon on Golden Willow beat 21 rivals to win the first running. Then, it was a matter a of "having a go" at a new sport on a decent hunter or army charger. Now horse and rider are athletes at the highest level. The course is a permanent fixture, run clockwise and counterclockwise in alternate years.

England's Badminton Horse Trials were first held in 1949 and provided the impetus for the formation in 1959 of the United States Combined Training Association (USCTA) to promote and regulate eventing in America.

Since then, under the leadership of the USCTA in partnership with the American Horse Shows Association and the United States Equestrian Team, eventing has continued to gain in popularity. The four competitive levels in Three-Day Eventing present horse and rider with increasing levels of difficulty. It begins on day one with

Dressage followed on the second day by the challenging Speed and Endurance phase. Two sessions of Roads and Tracks, a Steeplechase, and a Cross-Country test with as many as 30 obstacles all must be completed within a prescribed time. The final component is the Stadium Jumping phase.

The International Equestrian Federation (FEI) recognizes four US Three-Day Events: the Radnor Hunt International, the Kentucky Three-Day Event, the Essex Horse Trials, and the Fair Hill International Event.

Polo

History ✦ Rules ✦ Ranking

Polo is the fastest of all team sports, and one to be played with hot blood and a cool head. A good polo player must not only be an excellent rider, but excel at ball games. The basic skill, that of hitting a ball 3½in (9cm) in diameter with a long-handled, small-headed mallet from the back of a galloping horse, requires an unerring ability to coordinate hand and eye.

THE HISTORY OF POLO
Polo originated in ancient Persia, where it was known as *chaugan*, or mallet. It spread east across Asia to China, and from there, in the sixth century AD, to Japan. It found its way south in the 17th century, from Tibet to the mountainous Indian state of Manipur, where it was called *pulu*, the local word for a ball of willow-root.

Pulu spread to the West after it was adopted by the British Raj in the 19th century – the Cachar, the first European polo club, was founded in Assam in 1859. In 1869, polo was introduced

Above: Some protection for the rider is essential in what is a contact sport, with the additional hazards of flailing mallets and a flying ball. High boots, knee pads, and a helmet with faceguard cover the most vulnerable areas without restricting movement. Gloves help to prevent the reins from slipping. Horses wear leg bandages (wraps) or boots.

to England as hockey on horseback by cavalry officers of the Tenth Hussars, and in 1876 to the United States.

During the early 20th century, when polo was played at five Olympic Games, America, and Britain were the rivals. But by the 1930s Argentina – where the British had introduced polo in 1877 – had become the leading polo nation. Despite a blip during the Falklands War, it is still overwhelmingly the dominant force in terms of both riders and horses.

Polo began as the preserve of the ruling classes and the upper echelons of the army, an image it still retains. Though efforts are made to widen its appeal through movements such as the Pony Club in Britain (girls play as much as boys, but the higher reaches are the preserve of men), it is still largely a game for those with large bank balances. Teams are funded by wealthy patrons, who may ride themselves, and who usually recruit highly paid professional players.

The fortunes of any team rest on pony-power. A good polo pony (now horses; the 14.2 hand height limit was abolished in 1916) is fast, strong, athletic, handy, brave, durable and even-tempered, able to stop and turn on a coin. It must be ultra-responsive to the rider's leg or a shift of weight, and is usually severely bitted and bridled for instant control. Polo ponies, a type rather than a specific breed, are

Below: Back to basics in a rural game on ponies in Ladakh, India, at a height of 3500ft (1700m) above sea level. In Ladakh, tough, local Manipuri ponies are used to play the game.

Below: Wooden horses are the best way for novice players to perfect their strokes before playing the real game. These are outside – in an indoor polo pit the ball will keep returning, as on a squash court.

Above: High-speed action at the Palm Beach international ground, Florida. Polo is basically a summer sport, although year-round polo on artificial surfaces is gaining in popularity.

wiry and athletic. Most are Thorough-bred crosses – the best seem to have an innate ball sense and allow their riders to concentrate on the game.

RULES OF THE GAME

Polo is played by two teams of four on a pitch, or field, no more than 300yd (274.3m) long, and between 160 and 200yd (146.3–182.9m) wide, with a goal at either end with 10-ft (3-m) posts that stand 24ft (7.3m) apart. The ball, now plastic, weighs up to 4½ oz (127.5g) and the mallet has a wooden head and flexible bamboo or graphite handle up to 54in (1.37m) long.

A game is split into periods, or chukkas, of seven-and-a-half minutes, under the control of two mounted umpires. The usual game consists of six periods, although eight are allowed in internationals. Ties are resolved in a golden goal period, in which the

first team to score wins. No pony may play two consecutive chukkas or more than two chukkas per game.

RANKING

Each player is ranked, or handi-capped, according to ability assessed by his or her national association. The higher the handicap – from -2 to +10, expressed as goals – the better the player. Most tournaments are played on a handicap basis, with the lesser teams (based on the players' aggre-gate) given a starting goal advantage.

Only 55 players have ever been awarded the 10-goal accolade. A player with a handicap of 5 or more is "high-goal"– thus high-goal polo, is played by teams with an aggregate handicap of 19 or more.

RIDING OFF
◆

The art of riding-off is one of the most important aspects of polo technique. The idea is to ride alongside and push an opponent out of position, either off the line of the ball or to prevent an attack on another player. The trick is to get your pony's shoulder in front of that of the rival pony. Hooking an opponent's stick with your own to prevent a stroke is also permitted, but deliberate bumping or crossing a right of way are fouls, penalized by a free hit.

Hunting

History ✦ *Structure* ✦ *Season* ✦ *Hunting today*

*I*n its earliest days, hunting was one of life's necessities, to provide food or to protect livestock or crops and superior skill at the hunt was seen as something admirable. Eventually, the thrill and the fun of the chase on horseback became an end in itself.

HISTORY

The organized pursuit of game for sport, using packs of specially bred dogs that would hunt by scent rather than sight, was first known in France and was introduced into Britain in the 11th century, when wild boar, stag and even wolf were the quarry. These origins remain in many hunting terms – "Tally-ho!" for example, derives from the French, *Il est hault*, meaning "He is off."

Boar and stag hunting is still carried on in traditional style in France. However, in Britain, hunting began to change during the 18th century, when common land was enclosed by act of Parliament and became part of the gentry's estates. As a result, foxes, rather than stags or hares, became the primary target. This served a double purpose – they were considered a pest and, since they had a lesser scent than a stag and were possessed of natural cunning, they were considered to be more of a sporting challenge for the huntsman.

Hunting with hounds on horseback is now carried on mainly in Britain and Ireland, some European countries (the oldest tradition is in France), the USA and Australia.

THE HUNT STRUCTURE

The structure of a fox hunt is similar throughout the world. In effect, each one is a private club to which members pay an annual subscription. Funds are also raised by charging day visitors a fee. The hunt, usually run by a committee, owns a pack of hounds and employs professionals to manage it – the huntsman, the whippers-in, and kennel and stable staff. The unpaid position of Master (often shared by two or more people, male or female) is the top of the hierarchy.

During a hunt, the Master or the huntsman controls the pack, or "hunts hounds." Only the person hunting hounds carries a horn. This is used to communicate with the pack, the hunt servants and the mounted field. The hunt must gain permission from farmers and landowners to ride over their property.

There are more than 200 packs of hounds in Britain, run under the Masters of Foxhounds Association. Most are foxhounds but there are still some staghounds and harriers (for hunting hares), as well as drag packs. These follow an artificial, man-laid scent over a prearranged line. In France there are 75 packs of hounds, which are a heavier type than the faster English breed. Crossbreeding has improved on speed and stamina. In the USA, there are 150 packs, some of which hunt coyote.

Above: A stone wall typical of the rugged Galway countryside in the west of Ireland. The Galway hunt is known as the Blazers.

Below: The quintessential English hunting scene is provided by the Beaufort Hunt, a pack based in Gloucestershire.

The hunting season varies. Stags are hunted in late summer, autumn, and spring; hinds in midwinter and foxes, in Britain, from November 1 to the end of April. Before November, there is a period of informal early morning hunts to educate young foxhounds, which are called cubbing, or autumn hunting.

HUNTING TODAY

Hunting is one of the few recreational horse sports. Even so, it is a considerable challenge. Most people hunt to enjoy jumping, galloping, and pitting their wits against the terrain as they try to keep up with the pack.

Each pack makes different demands – open grassland and huge fences are the norm in the Shires; stone walls,

---

Ringwell cubbing days are among my happiest memories. These mornings now reappear in my mind, lively and freshly painted by the sunshine of …

autumn …

SIEGFRIED SASSOON, MEMOIRS OF A

FOX-HUNTING MAN, 1928

---

and rougher ground characterize the Derbyshire peaks; large dykes are typical in Essex. Horse and rider need to have courage, stamina, athleticism, initiative, common sense, and good manners, making the hunting field a good place to educate a young horse or rider. The type of horse needed depends on the country to be crossed.

Today, hunting is under fire, particularly in Britain. Those in favor of the sport claim that it represents the most efficient and humane method of

Above right: In France, traditional stag hunting is still practiced. Hunting live quarry is illegal in some parts of Europe, such as Germany and Holland, where drag hunting is substituted.

Right: Hunting with hounds was introduced into America by the British in the mid-17th century. Grey foxes are hunted, which are said to run less straight than the English red fox

controlling foxes (which can be a problem in some areas); those against consider it to be a cruel anachronism.

Many farmers still value hunts for controlling foxes on agricultural land and it provides and supports many jobs, in stabling and farriery. However, many objectors feel that it is unacceptable and if culling is required there are alternative, more humane means available. Whether hunting is, as Oscar Wilde put it, "the unspeakable in full pursuit of the uneatable" or, in the words of Robert Surtees' fictional huntsman Jorrocks, "the image of war without its guilt and only five-and-twenty percent of its danger" is up to the individual.

Western Riding

Methods of riding ✦ Western classes ✦ Rodeo skills ✦ First rodeos

What most sets Western horsemanship apart from European riding is its wholly American origin. It began with the horse culture of the Conquistadores (see page 242), which was then developed on cattle ranches. All of the modern Western riding disciplines can be traced to the practical applications and skills used by cowboys working on the cattle ranches of the American West.

Tack and clothing also differentiate Western from other styles of riding. On horseback all day long, the cowboy needed an animal that was a pleasure to ride and a saddle designed with the same comfort and practicality as his clothing (see page 245).

Western and European schools do have common objectives for the horse – lightness, self-carriage, obedience, and balance. The trained Western horse, however, is allowed to be more independent in thought and action.

Western training encourages a free self-carriage, with a minimal rein influence. The rider uses one hand and neck-reins, with an appropriate shift of body-weight – an important factor – to indicate a change of direction or speed. In ideal circumstances, the horse will be trained using a bitless bridle or bosal noseband, before it graduates to the apparently severe long-cheeked curb bit with its high ported mouthpiece. But by then the horse should be operating with only the lightest touch on its mouth, virtually by the weight of the reins alone.

By the late 1990s, the appeal of Western riding was increasingly international, and among the fastest growing disciplines were team roping, barrel racing, team penning, reining, and cutting.

REINING CLASSES

Reining classes are the Western equivalent of the European rider's dressage tests. In National Reining Horse (NRHA) competitions, the horse must perform one of 10 specified patterns, requiring suppleness, balance, and speed.

Each pattern includes small slow circles, large fast circles, flying lead changes, rollbacks over the hocks, spins done in place, and the spectacu-

Right: The against-the-clock objective in a calf roping event is to get any three of the calf's feet tied together, rendering it helpless.

Above: The steer wrestler slides from his horse, grabs the horns and drags his quarry to a standstill, wrenching its head sideways to force it to the ground.

Right: This cowpony, in complete balance with hocks engaged, performs the classic sliding halt. There is minimum mouth contact.

lar sliding halt from canter. All are maneuvers used when herding cattle. Judges give credit in their scoring for smoothness, finesse, attitude, speed, and authority in the performance of the several maneuvers. Like freestyle dressage, freestyle reining sets the maneuvers to music in a display designed by the competitor. In 1998, reining was accepted as first Western discipline of the United States Equestrian Team.

CUTTING COMPETITIONS
In one of the fastest growing equine sports, cutting horse and rider

partner each other in a demonstration of cattle handling. Under National Cutting Horse Association rules, they have two and a half minutes to cut a calf from a herd and keep it separated. It is the horse, on a loose rein once the calf has been cut, that controls the animal. A champion cutting horse needs no direction from the rider to react to the calf's movements with speed and agility to keep it from following its instinct to rejoin the herd. Most contestants will cut two or three cows in the allotted time.

PLEASURE CLASSES
The Western Pleasure class is the most accessible to the average rider. The aim is to demonstrate the paces, manners and obedience of the horse as a utility riding animal, including staying still if the rider dismounts, drops the reins and walks away.

BARREL RACING
Barrel racing is a competition that fully tests the agility and speed of the horse. Entering the arena at full speed, horse and rider trigger the clock as they start the cloverleaf pattern around three barrels positioned in a triangle; the clock is stopped by their leaving the arena. Touching and even moving the barrels is allowed, but there is a five-second penalty for an overturned barrel. Victory is measured in hundredths of seconds.

Barrel racing bridges the gap between Western classes at horse shows, which are open to hobby riders of both sexes, and rodeo events, which are confined to men who, more often than not, are professionals who travel the state fair circuit.

RODEO
The rodeo demonstrates the traditional skills of the cowboy: broncobusting, horseback riding, calf roping, and steer wrestling, as well as events unrelated to the Old West. The Professional Rodeo Cowboys Association recognizes 10 events: saddle bronc riding, bareback riding, bull

Above: Balance, agility and speed – and a sense of fun from both horse and rider – are paramount in order to scrape the barrels and gain precious seconds.

riding, calf roping, steer wrestling, team roping, steer roping, bullfighting, and barrel racing.

Riding the bucking bronco, saddled or bareback, is a classic rodeo event with roots in the competitions ranch hands would stage to see who among them had the best style with unbroken horses. The rider must remain on the horse, which wears a tight strap around its loins to make it buck, for eight seconds, but that alone is not enough to win. The rider, who synchronizes his spurring action with the horse's bucking, improves his score. Disqualification results if the rider touches the animal, himself, or his equipment with his free hand, or if a foot slips out of a stirrup, or if he drops the rein, or if his feet are not in the proper position over the bronco's shoulders at the start.

Calf roping requires harmony between horse and rider, who must rope the calf that has a head start out of the chute, dismount, and run to the calf, throw it to the ground, and tie any three legs. The rider throws his hands in the air as a signal to the judge and remounts. His horse, which had backed up to keep the rope taut, then rides forward to allow the rope to slacken. The calf must remain tied for six seconds. The event is directly tied to ranch work, when calves were roped for branding, veterinary treatment, or shipment to market.

Steer roping

On ranches, steer roping enabled the medical treatment of full-grown cattle. In modern steer roping, the cowboy ropes the steer around the horns, which are the only legal catch, tosses the rope over the steer's right hip, and rides to the left to bring the steer to the ground. Then the rider dismounts and runs to tie any three of the steer's legs. As in calf roping, the steer must remain tied for six seconds.

In team roping, a "heeler" and a "header" work together to catch the steer, with the header looping his rope over the horns of the steer and taking it in tow so that his partner, the heeler, can move in to rope both hind legs. In this timed event, the clock stops when both ropes are taught and the horses are facing each other with the steer in between. Champion teams have accomplished all this in less than five seconds.

Steer wrestling

In 1903, a new event was added to rodeo when Bill Pickett, a black cowboy from Texas, leaped for the horns of a steer to save his horse from being gored, wrestling the steer to the ground, biting its upper lip in a bulldog-style grip. Rodeo rules have eliminated lip biting, but steer wrestling is still known colloquially as "bulldogging."

Wrangling

In the most dangerous of rodeo events, bullfighting – or wrangling – the bullfighter is in the arena with the bull for a minimum of 40 seconds, with an option to stay for another 30 seconds. Points are won based on a combination of the bullfighter's control and the risks he takes. The bull can compete for years, learning from experience.

Denver, Colorado, is traditionally accepted as the birthplace of paid spectator rodeo, which first took place in October 1887. The Spanish *rodear*, to surround, is the origin of the word and the bucking horse comes from *potro bronco* – unbroken colt. The Calgary Stampede, first held in 1912 and held annually since 1919 is the most famous rodeo, but the oldest is the Cheyenne Frontier Days, presented every year since 1897.

Right: Broncos buck as a natural response to having a "predator" on their backs. Riders are generally required to survive eight minutes on board.

Showing

Categories ✦ Horse types

Above: A young competitor at a county show in Michigan, asks her pony, a Welsh-Arab cross, to stand up squarely for the judge. The handler's dress is as practical as that of her English counterpart (below).

*If one induces the horse
To assume that carriage
Which it would adopt
Of its own accord when displaying
its beauty,
Then, one directs the horse
To appear joyous and magnificent,
Proud and remarkable
For having been ridden.*

XENOPHON (C.430–355 BC)

Horse shows carry on the tradition of the country horse fair, where working as well as riding and driving horses could be judged, bought, and sold. The modern show, too, acts as a shop window for different breeds and types, maintaining standards as well as providing fun for amateur hobby exhibitors.

Showing today takes place all over the world, and hardly a weekend goes by that there is not a horse show happening somewhere in England, America, and Ireland. Horses of an almost bewildering variety come before judges at shows ranging from local riding club events to Major County and regional extravaganzas. At English county shows, the competitions are generally dominated by professional producers and breeders who make a living from horse dealing.

The American Horse Shows Association (ASHA) recognizes thousands of competitions nationwide each year, governing all aspects of competition at these events. Judging often takes into consideration not only performance but such attributes as quality, beauty, and style.

CATEGORIES

Horse shows are often organized by specialized associations around particular breeds: Arabians, Warmbloods, Quarter Horses, Appaloosas, American Hackney horses, American Saddlebreds, Tennessee Walking Horses, and British Isles natives like the Mountain and Moorlands. Classes for colored horses – piebalds, paints, skewbalds – are becoming increasingly popular. In-hand classes are the preserve of young stock and breeding stock.

Horses are shown either ridden or in-hand (led), depending on the category. Judges – usually two per class at the bigger shows – will base their opinion on conformation manners, and "presence." A horse with presence has that extra sparkle that says "Look at me."

In the UK and in the Eastern US, Hunter and Jumper events dominate. Western riding contests are, as one would expect, popular in the American West. Middle West states like Saddle Horses, Hackney, and Harness ponies, but these events turn up elsewhere. Within these groupings, there are numerous subdivisions. There are classes for Three-gaited and Five-gaited Saddlebreds, Hunter Hacks, Hunters Under Saddle, Hunt Seat Equitation, Western Pleasure,

Left: A handler at the Royal Windsor show is trying to persuade her yearling Arab to adopt a suitably flattering stance so that it can be judged. She is appropriately shod and, in a moment, will have to run to keep up as her horse displays its extravagant floating trot.

Right: David Tatlow, one of Britain's foremost showmen, launches the magnificent heavyweight hunter Skibereen into a gallop at Royal Windsor, one of the prestigious events of the summer circuit.

Below: Amazing grace at the Royal International Horse show in the sidesaddle *corcours d'élégance* where riding habits, ancient and modern, add a touch of theatre to the horsewoman's traditional style. Side-saddle riding requires great skill and is undergoing something of a revival.

Western Horsemanship, Equitation, Side-saddle, and many more. The classes under which horses are judged are so numerous, in fact, that there is sure to be a class suited to the abilities of just about any horse. There are dozens of possible classes for Working Hunters alone, with one of the most popular being for Amateur Owners.

For example, a class for hunters is generally is divided into lightweight, middleweight, heavyweight, referring to the type of rider the horse could be expected to carry. The term "hunter" refers to the type of horse, usually a quality sort with strength and athleticism. Proceedings begin with the horses circling the judges as a group, at walk, trot, canter, and gallop and in both directions, to provide an initial impression of their looks and paces, before being called to stand in a preliminary line-up.

After this, each horse is examined in detail by being asked to perform a short individual show before being ridden by the judge. The saddle is then removed so that the horse's conformation (see pages 22–3) may be inspected closely and, finally, it is run up in-hand to show off its action. The first attraction of a horse may be its looks, but great emphasis is placed on "the ride," the way it performs for the judge and its manners under saddle.

Show hunters do not have to jump in the ring, but working hunters must complete a course of rustic fences, over which their style and attitude is almost as important as whether or not they go clear. Ladies' hunters may be ridden sidesaddle. On the American circuit a difference is made between the various classes: hunt seat (English style), stock seat (Western style) and saddle seat (for the specially gaited breeds such as the Tennesee Walkers).

Below: The art of showing – the checkerboard is applied with a stencil or painstakingly with a short comb; the shark's teeth with sweeps of a soft brush. The patterns will show up only on a healthy, scrupulously clean coat.

Endurance Riding

Popularity ◆ *Trail riding* ◆ *Professional circuit* ◆ *Physical requirements*

Long-distance riding is the fastest-growing of equestrian sports for the good reason that it is accessible – at the simplest level, it is no more than a hobby rider taking their horse for a non-competitive, prolonged hack. However, at an elite level, it is an exacting sports, both physically and mentally, which involves careful training and conditioning of horse and rider.

TRAIL RIDING

Like many equestrian pursuits, endurance riding has military origins. Today, it has its greatest following in the USA, where the American Cavalry was the first body to organize such rides over inhospitable terrain, with

Above: The Tevis Cup, a national endurance riding competition, is held annually in the Sierra Nevada Mountains. Riders such as April Ott (above) compete on a 100-mile course through rugged and majestic terrain.

the aim of testing soundness and stamina and with the emphasis on horse management.

In the United States, the term "trail riding" covers three main categories: pleasure, competition, and endurance. In pleasure rides, as the terminology implies, there is no element of competition; the route, distance, and time taken are up to the participants. Competitive trail riding is held over one, two, or three days on marked courses, to be completed within a maximum

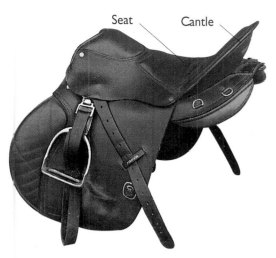

Seat   Cantle

Above: The long-distance saddle is a hybrid of English and Western styles. It has a flatter seat with a higher cantle and broader point of contact than a conventional competition saddle, thus distributing weight better, allowing maximum comfort for horse and rider.

and minimum time limit, with penalty points possibly deducted at veterinary checks. There is no racing element, but any horse that completes the course within set average speeds, with a clean veterinary, sheet will qualify for the top award.

However, in endurance rides, the horse that completes the course in the fastest time in satisfactory condition (as judged by a panel of vets) is the winner. Such rides, over marked trails, are generally 50 or 60 miles (80 or 100km) long.

INTERNATIONAL RIDES
The most gruelling ride in the USA is the Tevis Cup, a 100-mile (160-km) one-day ride from Tahoe City, Nevada, 6,000ft (1,829m) above sea level, to Auburn, California, at 1,000ft (300m). The route over the Sierra Nevada includes a climb of 9,500ft (2,896m) through Squaw Pass and extremes of climate from snow to temperatures of 100°F (38°C) in valleys. The winning time is usually 12 hours, but anyone who completes the race within 24

Right: Most sound, reasonably fit horses of any type or breed can tackle the less difficult rides. But in the top echelon, the Arab, purebred or crossed, like Peraz, the individual gold medallist at the World Equestrian Games in Holland in 1994 ridden by Valerie Kanary of the USA, comes into its own.

hours is awarded the coveted gold and silver belt buckle depicting a Pony Express rider (see page 244).

Australia's famous ride is the 100-mile (160-km) Tom Quilty Ride over the Blue Mountains in New South Wales. In Britain, the two-day Golden Horseshoe Ride, also over 100 miles, is the best known. The latter, however, is judged on the competitive trail-ride principle and is not a race.

FITNESS AND VET CHECKS
Every endurance ride involves stopping for veterinary checks at prescribed places along the course. The physical condition of the horse at these checks is the most important aspect of long-distance competition. Temperature, pulse, respiration rates, and dehydration are the factors that the vet will monitor, as well as any signs of lameness, injury, or chafing tack. Each horse and rider is serviced by a back-up crew at each stop. The sports is now a far cry from the rides, theoretically intended to improve standards, that were organized by Austro-Hungarian cavalry regiments at the end of the 19th century, in which horses were often ridden to death.

The fitness of the rider is as important as that of the horse, as rolling or slumping in the saddle, for example, can cause a sore back. Both horse and rider must become accustomed to long periods on their own

Above: A vet checks the feet and shoes at a gate. The horse must be in good condition if it is to be allowed to continue on the ride.

and must maintain concentration and alertness in such circumstances, particularly on uneven ground.

SPORTS ASSOCIATIONS
There are numerous Trail Ride associations in the USA and Australasia. In Britain, the internationally recognized representative body is the British Endurance Riding Association, in turn part of the European Long Distance Riding Conference. Team and individual championships are held at European and world level, with the possibility of inclusion in the Olympics on the horizon.

The Working Horse

Since the horse was first domesticated 5,000 to 6,000 years ago, it has played an important role in human history, often making and breaking whole civilizations. Initially herded and then used for riding and draft, its role barely changed until the early part of the 20th century with the advent of motorized transportation,

tanks, and farm machinery. Today, the horse is still a crucial element of life in areas of Eastern Europe and parts of Asia. In wealthier places, the emphasis is on sport. Even so, it plays an important part in state ceremonial, is often used by the police for street control, and there is no replacement to be had for herding cattle.

*Gypsy gold does not chink
and glitter.
It gleams in the sun and neighs
in the dark.*

CLADDAGH GYPSY SAYING
FROM GALWAY, IRELAND

*One stiff blind horse his every bone a-stare,
Stood stupefied, however he came there;
Thrust out part service from the devil's stud ...*

ROBERT BROWNING, CHILDE ROLAND TO THE DARK
TOWER CAME, 1855

*The horse is an
archetypal symbol
which will always find
ways to stir
deep and moving
ancestral memories
in every human being.*
PAUL MELLON, FORWARD TO THE
HORSE IN ART, 1980

This noble beast —
But why discourse
Upon the Virtues of the Horse?
They are too numerous to tell
Save when you have a Horse to sell.
No beast has done has much as He
To elevate Society.
How could Society Get On
(Or off), my Child, if He were gone?

OLIVER HERFORD, THE HORSE, 1906

'Wy it is that long-stage coachmen possess such insiniwations, and is always looked up to — adored I may say — by ev'ry young 'ooman in ev'ry town he vurks through, I don't know . . . . It's a regl'ation of natur — a dispensary, as your poor mother-in-law used to say.'

CHARLES DICKENS, THE PICKWICK PAPERS, *1837*

Soldiers are the noblest estate of mankind, and horsemen the noblest of soldiers.

SIR PHILIP SIDNEY, *1595*

PART 5

HORSE AND PONY BREEDS

Most equines of 14.2 hands (4ft 10in) or more, are described as horses, and those below are generally ponies. The purest bloodlines carried by the Arab, Barb, and Thoroughbred are known as "hotbloods," while the European heavy horses are "coldbloods." Warmbloods are any combination of the two. Now, with few horses left in the wild, most matings are planned to produce a particular breed or type and selection is increasingly scientifically based. A type with strong genes and dominant hereditary characteristics that become established may develop into a recognized breed. Stud books control the breeding lines and only horses acceptable to the breed's authority are eligible, to ensure continuing improvement. Horses and ponies not qualified for a Stud Book are grouped and described as "types."

Thoroughbred

The Thoroughbred was created by a relatively small group of Englishmen during the late 17th and early 18th centuries, a time when racing became ultra-fashionable because of the enthusiasm of royalty. In their search for faster horses, the nobility and gentry of the era crossed imported stallions – fiery Arabs, Barbs and Turks (see pp.184–5) – with tough native-bred mares like the Scottish Galloway ponies already used for sport.

The genetic qualities of each group proved an ideal match and it was soon apparent that a new, distinct breed had been developed, incapable of being improved by further crossing.

The first edition of the *General Stud Book*, which detailed the pedigrees of horses bred to race, was published in Britain in 1791 and contained the names of 354 mares. The 42nd edition in 1998 contained 23,237 and there are now 48 other recognized Thoroughbred stud books worldwide in countries as disparate as the USA and Cyprus.

Uses
The primary use of the Thoroughbred is for racing, in which sphere it provides the basis of a global industry that has expanded hugely with the development of ease of air travel. The vast majority of Thoroughbreds are produced for flat racing and the most successful or best-bred horses can command huge prices. The world record auction price stands at $13.1 million, given in Kentucky in 1985 for an untried yearling colt by Nijinsky.

The Thoroughbred is also a valuable cross with other breeds where an introduction of refinement, spirit, stamina, athleticism, or speed is required. Ex-racehorses can also make excellent competition horses in other sports, particularly eventing.

Appearance
The Thoroughbred is a fine-lined horse, with a varying amount of bone, length in the back and legs, and size of feet. The head, on a long, gently curving neck, is usually refined and alert with a bold eye. Shoulders should be long and sloping, with well-defined, sometimes prominent, withers. The body can be long and narrow, but the quarters should be strong, if angular. Limbs must be clearly defined, with well-formed knees and hocks, to withstand pressure at speed. Limb bones should be hard and flat. Thoroughbreds are always a solid color.

Characteristics
Thoroughbreds may be late to mature and nervous and excitable. Their action is long and low, although some have higher knee action. They need warmth, good food and regular attention, and cannot survive in the wilds in extremes of temperature. They are generally courageous, bold, enjoy galloping, jump well, and respond to kindness.

Height
14.2 hands–17 hands (4ft 10in–5ft 8in).

In England, the cradle of the Thoroughbred, racing takes place throughout the year both on the flat, over distances between 5 furlongs and 2¾ miles (1000–4400m), and over hurdles (above) and fences, between 2 miles and 4½ miles (3200–7200m).

Hackney Horse

The Hackney horse was once popular for riding over long distances on the road, and for light pulling. It is a fine-boned horse, descended from the Norfolk Roadster, a utilitarian breed with the same oriental blood as the Thoroughbred, which was then crossed with Thoroughbred blood. Trotting horses were popular in England during the 13th and 19th centuries – the Hackney Horse Society was founded in Norwich in 1883, and the breed was developed for trotting races, ridden and driven, and could trot at speeds of 16mph (25k/ph). Now they excel as harness horses, moving with dramatic knee and hock action, but with lightness, ease, and grace. It shares the same stud book as its relation the Hackney pony (see p.221).

Uses
Formerly popular for riding, the Hackney is now mainly a carriage horse. It is used for competitive driving and showing, and can prove a useful outcross in breeding.

Appearance
The Hackney horse has a straight or slightly convex profile to the head on a thick-set, crested neck, and very strong sloping shoulders to low withers. It stands with its hocks out behind, belying the strength displayed in action. Hackney horses are generally black, bay, brown, or chestnut, and often have white leg and facial markings (see p.23). The feet are extremely important and should not be flat and spreading but fairly upright with a strong wall, particularly at the heels.

Characteristics
The Hackney is a courageous horse with stamina and spirit. It has a brisk and elastic walk and a flowing, elevated trot, with dramatic knee and hock action. The trot covers the maximum amount of ground, and propels the horse forwards with incredible lightness. The action is hereditary, but showing enthusiasts train the Hackney to excel in its trot pace.

Height
14 hands–15.3 hands (4ft 8in–5ft 3in)

Above: A pair of Hackney horses, performing in a driving contest, give a typically spectacular display of trotting in unison.

Left: Here, a Hackney stallion is being shown in hand. In order to maintain the high standards expected of the breed, the judges scrutinize action, conformation and type, manners and temperament.

Welsh Cob

Largest and strongest of the Welsh breeds, the Welsh Cob is the result of Welsh Mountain ponies (see p.218) being crossed with Roman imports, including the Andalucian (see p.170), as far back at the 12th century. Originally known as the Powys Cob, it became a war horse, pulling guns, and carrying mounted infantry. The Pembroke Cart Horse, now extinct, is another probable ancestor, which was used to pull dairy and bakers' drays, and for shepherding and farming. In the 18th century, infusions of Norfolk Roadster, English trotting horses (see p.161), Arabian and Spanish blood combined to give the Welsh Cob its distinctive character and action.

Uses
A versatile pony, the Welsh Cob is popular for breeding, showing, competitive and practical driving, and riding. It is especially popular with light adults, but could carry a large man with ease. The Welsh Cob jumps very well and is in great demand when crossed, particularly with the Thoroughbred (see p.160), for a larger competition horse.

Appearance
The Welsh Cob has an attractive, slightly dished head, large bold eyes, small pointed ears and wide nostrils. The body is very strong, compact and deep, with a powerful loin area. The Cob tends to stand with its hocks out behind, and has silky, feathered heels and well-shaped feet. It may be any color, but is not often gray and never part-colored.

Characteristics
Brave, spirited and kindly, the Welsh Cob is known for its powerful, extravagant trot in which it extends the forelegs almost horizontally from the shoulder.

Height
Up to 15.1 hands (5ft 1in)

The Irish Draft

Irish-bred horses are renowned throughout the world for their soundness, jumping ability, and versatility. The Irish Draft, originally derived from the heavy horses of France and Flanders but given greater quality, speed, and stamina by Spanish imports, has evolved to become a substantial all-purpose horse, with a bold, willing nature. Much lighter than its ancestors, the Irish Draft is now established as Ireland's premier non-Thoroughbred horse breed.

Uses
Formerly a working horse, the Irish Draft is an ideal hunter, especially for the bigger rider. It has an even temper, which is ideal for horse trials, and excels at showjumping. It crosses well with the Thoroughbred (see p.160) to produce even greater speed, scope, and stamina.

Appearance
The Irish Draft combines substance with quality and strength. The old-fashioned type had a shortish neck, coarse head, and a rather straight shoulder, but the quality is now much improved, and the best make good show horses. The eye is kind and generous, the body deep and fine coated, not coarse. The limbs are very strong and clean boned, without feathers. The Irish Draft is mainly dappled gray, but any whole color is acceptable.

Characteristics
An ideal all-rounder, owing to its good temperament, soundness and athletic ability, the Irish Draft is also bold, sure-footed, versatile, and sensible. Generally straight in action, but not extravagant, the modern Irish Draft can really gallop. It is bigger than it was a century ago and matures at six to seven years old.

Height
16 hands–17 hands (5ft 4in–5ft 8in)

Cleveland Bay

The Cleveland Bay is the oldest of the English pulling horses, and has been recognized as a distinct breed since records began to be kept, more than 200 years ago. It originated as far back as the 16th century in the Cleveland area of Yorkshire, England, where it was known as the Chapman Horse or Yorkshire Pack, and carried goods for traveling merchants. Miners used it to carry heavy loads of ironstone from hill mines to the coast or rivers, so it had to be strong, sure-footed, and steady. In the 19th century, the Cleveland was in demand all over the world to improve other native breeds. By 1962, however, the breed's situation was critical with only four pure-bred stallions standing in Britain. The breed was rescued largely owing to judicious breeding by a stallion owned by the British Royal Family. Today it is a popular cross with the Thoroughbred.

Uses

Before motorized farming, the Cleveland Bay was a useful farm horse, powerful enough to work over heavy clay lands. It then became a popular coach horse until road surfaces improved and faster horses were used – often a Cleveland/ Thoroughbred cross. The Cleveland Bay is now used in driving competitions, but is more popular crossed with a faster, lighter breed, such as the Thoroughbred (see p.160), when it does well in showjumping and horse trials.

Appearance

The Cleveland Bay is always bay, with black points (mane, tail, lower limbs, and feet). No other color is allowed. It has strong, heavy bone (8½in–9in [21.6cm–24.1cm] below knee), and is never hairy-legged or heeled. The head is quite large, either straight or convex in profile, with long ears. A longish neck is often arched, on a wide, deep body. The back is strong, sometimes quite long, and the thighs and hindquarters are powerful. The limbs are fairly short, the feet reasonably wide, but not shallow.

Characteristics

The Cleveland Bay combines strength with activity to make it a versatile weight-carrying all-rounder. It is sure-footed, can be bold, but not fast. Its straight action is quite long striding, but rarely extravagant. A good jumper, it can carry a large man across heavy plow, or jump out of deep mud. It is sensible, docile, hardy, and proves an excellent riding and driving horse when crossed with Thoroughbred blood for greater agility and stamina at speed. It matures at five to six years old.

Height

16 hands–16.2 hands (5ft 4in–5ft 6in)

The Royal Mews keep many Cleveland Bay and Cleveland Bay crosses. The Queen's Cleveland stallion Mulgrave Supreme was used to rescue the breed in 1962. Put to pure-bred and part-bred mares, within 15 years there were 36 pure-bred stallions in the UK.

This Cleveland Bay stallion in Cleveland, Yorkshire, displays the typical characteristics of this ancient breed – the strong constitution of the heavier horse with the athleticism of the lighter type. Although today there are relatively few pure Cleveland horses being bred, they are instantly recognizable since no "outside" blood is allowed. This ensures that the breed's unique characteristics and bay coloring are retained. Poor specimens of the breed are also rejected by the *Cleveland Bay Stud Book*.

Friesian

The Dutch Friesian probably traces back to 1000 BC. Its ancestors were used by the Romans for pulling, and it carried knights during the Crusades, when it was influenced by Eastern blood. In the 16th century, when Spain occupied the Netherlands, Andalucian blood (see p.170) refined it further. The Friesian has influenced the breeding of Fell and Dale ponies (see p.216), the Oldenburg, possibly the Morgan (see pp.173 and 190), and through its derivative, the Old English Black, the Shire (see p.201). Its action caused it to be crossbred in the 19th century for a lighter type for trotting races. The breed almost became extinct, but was rescued and now flourishes.

Uses
The Friesian is a popular all-round working horse, often seen at shows and exhibitions, and particularly successful in driving teams.

Appearance
Smaller and faster than its heavier ancestors, the Friesian nonetheless retains their strength, courage, and willing nature. It has a fine head, carried erect on a high-arched neck, has an intelligent expression and a strong, compact, muscular body. The legs are feathered, the feet hard and the mane and tail full. Friesians are always totally black.

Characteristics
Friesians have an inherent high-stepping trot that makes them spectacular performers under saddle or in harness. Although docile, they are sensitive.

Height
15 hands upwards (5ft).

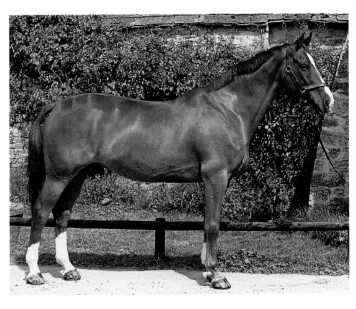

Dutch Warmblood

The Dutch Warmblood was founded in the 1960s. The aim was to develop an ideal competition horse, with quality, substance, and ability, that was also a pleasure to ride. It was founded on selected Gelderlander and Groningen mares, and these bloodlines were then mixed with lighter breeds to produce different breed categories, which are strictly controlled and graded. These categories are the "sport horse," the less ambitious riding horse, likely to have Anglo-Arab-type blood (see p.178), and the heavier carriage horse, which has more of the Dutch influence. Seven Lipizzaners (see p.175) were introduced to the breed the 1980s to produce a driving and riding type of horse.

Uses
The Dutch Warmblood is a powerful, all-round performer with athletic paces. It can excel at dressage, showjumping, horse trials, driving, and breeding "sport horses."

Appearance
The overall impression is of balance and strength, with no weaknesses, although in some cases the back can be long, and the head rather plain. It is strong bodied and strong-quartered, with ample bone and well-rounded feet. Bay or brown are dominant colors, although other solid colors occur.

Characteristics
The Dutch Warmblood has an equable temperament and almost invariably moves straight, with elastic paces and a willing, positive attitude to work. It matures early, at four or five years. Thoroughbred crosses are often used to produce greater speed and stamina for horse trials.

Height
16 hands upwards (5ft 4in)

Camargue

The Camargue horse, or pony, is an ancient breed that greatly resembles the primitive horses depicted in the cave paintings at Lascaux, France, which date from about 15,000 BC. The native stock probably remained fairly pure until the eighth and ninth centuries, when it was undoubtedly influenced by the Barb horses (see p.185) from North Africa that were brought to Europe during the Moorish invasion. Since then, however, the herds have been free from outside influence. The Camargue lives in southern France, where small herds still run wild. From 1968, when the breed was officially recognized, breeding became more selective and controlled.

Uses
These horses are used to herd cattle, work the black bulls of the region for the bullring, and carry groups of tourists across the rough terrain.

Appearance
Tough but rarely beautiful, the Camargue usually has a big, plain, head set on a short neck and upright shoulder. The back is quite short and strong. The quarters can be short, sloping to a wiry tail, and horses are branded with a "C" on the rear-side quarter. Limbs are short and very strong, with wide, very hard feet suitable for its native marshy environment. The feet are rarely shod.

Characteristics
The Camargue horse is slow to mature on the coarse, sparse grasslands of its habitat. Unusually, it survives on the salty water of this environment. As it is basically a wild horse, it can be wilful and independent, and difficult to catch and train. However, once "tamed," it is a willing, game form of transport over difficult terrain. The Camargue can live well into its 20s and is notable for a long, high-stepping walk, free canter and gallop but its trot is very uncomfortable, with short strides. A tough breed with stamina, the Camargue can cover long distances in a single day.

Height
Average 14 hands (4ft 8in).

Small herds of Camargue horses – stallions, mares and youngsters of up to three years old – roam the watery regions of the Rhône delta in southern France. They have adapted to their harsh surroundings over many centuries. Since 1968, the herds have been sorted and branded as foals and the less good colts gelded. They are protected from outside influence or alien blood. Although they are not, individually, a prepossessing breed, gathered together in herds or splashing through the water, the Camargue horses make a beautiful sight.

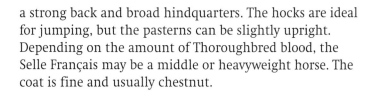

Selle Français

The Selle Français (French Riding Horse), originally known as the Anglo-Norman horse, was established as a warmblood breed in 1965. Its origins lie with the indigenous Norman Horse, a heavy pulling type that became a very useful and sturdy riding horse by outcrossing to Arab and Barb blood (see pp.184–5) from North Africa and southern Europe. In the 19th century, these Norman horses were crossed with Thoroughbred stallions (see p.160) and Thoroughbred half-breds with a Norfolk Trotter background, to produce the breed that became known as the Anglo-Norman. By increasing the Thoroughbred influence, the breed evolved into today's high-quality Selle Français. The term was first used in 1958 to describe the upgraded French riding horse, formerly a "*demi-sang*," or half-bred. The upgrading has continued and, such is the combination of speed and stamina, one group has now been allocated for non-Thoroughbred racing. The Selle Français Stud Book accepts various crosses, such as TB/French Trotter, Arab or Anglo Arab/French Trotter, and TB/Anglo Arab.

Uses
The Selle Français is well suited to all competitive sports, especially showjumping and horse trials. Some are selectively bred for racing, while another category is used in riding schools, for trekking, and the tourist industry in France, as well as for military work and training. Many famous showjumpers are Selle Français.

Appearance
The Selle Français has a quality, Thoroughbred-type head, which may be concave, like the Arab, or convex. It has strong, sometimes rather upright shoulders, a deep body, a strong back and broad hindquarters. The hocks are ideal for jumping, but the pasterns can be slightly upright. Depending on the amount of Thoroughbred blood, the Selle Français may be a middle or heavyweight horse. The coat is fine and usually chestnut.

Characteristics
The Selle Français usually has a sensible temperament. It is muscular, athletic, and quite close-coupled, with free active paces.

Height
Over 16 hands (5ft 4in)

This Selle Français horse displays the impressive paces and activity typical of the breed today. It is springing off the ground, showing the supple joints and athletic ability that make it much in demand as a sport horse in any sphere. An ancestry that includes Arab, Thoroughbred, Norman, and Trotter blood are all apparent in the Selle Français. Because of this diversity, the breed varies in appearance, size, and weight, but it also makes it versatile, with the ability to excel in all equestrian sports. Breeding is carefully controlled, depending on the use for which the horse is required.

French Trotter

The French Trotter originated in Normandy, which has been an important horse-breeding ground since the 12th century. It developed in the 19th century, when Thoroughbreds (see p.160) crossed with French half-breeds were then crossed with the Norfolk Roadster (see p.161) and Norman mares. Recently, some American Standardbred (see p.193) and Russian blood has been introduced into the breed in France. As the French favor Thoroughbred lines, most French Trotters descend from five dominant male lines originally of English stock. The breed was recognized in 1922, and since then trotting races, also thriving in America and other parts of Europe, have developed into a hugely popular sport and business. The French Trotter is raced both under saddle and in harness.

Uses

Most Trotters are raced in harness drawing a sulky, although 10 per cent of races are still ridden. Breeders may use trotting blood to enhance other breeds.

Appearance

The French Trotter has a bold head, with an alert expression, on a very strong neck and shoulders, with a broad, flattish wither. The body can be long with a round barrel, while the limbs must be perfectly formed to withstand hard work at extended trot, with large flat knees and good bone. The hindquarters must be extremely powerful and should slope back. Trotters are often black or brown, bay or chestnut.

Characteristics

The French Trotter is a big horse with a long, gliding trot. It makes an excellent jumper when crossed with the Selle Français, the Thoroughbred, or the Anglo-Arab (see p.178). The minimum speed required is 1 minute 22 seconds for 5 furlongs (1000m). They need courage and great stamina.

Height

Average 16.2 hands (5ft 6in)

Above: A French Trotter mare shows her exuberant natural action. She has substance and strength as well as speed.

Right: This stallion is being trotted up at the Haras du Pin, the French national stud in Normandy, an important breeding centre.

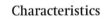

Salerno

The Salerno, a good all-round riding horse from the Maremma and Salerno districts of Italy, is derived from the Neapolitan of the Sorrento and Naples areas, which contained Spanish and Barb blood (see p.185). It first evolved as a breed after Charles III, king of Naples and then Spain, founded a stud at Persano, southern Italy, in 1763. This flourished as a foundation for beautiful riding horses in that region, which were capable of high-school work. Since 1900, Thoroughbred blood (see p.160) has improved the quality, and the Salerno is now a useful all-round riding and competition horse.

Uses
Some of Italy's best showjumpers derive from the Salerno breed, including the 1956 World Champion and the Olympic Individual Gold Medallist in Rome in 1960. The breed was formerly popular with the Italian Cavalry.

Appearance
With increased Thoroughbred influence, the Salerno is becoming more and more refined. Its head resembles a fine Andalucian (see p.170), the shoulder is well sloped, although the body may lack depth, and the limbs are well formed, with fine, hard bone and good joints.

Characteristics
A sensible type with good conformation, the Salerno is an athletic, free-moving horse, and jumps extremely well. It is less fiery and has lower knee action than before, but has kept its keen spirit and ability to withstand hot summers.

Height
Average 16 hands (5ft 4in); trends favor increased height.

San Fratello

The San Fratello, from Messina in Sicily, is founded on the Anglo-Norman horse (see p.166), imported to the island in the 17th century. Small numbers still run wild.

Uses
The San Fratello can be used for light pulling work or stock herding. However, the main aim of Italian breeders is to use it as part of a breeding program in which the San Fratello, Maremmana and Salerno are crossed with the Thoroughbred to establish one breed, the Italian Saddle Horse.

Appearance
Owing to mixed breeding, the appearance of the San Fratello varies. A larger type is being established for competition work.

Characteristics
The San Fratello is hardy, surviving hot, humid summers and cold, sparse winters in the Sylvan region near Messina.

Height
15.3 hands–16 hands (5ft 3in–5ft 4in)

Maremmana

Also known as the Maremma, the Maremmana is almost extinct in its original form, but still exists as a modified breed type. Evolved from Neopolitan and other European lines, it was originally used for farm and stock work in the Tuscan region of Maremma, north of Rome, where semi-wild horses were crossed with any suitable horse or pony that came to those parts. It is an Italian native, although not originally indigenous.

Uses
A versatile horse, the Maremmana is suitable for light farm tasks, especially working cattle, and general-purpose riding. It is still used by the Italian Mounted Police.

Appearance
Not a beauty, but workmanlike, the Maremmana is solid, very steady and hardy. Its neck is short, and the general impression is of weakness, but the hocks are strong and the all-important feet are durable and a good shape. All whole colors can be found in this breed.

Characteristics
The Maremmana has a dependable, calm and steady character. It is willing and good-natured, possessing endurance and some speed, but it is not known for its jumping ability. It can be crossed with the Thoroughbred (see p.160) to obtain a quality riding horse with more size, better paces and greater speed. The true Maremmana is hardy, economical to keep and stolid in character. Their reliable character makes them popular for police work in Italy.

Height
Average 15.3 hands (5ft 3in)

Above: The reliable temperament of Maremmana horses and their affable nature make them popular with the Italian police for police duties, parades and patrols. Although they are quite small, their sturdiness and toughness make them useful riding horses for many purposes.

Right: Italian cowboys, or *butteri*, use the Maremmana horses to round up and work cattle in the rugged country of southern Italy. The Maremmana is well known for its natural, instinctive ability to herd cattle, and its strong hocks enable it to work hard for long periods of time, often in fierce heat.

Andalucian

The Andalucian, an ancient breed from southern Spain, is a descendant of the Iberian horse that was valued so highly by the Romans. Similar horses can also be seen in cave paintings in southern Spain dating from *c.* 18,000 BC. Arab and Barb blood (see pp.184–5) was introduced in the eighth and ninth centuries during the Moorish invasion of the Iberian peninsula, and the resulting horses were sought after all over Europe until at least the 18th century. The breed was kept pure by the Carthusian monks of Jerez de la Frontera who set up a stud specifically for this purpose in 1476. Today, Andalucian breeding is carefully promoted and controlled in Seville, Córdoba and Granada, flourishing where the breed originated so long ago.

The Andalucian has been a major influence in founding many famous breeds; the Lusitano and the Alter-Real are closely related and the Lipizzaner, Kladruber, Nonius (see pp.175 and 182) and many of the German breeds are descendants. Most of the American breeds (see pp.190–7) trace back to the Spanish horse, as do the Welsh Cob, Cleveland Bay, and Connemara pony (see pp.162–3 and 220) in Britain and Ireland.

Uses
The Andalucian is famous for its prepotent influence on breeding since ancient times. Popular for performing high-school dressage and as a parade horse, it is also still used in the bullring and for herding cattle. It is a pleasure to ride, and although its rounded action is not generally considered well suited to conventional dressage, it can be a brilliant jumper. It is increasingly popular for competitive driving.

Appearance
The Andalucian is a short-coupled, very strongly made horse, with slightly sloping quarters and a long, wavy, flowing mane and tail. The head is fairly large with a convex profile and flared nostrils, while the neck is high and arched, giving great presence as well as natural balance. The shoulder can be fairly straight and the wither rather flat as part of the strong, short back, with powerful loins and hindquarters. The feet are very hard, adapted to their hot, dry environment. The color is predominately gray, with some bays, golden duns or roans.

Characteristics
The Andalucian is a striking horse, appearing bigger than it really is. It has very active springy gaits and a proud self-carriage. The walk is rhythmically pronounced, the trot high and rounded, and the canter smooth but rocking. The gallop does not cover much ground, but like all the paces can be spectacular. This breed is supple and athletic, combining a gaiety of spirit with gentleness and docility.

Height
Average 15.2 hands (5ft 2in)

Andalucian horses perform *haute-école*, or high-school movements, as they have done since the 16th century, when classical riding became popular with the nobility of Europe. The precepts of classical riding go back to the writings of the Greek general Xenophon (*c.* 430–355 BC) and beyond, when such skills were necessary for the battlefield. Today, some Andalucians are trained for displays of advanced dressage movements and many of them excel at jumping.

Lusitano

Similar to the Andalucian, the Lusitano (from *Lusitania*, the Latin for Portugal) is likely to share the Andalucian's oriental ancestors and is believed to be an ancestor of the Lipizzaner (see p.175). It was officially established only in 1966 in order to safeguard the important bloodlines. Formerly used by the Portuguese cavalry, it is now valued by bullfighters (*rejoneadores*), who train their horses to an advanced standard of *haute-école*, so they can give an artistic display while also skilfully controlling the fight.

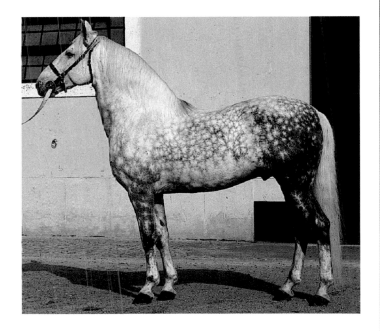

Uses
The Lusitano has the agility to be a versatile riding horse, whether for pleasure, competitive work, or in the bullring and similar displays. It is useful for farm work and also makes an ideal driving horse, being intelligent and willing.

Appearance
Despite a similar breeding history, the Lusitano is distinctly different from the Andalucian. The expression is alert, but the profile tends to be more convex and the forehead broader. The neck is thick and quite short, set on powerful shoulders, and the quarters tend to slope to a low-set tail. Its body can be "tubular," lacking girth, making it seem rather leggy. It shares the long mane and tail of the Iberian horse. It is usually gray, but other solid colors do occur.

Characteristics
The Lusitano has much the same personality as the Andalucian, and despite being a little bigger and heavier in the front, is just as agile. It is also less "showy," but has slightly elevated paces, well suited to collection and tight turns, and enormous courage and generosity of spirit.

Height
Average 15 hands–16 hands (5ft–5ft 4in)

Alter-Real

The Alter-Real was founded in the 18th century, using 300 Andalucian mares, at Vila de Portel Stud in Portugal. Fine, handsome and proud, it excelled at the fashionable *haute-école* skills of the era and flourished until the stud was sacked during the Napoleonic invasion of 1809–10. The breed was then spoilt by foreign outcrosses, but restored to true type in the early 20th century when Andalucian stallions were reintroduced. Although *haute-école* was not popular once Portugal became a republic, and the breed records were destroyed, the government set up a breeding program using the best mares and two selected stallions.

Uses
The Alter-Real specializes in classical *haute-école*, or high-school, work. It is also a useful riding horse, although it can be too spirited for the inexperienced rider.

Appearance
The Alter-Real has an intelligent, quality head, typically Iberian in shape, with a broad forehead. The neck is muscular and raised on a sloping shoulder, with a more pronounced wither than most of its Spanish relations. The chest is also wider, generally, and the body has greater depth. The Alter-Real has a fine, long, flowing mane and tail, the latter on sloping quarters.

Characteristics
Like all Iberian horses, the knees and hocks of the Alter-Real have exaggerated flexion, making them well suited to high-school movements, but less able to extend the stride. It generally has a biddable nature and is easy to train. The principal colors are bay, brown, and occasionally gray.

Height
Average 15 hands–16 hands (5ft–5ft 4in)

Hanoverian

The Hanoverian is a warmblood renowned for providing some of the best showjumpers and dressage horses in the world. It was officially bred from 1735 for farm, pulling and military work at the newly opened State Stud at Celle in North Saxony, Germany, although pedigrees were not listed until 1790. Fourteen black Holstein stallions formed the base stock and, crossed with local mares, produced a good working horse. Thoroughbred and Cleveland Bay blood (see pp.160 and 163) was added to create a lighter horse with more courage and stamina that was also suitable for pulling coaches and performing army duties. In recent times, Thoroughbred and Trakehner blood (see p.174) has been introduced to adapt to sporting demands.

Uses
The Hanoverian is not bred for speed and stamina, but its natural impulsion and willingness make it perfectly suited to top-class showjumping and dressage. There have also been many successful teams in international driving events and it is used extensively as a general riding horse. The faster Thoroughbred cross can excel in the three-day event.

Appearance
The Hanoverian can vary considerably in size and weight, but the conformation is correct. An arresting horse, the head is medium-sized, alert and set on a fairly long, muscular neck. The strong shoulders are well sloped, and the withers clearly defined. Deep bodied, with a rounded rib cage, the back broadens to extremely powerful loins, while the hindquarters can be almost flat along the croup, with the tail set high. The Hanoverian has large, well-formed joints, short cannons and strongly muscled forearms and second thighs. The feet are well shaped and hard. Any whole color is acceptable.

Characteristics
All registered Hanoverians are branded with the "H" symbol introduced at Celle in 1735. To merit this distinction, they must have a good, honest temperament, natural rhythmic paces, straight, energetic action and a long stride.

Height
15.3 hands–over 17 hands (5ft 3in–5ft 8in)

Two hundred Hanoverian stallions now stand at Celle, including a few Trakehners and Thoroughbreds still used to refine certain lines. These horses serve more than 8,000 mares at the "stallion stations" around Germany. All breeding stock is strictly selected using organized performance-testing. Great emphasis is also placed on a reliable, willing nature, as well as sound conformation and action. Hanoverians are popular throughout the world, although they can be too heavy for very dry countries.

Holstein

Probably the oldest German breed and originally used as a war horse, from 1680, the Holstein was bred as a strong, reliable carriage horse and army remount. In the 19th century, Cleveland Bay (see p.163), Yorkshire Coach, and Thoroughbred blood (see p.160) was introduced to produce a lighter, but still strong horse, that could also be used to improve other German breeds. With continued use of Thoroughbred blood, the Holstein has become an ideal all-round performance horse. Like all warmbloods, it is performance-tested before entry into the Stud Book.

Uses
The modern Holstein is suited to all equestrian disciplines. It is still one of the best carriage horses, is world class at dressage and showjumping, and is probably the best of the German breeds for eventing.

Appearance
The Holstein is tall, elegant, with a fine head and bright, intelligent eyes. The long neck is arched on a well-sloped shoulder, and the wither is well shaped. It is deep chested, with powerful loins and quarters, and well-muscled thighs and forearms. The limbs are superior, with dense, hard bone, well-formed joints and short, strong cannons. Any whole color is acceptable, with black, bay and brown favored.

Characteristics
The Holstein has abundant quality, a willing, bold temperament, correct conformation with bone and substance, and the ability to gallop and jump. Its action is free, straight and long-striding, and it possesses a natural balance and rhythm. Pronounced knee action has been bred out along with the rather straight shoulder suitable for carriage horses. It has now also developed the stamina for covering long distances at speed.

Height
16 hands–17 hands (5ft 4in–5ft 8in)

Oldenburg

It is now a capable sport horse. The breed society is strictly selective, to safeguard tractability, size and strength, and all stallions are performance-tested. Now uniformity is well established, and little outside blood is allowed.

Uses
The Oldenburg is used for riding, driving, and dressage. It is bred for fertility and longevity and may be used to improve other breeds, such as the Kladruber (see p.175).

Appearance
An impressive horse, the Oldenburg has a strong, long neck, a broad chest, muscular hindquarters and hind limbs, well-formed joints and well-shaped feet. The body can be long. The breed brand is an "O" below a coronet on the near-side quarter. Colors are usually black, brown, bay or gray.

Characteristics
For its size and scope, the Oldenburg is an early maturing breed. An equable horse with correct and vigorous paces, it is not very fast, not having a very far-reaching stride, and may retain some knee action. Powerful and surprisingly agile, it is usually an excellent jumper.

The German Oldenburg, based on its neighbor, the Friesian (see p 164), is a heavy warmblood and was first bred for farm work. Its strength, size and high knee action made it a suitable coach horse, and in the 17th century Count Anton von Oldenburg imported the best Neapolitan and Spanish lines and put them to this local stock. The breed society began in 1819, when Thoroughbred (see p.160), half-bred, Hanoverian, and Norman blood was introduced.

Height
16.2 hands–17.2 hands (5ft 6in–5ft 10in)

Trakehner

The Trakehner is one of the oldest of the warmblood breeds and the most elegant. It is partly based on the East Prussian Schweiken, a tough little native known to have been used in 13th-century farming. The Trakehner Stud was founded in 1742 in East Prussia, by Frederick William I. Here, robust horses were bred to supply the army and the royal stables. Eastern blood refined the breed, and the Thoroughbred (see p.160) was a major influence, notably after the importation of the stallion Perfectionist, born in 1899. In just three seasons, he sired 131 foals, of which 32 were accepted into the Stud Book as stallions and 37 as brood mares. Tested at each stage of development, only the best horses were registered to become cavalry horses, renowned for endurance, courage, agility, and speed. In World War II the stud was evacuated for the fifth time since 1812 and numbers were devastated. Roughly 1,000 horses arrived in West Germany after a three-month trek, and today the Trakehner is bred on private studs.

Uses
The Trakehner is a famous all-round competition horse, responsible for many champion showjumpers, dressage horses, and three-day eventers. Its distinctive characteristics, which are always reproduced, are sought to improve many of the other competitive breeds, particularly the Hanoverian (see p.172), and it is a popular import to the USA, Sweden, and Britain. It is also used for competitive driving.

Appearance
The finest of the warmbloods, the Trakehner retains both Thoroughbred and Arab traits (see pp.160 and 184), combined with the native Schweiken substance and toughness. Its head is finely shaped, with a distinctive and alert expression and well-shaped, mobile ears above the broad forehead. The neck is fairly long and elegant, on usually well-sloped shoulders, while the medium-length body has a well-sprung rib cage and good depth. The quarters tend to be more rounded than those of other warmbloods, and the feet are generally better, being perfectly shaped and durable. The Trakehner has excellent limbs. Dark colors are favored, although any color is allowed.

Characteristics
The Trakehner is bred to be a top-class athlete. It has ideal conformation, action, stamina, and courage, while its talent for jumping is inherent. It combines a tractable temperament with spirit, and has greater endurance ability than other German breeds, with a longer, flowing stride that resembles that of the Thoroughbred.

Height
16 hands–16.2 hands
(5ft 4in–5ft 6in)

The Trakehner breed is controlled by the Trakehner Verband, formed soon after World War II, in 1947, when about 1,200 survivors from 25,000 registered mares provided a foundation from which the breed was re-established. Trakehners are branded on their near-side quarter with an Elk-horn motif.

Lipizzaner

The Lipizzaner was founded on nine Spanish stallions and 24 mares imported to Lipizza in Austro-Hungary (later Slovenia) in 1580 and crossed with Arab and Barb blood (see pp.184–5). Intended for royal use, it proved ideal for the Spanish Riding School, which had been set up in 1572 to teach classical riding to the nobility. Lipizzaners are now bred in several countries, although the School stud at Fiber, Austria, produces the best stock. Types vary slightly, but the stud book is strictly controlled. All trace to five stallions of Andalucian descent (see p.170). The purest lines have best preserved the breed's unique characteristics.

Uses
The Lipizzaner performs high-school displays all over the world. It competes in dressage and is becoming popular for competitive driving. At the Spanish School (in Vienna since 1735), it is used to train classical riders. It is crossed in parts of Europe with local mares to produce farm horses.

Appearance
The Lipizzaner is short, compact, unusually strong, but graceful. The head, typically Spanish in shape, is set on a short muscular neck. The shoulders are strong, and an undefined wither runs into a short back, broad loins, and powerful quarters. The body is very deep, the legs short with strong joints and tough, hard feet. The mane and tail are fine and silky. Gray is usual but black, brown or bay occasionally occurs.

Characteristics
The Lipizzaner matures slowly and is rarely white before the age of ten. Its agility and athleticism develops slowly, and belies a rather "cobby" conformation, but it is long-lived, often working well into its twenties. The Piber Lipizzaner tends to be smaller and more powerful and docile than others in Europe, where the Thoroughbred influence gives greater size and length of stride, but with some loss of power, and often forfeits the docile temperament that makes this breed so trainable.

Height
15 hands–16 hands (5ft–5ft 4in)

Kladruber

The Kladruber was developed in the western Czech Republic from Spanish horses as a very tall and powerful coaching horse to draw the Imperial carriages. It was first registered in the early 18th century, when 1,000 horses were recorded at the royal stud at Kladrub. Some exceeded 19 hands (6ft 4in). A fire destroyed the stud and its records in 1770, but the breed was rescued and now produces smaller, but still impressive, horses that continue to be in great demand. The Kladruber is the only "native" of former Czechoslovakia, although a warmblood breed is evolving, based on lines including the Furioso (see p.183), Gidran, and Thoroughbred (see p.160), to create an all-round riding horse.

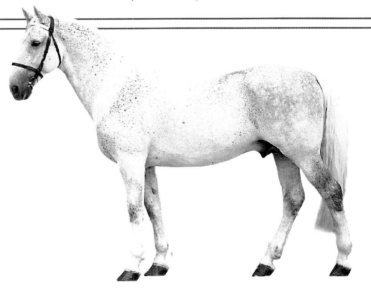

Uses
An outstanding carriage horse, the Kladruber is popular in eastern European and at international driving events, driven in teams of up to eight pairs, with teams of ten or eight quite usual. It is used increasingly for riding.

Appearance
The Kladruber is a strong, tall, impressive horse, similar to the Lipizzaner and Andalucian. The head may be convex in profile, reflecting its Spanish descent, and it is carried high on a crested, muscular neck and powerful, sloped "driving" shoulders. The body is long and tubular rather than deep, with strong, rounded hindquarters and good, clean limbs. The horses from Kladrub are gray and a black variety is raised at the state stud at Slatinany.

Characteristics
The Kladruber has an even temperament, and its strength makes it ideally suited for driving work. It has a majestic walk and all the paces are fairly short, with a raised knee action. Its size makes this breed impressive.

Height
Average 16.2 hands–17 hands (5ft 6in–5ft 8in)

Knabstrup

This Danish breed is based on a gray-spotted Spanish mare called Flaebehoppen that was left in Denmark (among many others) by Spanish troops during the Napoleonic Wars. Known for speed and endurance, she was crossed with a Danish Frederiksborg stallion. The stud book was opened in 1808, but the modern Knabstrup is somewhat different. Owing to uncontrolled breeding over generations, the spots all over the body and legs are far more difficult to reproduce. However, what has been lost in color has been gained in quality and conformation.

Uses
The Knabstrup is an all-round riding horse, and is also used for circus work and driving and vaulting competitions.

Appearance
The Knabstrup is now more like the Appaloosa (see p.192) than the original, which, despite the true spotted coat, had a coarse head and neck, an upright shoulder and angular quarters. Attempts to reinstate the pattern by introducing other blood means that conformation varies. The Knabstrup is now more substantial, has a finer head and neck, a better riding shoulder, rounder hindquarters and improved conformation. The mane and tail are still sparse. There are often large patches of roan as well as spots.

Characteristics
The Knabstrup has a gentle nature and inherits the intelligence and toughness of its forebears, which, together with their coloring, made them so popular for circus acts, demonstrations and exhibitions. It is suitable for children to ride.

Height
Average 15.2 hands (5ft 2in)

Frederiksborg

The Danish Frederiksborg has altered greatly since 1562 when King Frederik II founded the Frederiksborg Stud, based on Spanish stock, with later additions of Italian, British, and Arab bloodlines. Valued as a charger and school horse, the early breed was elegant and kind, with high-stepping action. It was used to lighten local Jutland heavy horses, and one white stallion, Pluto, founded an important Lipizzaner line (see p.175). Later, out-crossing weakened and depleted the breed and the royal stud was disbanded in 1839. It is now bred privately in Denmark. Friesian and Oldenburg blood (see pp.164 and 173) were introduced in 1939, and Thoroughbred and Trakehner (see pp.160 and 174) have since added scope and quality, making it a more typical warmblood.

Uses
Mainly used for driving, the Frederiksborg is an excellent horse for light pulling and riding. It is increasingly used to improve the Danish Warmblood.

Appearance
The Frederiksborg is strong-shouldered, has a prominent, broad chest and good limbs with well-formed joints. The head, although plain, is alert and carried high. The neck is upright and muscular, but long enough. A rather flat wither runs into a longish back, and flat-topped quarters continue straight to a high-set tail. The limbs are often rather upright, but the feet are well shaped and hard. This breed is chestnut.

Characteristics
The even-tempered Frederiksborg boasts a straight, high vigorous trot well suited to modern driving. Although not built for speed, it moves with freedom and energy at all paces, and has excellent natural balance.

Height
Average 16 hands (5ft 4in)

Danish Warmblood

The Danish horse population was severely depleted after World War II and horse-owners generally imported their stock from abroad. In 1960, when demand for a Danish competition horse was already high, the Danish Sports Horse Society was formed. Thoroughbred, Trakehner, Polish, and Anglo-French stallions (see pp.160, 174, and 178–9) were used on selected local Frederiksborg mares, and the Danish Warmblood, a handsome and courageous performance horse, evolved. It is now well established and has produced international champions in horse trials, showjumping, and dressage. It is one of the country's best exports and, inevitably, is very expensive.

Uses
The Danish Warmblood is bred specifically to excel as a competition horse, whether in dressage, showjumping or three-day eventing.

Appearance
The Danish Warmblood combines the beauty of a Thoroughbred with the substance and sensible nature of its less rarefied ancestors. It has a quality head, the long, slightly crested neck flows into prominent withers set well back on a sloping shoulder. The back is of medium length and there is ample depth at the girth. The limbs are excellent, with good bone and well-defined joints, and the feet are also hard to fault. Bay is common but any whole color may occur.

Characteristics
This horse possesses the soundness, temperament, and ability that makes a top competition horse. Unlike most registered warmbloods, Danish horses generally have the courage, spirit, speed, and scope to become international eventers, as well as to excel in other areas. They should have natural balance, move straight with elastic paces and be talented jumpers.

Height
16.1 hands–16.3 hands (5ft 5in–5ft 7in)

Swedish Warmblood

The Swedish Warmblood is based on the Swedish 17th-century army riding horse, the result of Spanish, Friesian, and oriental horses put to local stock. Thoroughbred, Hanoverian, Trakehner, and Anglo-Arab crosses (see pp.160, 172, 174, and 178) upgraded the breed and a Stud Book was opened in 1874. As demand grew, two stallion depots were set up at Stromsholm and Flyinge. All horses were tested before acceptance by the Stud Book. Selection is even stricter today – a stallion must prove itself in dressage, jumping, and in harness, and if, later, its progeny fail on any point, it must stop breeding. Mares are also carefully screened – new blood is allowed to counteract any weakness that may appear in a given line.

Uses
The Swedish Warmblood is in world demand, especially for dressage and showjumping. It has a brilliant record in every Olympic equestrian sport, winning gold medals in each. It also excels at driving.

Appearance
The Swedish Warmblood has a fine, attractive head, with a bold eye and outlook. The conformation must be correct, with a well-sloped shoulder, somewhat crested neck, good depth at the girth and powerfully rounded quarters. Above all, it must have strong, sound limbs of ample bone, well-formed joints, and perfectly shaped feet. Anything less is not acceptable to the Stud Book.

Characteristics
This horse is an athlete, capable of the ultimate tests. Its springy, powerful paces, natural impulsion and generous temperament make it an exceptionally good dressage horse. The breed varies considerably in size and weight, and the largest can carry a heavy person with ease at top levels of competition.

Height
15.2 hands–16.3 hands (5ft 2in–5ft 7in)

Anglo-Arab

The Anglo-Arab originated in Britain but is now widely bred, especially in France. It is descended from the Arab and its derivative, the Thoroughbred (see pp.184 and 160). In Britain, the Thoroughbred parent must be registered in the *General Stud Book* and the Arab in the *Arab Horse Stud Book*. Recrossings are allowed, but the progeny must be at least 12.5 percent Arab. The French Anglo-Arab horse requires 25 percent Arab blood. In France, selective breeding began in 1836, when two Arab stallions and three Thoroughbred mares were chosen for breeding at the Pompadour Stud in southwest France. In Navarre, Gascogne, and Limousin, other Arab or oriental-type mares were used. Gradually a type developed, and studs at Pau, Gelos, and Tarbes became breeding centers.

Uses

Anglo-Arabs are versatile riding horses, suitable for all types of competitive work. In Britain, they are popular in the show ring, first-class for long-distance riding and an excellent cross to improve other breeds. In France, an outstanding riding and competition horse has evolved that is consistently successful in horse trials, dressage, showjumping, and racing. In France, the stallions are more often used to produce the Selle Français (see p.166) and Cheval de Selle than other registered Anglo-Arabs.

Appearance

The British Anglo-Arab has more size and substance than its forebears, owing to larger Thoroughbred mares being put to Arab stallions. However, there is still a wide variety within the breed, and reverse mating (Arab mare × Thoroughbred stallion) may produce a much smaller, more Arab type.

The French Anglo-Arab is generally larger and more muscular than the British type. Its outline is more like that of the Thoroughbred than the Arab. In southwest France it has a lighter frame to cope with racing on dry, often firm ground.

The Anglo-Arab head has a straight profile, with an alert, intelligent expression and mobile ears. The neck is longer than the pure Arab, the shoulder more sloping, the wither better defined, the body shorter and the croup less flat. It is more solid and substantial than the Thoroughbred and can, therefore, carry more weight. Although the limbs may seem light of bone, they are generally tough and sound and the feet are strong and hard. Anglo-Arabs can be any full color, but gray and chestnut are the most common.

Characteristics

In general, the Anglo-Arab should inherit the size, speed, substance, and longer galloping stride of the Thoroughbred, especially if the dam is a Thoroughbred, and the soundness, endurance, easy temperament, and intelligence of the Arab. Although not as fast as the Thoroughbred, the Anglo-Arab is tough and athletic, with great agility. The best are very bold and talented jumpers, for both cross-country and showjumping. They also move freely and straight, and are capable of impressive extended paces, making them good dressage prospects. French Anglo-Arabs have excelled as competitors in all the Olympic disciplines.

Height

16 hands–16.3 hands (5ft 4in–5ft 7in)

Jennie Loriston Clarke rides the Anglo-Arab Prince Consort in the dressage competition at the 1984 Olympics. Other Anglo-Arabs have competed at international level in the three-day event, showjumping, and long-distance events.

Malapolski

This breed, largely of Arab descent, is bred mainly in the south of Poland as a riding horse. It originated from primitive native horses, crossed with both oriental and Thoroughbred blood (see p.160). Hungarian and Austrian breeds were also used to produce a better riding horse, including the Arab-like Shagya and Furioso (see p.183), the Gidran, the Lipizzaner (see p.175), and the Wielkopolski. There is now wide demand for this useful horse in Poland, and 300 Malapolski stallions stand at the state studs alone. Another 800 stallions are used from private studs, which indicates that this comparatively newly established breed is flourishing.

Uses
The Malapolski is used as a riding horse, in harness and for light tasks on the land. It is popular with Polish farmers owing to its honest and willing attitude to work, ranging from pulling a cart to herding animals and transporting laborers and their goods.

Appearance
The Arab blood is noticeable in the slightly dished, or concave, profile of the head, wide forehead and bright, bold eyes. The neck is slightly crested, on a lean, "tubular" body that lacks depth. The Malapolski is an elegant horse, its slight appearance belying its strength. It can be any full color, with bay, gray, chestnut and black being the most usual.

Characteristics
This breed is a quality riding horse, versatile enough to adapt to driving work. It has a kind, willing disposition and great stamina. It is renowned for soundness and for being economical to keep, since it maintains its body-weight well and stores energy reserves efficiently.

Height
15.3–16.2 hands (5ft 3in–5ft 6in)

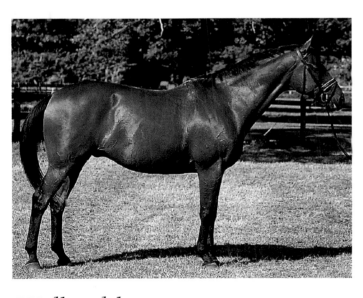

Wielkopolski

The Wielkopolski, based on the Masuren and Poznan horses, is not well known but deserves recognition as a talented warmblood. The substantial Poznan, suitable for farming and riding, is Konik pony mixed with oriental, Hanoverian, and Trakehner blood. The Masuren was a Trakehner breed of oriental and Thoroughbred blood. The Wielkopolski evolved when the two were brought into one stud book. It is now bred at 13 Polish state studs, five of which specialize in the high-class "sports horse."

Uses
The Wielkopolski is a useful riding horse that can perform all equestrian disciplines to a high standard. It is still used for light pulling, but its bloodlines are continually upgraded to meet competitive demand. It is an excellent harness horse and jumps very well, making it suitable for both showjumping and cross-country.

Appearance
The Wielkopolski is a handsome, deep-bodied horse, with good bone and feet. It has a quality head, a long, well-shaped neck and a sloping shoulder. The hindquarters are muscular, with strong hind legs.

Characteristics
A versatile horse, the Wielkopolski is well proportioned and has natural balance. It moves extremely well, is active and powerful, has a free, long-striding walk, rhythmic trot, and a ground-devouring gallop. It has a sensible temperament and adapts equally well to harness or farm work. The heavier type is best suited to dual-purpose activities, and the competition horse can excel in any of the equestrian disciplines, possessing speed, scope, courage, and athleticism.

Height
Average 16.2 hands (5ft 6in)

Russian Trotter

There are more breeds of horse and pony in the former USSR than in any other country, the most famous of which is the Russian Trotter. It evolved from the long-established Orlov, which was bred for various uses, with heavy and medium-built types, as well as a sporting type, which was probably the best trotting horse in the world until the coming of the American Saddlebred (see p.194). The Orlov was named after Count Alexis Orlov and was founded on a stallion, Bars I, the progeny of a heavily built Dutch-bred mare and an Arab × Danish cart-mare stallion, born in 1784. All Russian Trotters descend from three sons of Bars I.

When trotting became increasingly popular after the first races in Moscow in 1799, much inbreeding took place to try to upgrade the existing mixed breeds and produce faster, better horses. Arab (see p.184), Mecklenburg, and Thoroughbred blood (see p.160) were added to improve the Orlov's speed, size, and power. Between 1890 and 1917, when the American Saddlebred was proving so successful, Russian breeders imported 156 American stallions and 220 broodmares in an attempt to upgrade the Orlov. However, when crossed, the progeny was rather small, with conformational defects. The incentive to improve the breed was becoming intense, and the state studs began to breed selectively again. They wanted to increase the size, while retaining a light but powerful frame, to minimize any potential unsoundness, and, above all, they wanted to improve performance. The result, the Russian Trotter, was recognized as a breed in 1949.

The modern Russian Trotter, now a spectacular trotting horse, is a faster, bigger version than its forebears and can take on the best trotters in the world.

Uses
The Russian Trotter is mainly a harness horse bred for trotting races. It is also popular as a carriage horse and for all forms of driving, and makes a good riding horse.

Appearance
Russian Trotters are muscular but light framed. They are more elegant than their ancestors, but they are built for performance rather than beauty. Some inherit an attractive Arab-like head, but others are small and coarse. The shoulders are powerful, but rather straight, the back quite long, which is a Trotter's characteristic, and the hind legs and hocks are extremely strong, for propulsion. The better individuals have plenty of depth through the girth and good bone. Others tend to be leggy, lacking depth. Some inherit the sickle hocks and sloping croups of native forebears, and all retain some feather at the heels. However, selective breeding continues to improve the breed.

Characteristics
The Russian Trotter tends to mature early and is fully grown at four years. It usually achieves its maximum trot speeds at five or six years old. Despite its precocity, it is generally long-lived. The stride is long and low, and this horse has great stamina. Some will tend to pace, instead of their natural diagonal gait, which is a trait inherited from the American Standardbred. The temperament is easy.

Height
15.3 hands –16 hands (5ft 3in–5ft 4in)

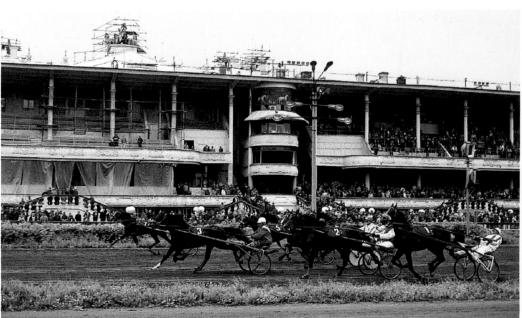

The Russian Trotter is performance-tested on the raceway before being allowed to compete. Here, the horse at the back has broken into a canter, which may mean disqualification.

Budyonny

By 1914, Russia's horse stock was sorely depleted. As a result, a cavalry commander, Marshal Budyonny (or Budenny), crossed the best horses available, local Don mares and Thoroughbred stallions (see p.160), to produce a cavalry mount. This resulted in the Budyonny, which may also be called a Russian Warmblood. The breed was named in 1949 and has since been regulated by performance-testing. Increasing amounts of Thoroughbred blood have refined and adapted it to modern needs. Although not as fast as the Thoroughbred, the Budyonny often competes in Russia, and a Budyonny has won the famous Pardubika Steeplechase in the Czech Republic. It is now bred in the Ukraine, Kazakh, and Kirghiz republics in the southern part of old Russia.

Uses

The Budyonny is well suited to long-distance riding, cross-country, and steeplechase. It is used as a competition horse or general-purpose riding horse and does well at dressage.

Appearance

The Budyonny has good conformation and an attractive head with a bold outlook on a long, elegant neck. The body is strong and quite deep, while the shoulders and quarters are strong and good. The legs are correct, with plenty of bone, and the feet are well formed. Most Budyonnys are chestnut, often with a golden sheen on their fine coats. Bays and grays are also seen.

Characteristics

The Budyonny is a calm, sensible, and versatile breed. Its paces are regular and smooth, if not spectacular, and it makes a good dressage horse. It is renowned for its toughness and stamina – one stallion, Zancs, covered 192 miles (309km) in 24 hours.

Height

15.2 hands–16 hands (5ft 2in 5ft 4in)

Don

The Russian Don originated on the Steppe near the Don River and is descended from the Turkmene, a desert Arab, and the mountain Karabakh (see p.189), both of which had been let loose with the native herds. A tough horse, it rose to world fame in 1812 when 60,000 Russian Cossacks rode Dons to drive Napoleon back to France. Most of the French horses died, but the Dons survived. They were then upgraded with Orlovs, Thoroughbreds (see pp.180 and 160), and Strelet Arabs. No other blood has been added since the early 20th century. One of the toughest breeds, it is performance-tested and is expected to travel 170 miles (275km) in 24 hours.

Uses

The Don, long used as an army remount that also goes well in harness, is now used for general riding. It is also crossed with the Thoroughbred and then outcrossed to improve other breeds. It is still a hard-working horse, used by local herdsmen, and many still live in herds.

Appearance

Wiry, long-legged, and often lacking bone, the Don defies its looks and is a sound breed. Its head-profile, set on like that of an Arab, is straight, as is the neck. It has low withers, a broad, straight back, sloped quarters, and straight shoulders, but the chest is broad and quite deep. Although it may have sickle hocks, small joints and upright pasterns, the feet are usually sound and hardy. The fine coat is generally golden dun or chestnut, with a bronze sheen, but bays and grays are also seen.

Characteristics

The Don is a good-natured, calm and tractable breed. However, owing to conformational defects, it is not a free mover, and, although the paces are regular, they are not particularly comfortable. The high level of endurance and economy of needs make it a popular work horse.

Height

15.3 hands–16.2 hands (5ft 3in–5ft 6in)

Nonius

Horse-breeding has been a national pastime in Hungary since at least the 9th century. From the 19th century until World War I, Hungarian horses were considered the best, after the British and French, and were in great demand all over Europe. The Nonius is a distinctive Hungarian breed. Formerly a heavy horse, it is now a more refined middle-weight. Its foundation sire was an Anglo-Norman stallion named Nonius, which was born in 1810 and captured in Normandy during the Napoleonic Wars and taken to Hungary. Based on his bloodline, the breed was established at the the famous Mezöhegyes Stud, founded by Emperor Joseph I in 1785, where up to 12,000 horses were once kept. Although Nonius himself was far from handsome, having a large, plain head, long ears, small eyes, a short neck, and a long back, his merits as a sire made him famous. He bred 15 excellent stallions from a variety of mares that included Arab, Holstein, Lipizzaner, and Anglo-Norman breeds (see pp.184, 173, and 175). The original Nonius died in 1832, but 40 years later his progeny included 2,800 stallions and 3,200 registered broodmares. The Nonius remains a useful and popular breed, which has been improved over many generations, mainly by using Thoroughbred blood (see p.160). The breed varies in size, the smaller types are lighter and have more Arab blood.

Uses

The Nonius, especially the larger type, is still used for agricultural and light pulling work. It also makes an excellent carriage horse and is now sufficiently refined to make a useful riding and competition horse, particularly when crossed with the Thoroughbred. The smaller Nonius is a good worker, both when ridden or in harness.

Appearance

A very sound horse, the Nonius has a stocky appearance, with ample bone and short strong limbs. The head reflects an honest, willing expression, while the shoulders and back and quarters show strength and power. There is good depth through the girth, the limb joints are well formed, and the feet good. The Nonius is often bay, black, or dark brown, but may also be chestnut.

Characteristics

The Nonius is known for its equable temperament and willing nature. It is a genuine all-rounder and, although not fast, is suitable for all competitive work, especially when crossed with the Thoroughbred. Its paces are active and free, but not extravagant, and it jumps very well. The Nonius continues to be a popular driving horse, both for practical purposes and in competition.

Height

15.3 hands–16.2 hands (5ft 3in–5ft 6in)

A pair of typical Nonius carriage horses demonstrates active paces and a bold outlook. The breed tends to develop slowly and does not mature until it is around six years, but it will go on working until well into its 20s.

Furioso

The Furioso is based on Furioso, an English Thoroughbred born in 1836, and North Star, a near-Thoroughbred with Norfolk Roadster blood (see p.161). Both were imported to the state stud of Kosber in Hungary and put to local mares of Nonius type. Arab crosses were also used with the aim of producing a beautiful all-purpose breed that would retain the strength and hardiness of the Nonius. Furioso was a great success and sired 95 stallions, which were used by many of the imperial studs. The two lines were kept separate until 1885, since when the Furioso line has flourished best. It is now bred from Austria to Poland.

Uses
This attractive horse is versatile and can be used in all the equestrian disciplines. Together, the Nonius and Furioso are Hungary's warmbloods. It is developing into an excellent sports horse and has the necessary scope and speed to race in the steeplechases of Central and Eastern Europe.

Appearance
The Furioso generally has good conformation. The head is alert and of Thoroughbred look, but with wider ears. The muzzle is almost square, with flared nostrils. It has a good length of neck, well-sloped shoulders, and adequate depth through the girth. The quarters tend to slope down from

the croup, but are powerful. The limbs are correct, with large, well-formed joints, but with a tendency to weak hocks and upright pasterns, inherited from the coaching traits of its ancestors. It is black, dark brown, or occasionally bay.

Characteristics
The Furioso is intelligent, good-natured, and full of stamina. It moves freely, still retaining some lift in the knees, and is capable of impressive extension. A sound horse, it inherits the hardiness of its ancestors and the speed and quality of the Arab (see p.184) and the Thoroughbred (see p.160). It is very athletic and jumps extremely well.

Height
Average 16 hands (5ft 4in)

Shagya Arab

The Shagya Arab was developed at the Bábolna Stud in Hungary from Shagya, a six-year-old Syrian horse that was bought from the Bedouins in 1836. A striking, cream-colored horse, half pure Arab, out of an oriental mare of Thoroughbred, Spanish, and Hungarian blood, at 15.2 hands (5ft 2in), he was taller than a pure Arab. The breed was established in six years.

Uses
Originally a popular cavalry horse used by the Czech, Polish, Austro-Hungarian, and Hungarian armies, the Shagya now flourishes as an all-purpose riding horse. It is used for all equestrian sports, especially driving, excelling where endurance is important.

Appearance
The Shagya has a fine, silky coat and a flowing mane and tail, both of which are untrimmed. The Arab influence is clear in the beautiful, slightly dished head tapering to flared nostrils and a small muzzle, the large eyes, wide forehead, lively ears, and alert, intelligent outlook. However, it is more substantial than the finer type of Arab seen today, and unlike some Arabs, has a well-sloped riding shoulder and defined wither. The hind legs are correct and strong, and the feet of good size and shape. Usually gray, all registered Shagyas are branded to identify the stud and family of origin.

Characteristics
Lively and good-natured, the Shagya has brilliant, free paces and is fast over long or short distances. It makes a tireless, practical horse, particularly for coach or light pulling.

Height
Average 15 hands (5ft)

Arab

The Arab is the oldest pure breed, and evidence suggests that it existed on the Arabian peninsula around 2500 BC. It first came to Europe with the invading Muslim armies in the eighth and ninth centuries and soon influenced local breeds. Arab blood is the chief and dominant source of the Thoroughbred (see p.160) and has restored the most desirable qualities to countless breeds. Arabian soundness, hardiness, and resilience, coupled with a spirited character and free action, are still the time-honored combination. An official "International breed," the Arab is bred all over the world, with pedigree-controlling registration with the Arab Breed Society.

Uses
The Arab is a versatile and varied breed. It is raced and, although its action is not ideal for dressage or to jump big fences, it is well able to compete in the full range of equestrian sports and excels at long-distance or endurance riding. Arabs are also often shown in hand or under saddle. However, outcrossing to other breeds remains the primary use. The Anglo-Arab (see p.178) has become a registered breed in its own right.

Appearance
The Arab is a light-boned, small, muscular horse with fine bone structure. It has a fine, dished profile, mobile, neat ears that point in slightly, and large, bright, widely spaced eyes, tapering to flared nostrils and a small muzzle. The coat, mane, and tail are fine and silky. The shoulder can be fairly straight, but proportionate to the short back, while the chest is deep and broad and the wither rather flat. The Arab has a unique bone formation of 17 ribs, 5 lumbar bones and 16 tail vertebrae (as opposed to 18-6-18 for most other horses), which results in the croup being flat to the tail, which then extends straight from the spine. The limbs are very clean, with well-defined bone, joints, and tendons. The hocks, formerly a weakness of the modern, light-boned Arab, have improved.

Characteristics
Arab horses are adaptable to every type of environment or climate and can exist on a sparse diet. They have great powers of endurance, are sure-footed on the roughest of ground, and are blessed with an inherent soundness and intelligence that sets them apart. Arabs are generally kind and friendly, but can be high-spirited, even neurotic. Many are naturally suspicious of water. Thanks to their economical action, which is straight, low and free, Arabs can carry heavy weights over long distances.

Height
Average 14.3 hands (4ft 11in)

Left: The Arab is noted for its free and "floating" action. It is lean and muscular, and extremely fast over short distances. It has been raced for centuries and is now raced for big prizes worldwide.

Right: The Arab is highly intelligent and is said to have a love of human company that is unique among horses.

Barb

The Barb is an ancient North African desert breed that may be even older than the Arab. Like the Arab, it has had a huge influence on other breeds, but physically the two are distinctly different. Like the Arab, the Barb, Berber, or Barbary horse came to Spain and Portugal in the eighth and ninth centuries. It influenced the Spanish breeds, especially the Andalucian (see p.170), and eventually influenced many others. The purest blood is found in Morocco, Algeria, and Tunisia.

Uses

The Barb is ridden in North Africa and will survive harsh conditions and hard work on sparse rations. It is a capable jumper and can be a useful sports horse, but there is little demand for such talents in North Africa.

Appearance

Despite apparently similar backgrounds, the Barb and the Arab do not seem to share the same ancestry. Fine-skinned, lean, and hard like the Arab, the Barb's head is long and the profile convex (or Roman-nosed). It has an arched neck and prominent withers, and the shoulder tends to be upright. The chest is narrow, but the short-coupled body is fairly deep. The Barb has angular hindquarters, sloping down from the croup to a low-set tail. The limbs are hard and sound, but the breed is often cow-hocked. The feet are hard-wearing but the shape is often narrow and boxy. Barbs are rarely shod in Africa. They are usually gray or black, but dark brown, bay and dark chestnut also exist.

Characteristics

This is a breed of unusual toughness and resilience. It can withstand extreme heat and drought conditions. Like the Arab, it is exceedingly fast over short distances, yet has great stamina over very long ones. It is economical,

surviving on sparse rations and little attention. The Barb is sound and agile, hence its survival to the present day. It also moves well, although without such a floating quality as the Arab.

Height
14.2 hands–15.2 hands
(4ft 10in–5ft 2in)

Above: The Barb is second only to the Arab in terms of influencing the world's breeds and may be descended from wild horses that escaped the Ice Age on a fertile coastal region. Initially, it influenced the Spanish horses, but over time, as Barbs and Barb crosses were imported elsewhere, their influence spread throughout Europe.

Left: This Moroccan *fantasia* puts the agility and toughness of the Barb horses to the test. They are "desert" horses, which have adapted to harsh climatic conditions on limited food over thousands of years.

Kabardin

The Kabardin, a native of the northern Caucasian Mountains, probably descends from the Asiatic Wild Horse and the Tarpan (see pp.18, 230, and 228) and developed by being crossed with the Karabakh and other oriental types. Typically hardy, it is used in some parts of the former USSR to improve local breeds. Two-year-olds are performance-tested on the racecourse.

Uses
The Kabardin is used under pack, in harness, for local games and races, and for competitive riding. The mares provide good milk and some are crossed with the Thoroughbred (see p.160) to create the Anglo-Kabardin – a taller, finer, faster, version.

Appearance
Fine-skinned but thickset, the Kabardin has a long, attractive, Roman-nosed head and sharp, lively ears. The short, muscular neck is set on a rather straight, undefined shoulder with a short, level back. Broad quarters slope down from croup to tail. The strong loins are slightly raised and the limbs short, fine, and strong. Joints and bones are well defined, although the hind legs can be sickle-hocked. Feet are extra hard, correctly formed and rarely shod. Colors are bay, dark brown, black, and occasionally gray.

Characteristics
The Kabardin is strong, intelligent and obedient. It is also sure-footed, agile and docile, and can track in the dark, across the rocky terrain and through rivers and deep snow. It can carry huge weights over long distances, but is also a good riding horse, with an even, regular walk and light, smooth paces. Some are pacers from birth. The Kabardin is known for its energy, high fertility, and longevity.

Height
15 hands–15.2 hands (5ft–5ft 2in)

Tersk

The Tersk was bred at the Tersk stud in the northern Caucasus in the 1920s from two Strelets Arabian stallions (a breed that was virtually extinct by then) and three pure Arab stallions (see p.184), crossed with Strelets × Kabardin and Arab × Don mares. The aim was to produce a tough, native-type performer, with the Arab lightness and stamina. The Tersk was recognized as a breed in 1948.

Uses
The Tersk is raced and compares well over long distances with the Thoroughbred. It is a top-class endurance horse, successful in both eventing and dressage. It is also used in farming, by the army, and in the circus. To increase its size, it is often crossed with the Lokai, a mountain breed of Arab and Turkmene descent, the Thoroughbred, or the Karabakh.

Appearance
The Tersk looks like an Arab with more substance. It has a straight or slightly concave profile, large, bright eyes, long ears, a short back, and a deep body. The shoulder is well sloped, the quarters broad and strong, and the tail is set and carried high. The limbs are fine boned, but strong and with well-defined joints. The feet are well shaped and hard. The Tersk has the sparse mane and tail of the Arab and the same fineness. The color is often gray with a silver metallic sheen. Bays and chestnuts also occur.

Characteristics
The Tersk is a tougher version of the Arab. It is agile and athletic, with smooth, flowing paces. It is a gentle and intelligent horse, jumps well and boldly, and is capable of great stamina and endurance.

Height
14.3 hands–15.1 hands (4ft 11in–5ft 1in)

Karabakh

The Karabakh is a pony-sized horse. It originates from the Karabakh mountains of Azerbaijan, between the Black and the Caspian Seas and is a neighbour to the Kabardin. It has oriental forebears, notably the Arabian and the primitive Mongolian steppe horse (see pp.184 and 231). It was mixed at different times and to varying degrees with other oriental blood, from Turkey, Iraq, Iran, and Kurdistan, until the breed became established. The best Karabakhs are now found at the Akdam stud, where they are crossed with Arab stallions. The breed still retains the versatile, hardy character of the native mountain horse. The Iranian Karadagh and the Deliboz from Azerbaijan both seem to be closely related. Like so many of the eastern European breeds, the young Karabakh must undergo performance trials on a racecourse, to test for speed, stamina, temperament, and correct type.

Uses

The Karabakh is basically a working horse used by tribesmen for herding, agriculture, transport, pack-carrying, and trading. It adapts to all types of terrain. It is also used for playing *chargan*, a version of polo, and *surpanakh*, a form of basketball on horseback.

Appearance

The Karabakh is a very small, elegant-looking horse of obviously Arab origins. It has a fine, attractive head, which is broad and slightly prominent between its large, bright and intelligent eyes. The arched neck is of medium length, running into a straight shoulder, which is better suited to climbing than to galloping. It is quite deep through the chest and has muscular quarters. The limbs are clean and hard, with a tendency to sickle hocks, a typical feature of mountain horses. The colors, mainly chestnut, bay and dun, have the golden metallic sheen that is characteristic of eastern Russia and suggestive of Akhal-teke ancestry (see p.184). Gray is also seen.

Characteristics

The Karabakh is very agile and well balanced, as might be expected. It is a docile, willing and energetic worker and moves well, although not fast. However, it is not particularly comfortable to ride, being small with an upright shoulder and a brisk trotting action.

Height

Average 14 hands (4ft 8in)

In this mountain setting, a Karabakh horse and rider present a timeless picture. Referred to as far back as the 4th century, the Karabakh horse was decimated during World War II, but has since been revived. Used for herding cattle, it now flourishes as an important part of its country's culture.

Morgan

All Morgan horses descend from one stallion from Massachusetts, which was originally called Figure but renamed Justin Morgan after his owner. Born around 1790 in Vermont, Justin Morgan was only 14 hands and led a hard working life, but was remarkably successful in all local competitions of strength and speed. As a result, he was much sought after as a prepotent sire. He was probably a combination of Thoroughbred, Welsh Cob, and Arab/Barb, blood (see pp.160, 162, and 184–5), although no records exist to verify this. There are now Morgan breeding farms throughout America and in other countries. The Standardbred, Saddlebred, and the Tennessee Walking Horse (see pp.191 and 194) have all benefited from Morgan blood.

Uses
The modern Morgan is taller and finer than the original type. It used to be the US cavalry mount, but is now in demand for showing, both ridden and in harness, for driving events, pleasure riding, Western-style, and trail riding. It may also compete in jumping and dressage events. It is still used for ranch and farm work in some areas and is very popular for breeding and crossbreeding.

Appearance
A sturdy horse, the Morgan has good conformation, a quality head with a straight or slightly concave profile, a tapered muzzle, wide nostrils, large, bright eyes, pointed ears, and an alert expression. The neck is crested, the wither high and defined, and the shoulders sloping. The back is very strong, the body round-barrelled, and the chest wide and deep. The hindquarters should be powerful and well shaped, and the hind legs should have strong hocks. Cannons are short, joints strong and the feet good. The mane and tail are soft and silky, and in motion the long, untrimmed tail is carried high. The Morgan is bay, brown, black or sometimes chestnut. White markings are minimal.

Characteristics
A courageous, spirited breed, the Morgan is intelligent, kind, and easy to train. Famously tough and versatile, with great endurance, it has straight action, a long, active walk, a free trot (both collected and extended), and excellent balance. Special shoeing techniques are sometimes used to make the trot more elevated for specific show classes. The Morgan enjoys jumping.

Height
Average 15.2 hands (5ft 2in)

A pair of Morgan horses parade in harness at a big show. The distinctive appearance of the Morgan, which breeds true to type, suggest the strong genes of the purest bloodlines, probably dominated by Arab and Thoroughbred ancestry. The Morgan was the first American trotting horse but now excels in many spheres, making it a popular all-rounder. The breed has two divisions, the Pleasure Morgan, seen left, has a lower action and is easier to train than the high-stepping Park Morgan.

Missouri Foxtrotter

The Missouri Foxtrotter, based on Spanish Barb, Arab, Thoroughbred, and Morgan blood brought into Missouri by the Pioneers, has existed since the early 19th century. The Tennessee Walking Horse, Saddlebred, and Standardbred (see pp.191 and 194) were introduced later. The resultant breed has a peculiar and very comfortable broken gait, like a "foxtrot." The Breed Society was founded in 1948. The Foxtrotter was developed by selective inbreeding and is popular throughout the USA.

Uses
The Foxtrotter was a popular horse for tradesmen, stockmen, doctors, and the law, but is now a pleasure and show horse, ideally suited to trail riding, usually ridden Western-style. No artificial training aids are allowed.

Appearance
The Missouri Foxtrotter is very strongly made. It has a neat, intelligent head, pointed ears, large eyes, and a tapering muzzle. The neck is thick but well shaped, the shoulders sloping, the chest wide, the body deep, and the back short and strong. It has powerful, muscular hindquarters and upper hind legs, with good bone. The feet are good, and the mane is clipped, or hogged, well back from the poll. Any color is allowed.

Characteristics
The Foxtrotter's unique gait is sometimes described as a "shamble", as its front legs move in a quick walk while its hind legs seem to trot. The action is fast, low, and very smooth and comfortable. It can cover 10 miles (16km) per hour, and moves tirelessly over a long distance. The breed is docile, gentle, and easy to keep, ride, train, and handle.

Height
14 hands–16 hands (4ft 8in–5ft 4in)

Standardbred

The Standardbred was established around 1800 in the northeastern states of the USA and is probably the world's best harness-racing breed. The foundation sire was an English Thoroughbred, Messenger, which was crossed with imported Dutch horses to produce progeny with great trotting ability. These were crossed to the influential sire Hambletonian (born 1849). Almost all Standardbreds descend from four of Hambletonian's sons. The breed takes its name from the time standard required for entry into the American Trotter Register, originally three minutes for one mile (0.6km) but now nearer two minutes. Standardbred pedigrees include some Barb (see p.185) and Morgan blood.

Uses
Bred for harness racing, which thrives in the USA, Canada, Eastern Europe, and Australasia, the Standardbred is used to upgrade other trotting and non-trotting breeds and thus has a huge influence on racing performance and breeding. It is bred on a large scale in Puerto Rico and the USA.

Appearance
The Standardbred has a plain head, fairly long body and a long neck. It is very deep at the girth, and has the well-developed chest that is required for trotting horses. The hindquarters are extremely powerful, and the croup can

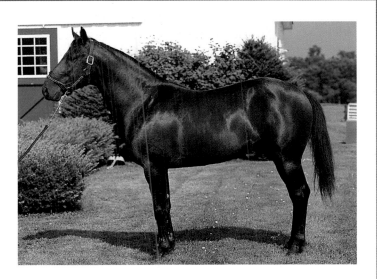

be higher than the withers. The upper limbs are muscular and iron-hard, with very strong hock joints. Standardbreds are mostly bay, brown, black, or chestnut.

Characteristics
The Standardbred is renowned for its courage and toughness. Its action is straight and free. Some trot and pace (when the legs move in lateral rather than diagonal pairs). Natural pacers are encouraged in this gait.

Height
15.2 hands–16 hands (5ft 2in–5ft 4in)

Mustang

The Mustang is the original "Wild West" pony and descends from the 16th-century Spanish horses introduced by the Conquistadores. Its name derives from the Spanish *mestena,* "a herd of wild horses." Turned loose, the Mustang moved north to be adopted by the Indians and cowboys of Texas, New Mexico, and California. A natural cow-pony, it was also used for trade and pack. By 1900, there were about a million feral Mustangs. However, many bloodlines became diluted by crossbreeding to larger imported breeds, the best Mustangs becoming foundation stock for new developing breeds.

Uses
When the wild Mustang became redundant, and it was competing with cattle for grazing, its only use was for the meat trade. Now, an "ancient breed," it is protected by law, although its numbers are controlled.

Appearance
The modern Mustang has a longish head with thick cheeks and a convex profile, ears rimmed with black hair, a deep, narrow body, quite short legs, and fairly flat withers. The shoulder is less straight than it was, and the quarters slope from the croup to a low-set tail. A dorsal stripe is common. Mustangs are any color but tend to have black points.

Characteristics
The Mustang is innately suspicious of humans and has a reputation for being difficult to tame and train, although many have become more "domesticated" and tractable in private ownership. They are very tough and hardy, and economical to keep and feed. They are seldom comfortable to ride, but usually agile and quick. Some "wild" Mustangs are maintained in California.

Height
13.2 hands–15 hands (4ft 4in–5ft)

Appaloosa

The Appaloosa is recognized as a breed in the USA and Canada, but considered elsewhere to be a horse or pony type distinguished by its coat patterns. Bred in Oregon by the Nez Percé Indians from descendants of spotted horses brought to Mexico in the 16th century, its name derived from the Palouse river. The breed was almost wiped out in 1876 when the Nez Percé were evicted from their lands. The Appaloosa Horse Club was formed in 1938. Some Arab blood (see p.184) has been allowed and, more recently, it has been outcrossed to the Quarter Horse (see p.195).

Uses
Originally used for hunting and warfare, the Appaloosa is a popular ranch and pleasure horse, ridden Western-style in shows, on endurance rides, and in cow-pony contests. It jumps well, goes well under harness, and is successful in showjumping, eventing, and dressage competitions.

Appearance
Although diversity of type and coat pattern (of which there are five) ensures that no two Appaloosas look identical, the breed is generally compact, has good limbs, a short strong back, a quality head with mottled skin around the muzzle and a white ring around the eyes. The feet are very good and hard, sometimes striped, and the mane and tail

are thin and short. The forehand can be any color, blending into a white area spotted with the same color; white Appaloosas may have spots of any color (see p.242).

Characteristics
The Appaloosa is bred to work hard. It is agile, handy, willing, and sensible, a typical cow-pony, but with quality. It also has stamina and endurance, jumps well and the paces are often good enough for dressage.

Height
14.2 hands upwards (4ft 10in)

Pinto

The Pinto, also known as the Paint or Calico horse, descends from the Spanish horses of the 16th century. Although primarily an American horse, the Pinto Registry, started in 1956, includes many from Canada, Europe, and Asia. A Pinto is more often categorized as a color, like the Palomino (see below) and the Albino, but the color gene is dominant, and it has been selectively bred in the USA, having been recognized as a breed since 1963. There are two distinct Pinto color patterns: the Overo, which has a dark base coat with white patches and is found mainly in South America; and the Tobiano, a white base coat with dark patches, which prevails in North America. The Pinto comes in four main types: the Stock horse; the Hunter, which has more Thoroughbred blood; the Saddle Pinto, with a high head carriage and knee action like the Standardbred, Tennessee Walking Horse, and Saddlebred (see pp.191 and 194); and the Pleasure type, which resembles the Arab or the Morgan (see pp.184 and 190). There are also four categories of Pinto pony. A separate American Paint Horse Registry exists for Pintos with Thoroughbred and Quarter Horse breeding and conformation (see pp.160 and 195). Pure Thoroughbreds and Arabs are never of mixed color.

Uses

The Pinto used to be favored by American Indians for its color, and was later similarly favoured by producers of Western films. In coaching days, it was popular in harness, particularly in tandems and four-horse carriages. It is now a general riding horse or pony. Breeders aim more for correct color than a specific type. It is also used in cowboy displays and historical pageants as part of the American heritage, and there are show classes for the Pinto, often ridden Western-style.

Appearance

The Pinto varies in type, shape, quality, and size. It may be piebald (broken patches of black and white anywhere on the horse) or skewbald (white with any color except black). In earlier days, the coloring was valued for its natural camouflage. The best Pintos have Thoroughbred type heads, strong Quarter Horse backs, a muscular topline, and strong limbs and feet. Manes and tails are sparse.

Characteristics

Pintos are generally good, all-round riding horses or ponies. They should move straight, be active and agile, and have smooth, easy paces.

Height

There is no uniformity of height.

The Palomino is promoted as a breed in the USA, although elsewhere it is considered more a type of horse or pony identified by its color. It has a golden coat, ranging from pale to darkest bronze, and a flaxen or almost white mane and tail. Most are registered with the Palomino Horse Association Incorporated, which limits entry in the Book to acceptable color, minimal white markings, and at least one registered Palomino parent, the other being Thoroughbred, Quarter Horse or Arab.

Tennessee Walking Horse

The Tennesee Walking Horse was developed by plantation owners to carry them around their estates. It is a "gaited" horse, moving in an unusual four-beat pace that is half walk, half trot and is smooth and comfortable to ride. The foundation sire, Black Allan, a Standardbred failed harness racer (see p.191) born in 1886, moved naturally in this gait and passed it on to his progeny. The modern breed also has Thoroughbred, Arab, and Morgan blood among others (see pp.160, 184, and 190). The breed was recognized in Tennessee in 1935 and officially recognized in 1947.

Uses
The Tennessee Walking Horse is a popular family horse. It is used for showing, particularly in the southern states, and can be seen in displays and parades all over the USA.

Appearance
The Tennessee has good conformation, a plain head, but a kind expression. The ears are long and fine, the neck arched, the shoulders and hindquarters very powerful, and the limbs fine boned but strong. The body is deep, and short-coupled. The flowing mane is left untrimmed except at the poll, while the tail is traditionally "nicked," giving it an unnaturally high tail carriage. The coat can be any color, but black, bay, and chestnut are usual.

Character
Kind, steady and reliable, this popular horse is suitable for any rider. Said to be more comfortable than other breeds, its unique action is bred into it, although in many cases, the front feet are grown long and "high-heeled," weighted shoes are used to encourage very elevated action. The hind shoes have elongated heels, encouraging the hind legs to glide with little elevation, and to step under the body, over-tracking the fore feet by around 12in (30cm). The head nods up and down in time. The canter is high and rocking.

Height
15 hands–16 hands (5ft–5ft 4in)

Saddlebred

The American Saddlebred is a descendant of the Kentucky Saddler, a horse developed by 19th-century pioneers from the now extinct Narragansett Pacer of Connecticut, and from Thoroughbred, Morgan, and Trotter bloodlines. However, it clearly traces back to Spanish pacing horses.

Uses
The Saddlebred was initially bred to carry landowners in comfort and at speed around their properties. It was also used in the Civil War (1861–65). It is now bred mainly as a show animal, ridden and in harness, when it competes in three-gait and five-gait classes. It is also used for pleasure, trail riding, and pulling buggies. Its unusual gaits make it a popular parade horse, but it can also jump and compete in dressage when correctly trained. It is strong enough to pull a plow and fast enough to race.

Appearance
A striking horse with substance and quality, the Saddlebred has a fine head, small ears, wide-set eyes, large nostrils, and a long, arched neck. Its withers are narrow, its shoulders slope and it has a short back, a level croup, high-set tail (often nicked) and muscular quarters. The pasterns are usually long and flexible, and the hooves sound, although heavily shod for showing. All solid colors are found.

Characteristics
The Saddlebred looks fiery in action, with elevated, agile paces, but has a docile temperament and is intelligent to train. It is also very versatile, has stamina, and is comfortable to ride. The five gaits can be inherent, but a good trainer will develop this trait. The natural gaits can be abused by putting weights around the feet or fetlocks to gain more elevated paces. The extra two gaits have four beats and are the "slow gait," a prancing motion, and the "rack."

Height
Average 16 hands (5ft 4in)

Quarter Horse

The American Quarter Horse was the first breed to be developed in the Americas and was recognized in 1611. It was derived from the existing American stock (originally Spanish horses that had then been put to Arabs, Barbs, and Turks) and crossed with imported, English "running" horses (the basis for the English Thoroughbred – see p.160). The result was a very fast, powerful sprinter. The settlers in Virginia and the Carolinas adopted these horses for their hobby of racing, using the village street, or lanes between their estates. These horses excelled over a quarter mile (400m), hence the name "Quarter Miler." Although Thoroughbred racing overtook this sport, it is still popular as a business as well as for fun. The Quarter Horse Association was founded in Fort Worth, Texas, in 1941. Most Quarter Horses remain in the USA, with around one million registered, but they are extremely popular all over the world.

Uses

The Quarter Horse was used by the pioneers in their trek West. Ideal for ranching and cutting out cattle, it was a useful harness horse for haulage and transport. It has become an all-purpose riding horse, used especially for Western riding contests such as barrel racing and steer-roping, for rodeo shows, and trail and pleasure riding. It jumps well and is a top-class showjumper or event horse, particularly when crossed with the Thoroughbred.

Appearance

The Quarter Horse, with its muscular physique and massive hindquarters, is built for sprinting. An attractive, compact horse, it has good conformation. The head is quite short and wide, and the neck can be long, set low on to strong shoulders and a well-defined wither. It has a wide chest, a short back, and well-muscled thighs and gaskins. The hocks must be very strong, and the pasterns should slope to act as shock absorbers at speed. Any solid color is allowed, but chestnut is most common.

Characteristics

Fast, strong, intelligent, and kindly, this is a versatile and popular breed. Although built for straight speed, with low action, it is also agile and surprisingly well balanced. It is an instinctive cattle work horse, with innate "cow-sense."

Height

Average 15.2 hands (5ft 2in)

There are more Quarter Horses registered in the USA than any other breed. They are bred to turn more quickly and accelerate faster than any rival, having particularly muscular hindquarters and hind legs, which come well under the body at speed. They can easily carry large men for ranching or pack work. Racing continues to be very popular, especially in the USA and Canada, where rodeo events such as cattle cutting, steer roping (above), and barrel racing (right) are specialities of the breed.

Criollo

The Criollo is the native horse of Argentina. It derives from Spanish horses thought to have arrived in Argentina with the Spanish cavalry in 1535. Following Indian attacks, the horses later took flight and ran free, mixing with others and becoming native survivors. The Criollo has since spread all over South America, with minor variations in character, depending on different habitats. The Brazilian version, with similar antecedents, is the lighter-framed Crioulo while Venezuela has the Llanaro, Chile the Caballo Chileno, and Peru the Costeno, the Moruchuco, and the Chola.

Uses

The Criollo is the cow-pony of the Argentinian *gauchos*, or cowboys. It is well suited to cattle herding and cutting out, and is used for farm work and pack carrying. Ideal for endurance rides and long distance treks, it is used by ranchers to travel around their *estancias*. The Argentinians hold an annual long-distance ride for Criollo breeders, covering over 470 miles (750km) in 15 days. Each horse must carry 242lb (110kg), and no treatment or extra food, apart from browsing en route, is allowed. The winners of this tough "performance test" increase their breeding and commercial value. The Criollo is also crossed with the Thoroughbred (see p.160) to breed good polo ponies.

Appearance

More pony than horse in appearance, the Criollo is short and stocky. It has a plain, broad, straight head and a short, muscular neck. The body is deep and compact, the croup sloping, and the limbs have ample bone and short cannons. The joints are strong and the feet quite small, but well shaped and very hard. No shoes are needed. It has a coarse mane and tail. It is often dun in color, but also chestnut, roan, palomino, and bay. Many have a dorsal stripe, a Spanish legacy and useful camouflage in earlier days.

Characteristics

The Criollo is extremely tough and sound. A quick and intelligent horse, it has great endurance, is adaptable to extreme temperatures, and capable of surviving on small quantities of food. It is very willing and carries large weights despite its small size.

Height

14 hands–15 hands (4ft 8in–5ft)

Above: This Criollo, tacked up in traditional "Western" gear, is typical of these horses, renowned for travelling long distances in the fiercest extremes of climate and terrain – ranging from desert to snow-capped mountains.

Right: The Criollo is a very hardy breed that has survived the harsh conditions of its native habitat over centuries. It retains some similarities in appearance with the Barb and Andalucian (see pp.185 and 170) from which it is believed to be descended.

Paso Fino

Of the three horse types in Puerto Rico, the Paso Fino is the only "native," the others being the imported Spanish Andalucian (see p.170), and the Thoroughbred (see p.160), which is mainly used for racing. The Paso Fino has the same origins as the Peruvian Paso, following the arrival of Columbus in 1492, when horses of Andalucian, Barb, and the Spanish Jennet breeds were crossed with local horses. The "ambling" or four-beat gait of the Jennet was passed on and became known as the Paso or "step." This gait is inherited, never taught. Similar horses of Spanish origin were discovered breeding on several Caribbean islands during the 16th century, but were then confiscated during later invasions and used to carry occupying armies in Peru, Mexico, and further lands. The Paso Fino is based mainly in Puerto Rico, Colombia, and the Dominican Republic, but it is also in demand in North America.

Uses
The Paso Fino is used for trail riding and for pleasure. It can also jump and canter, but is less suited to these movements. It is popular for showing, in which it exhibits the Classic Fino, a slow, four-time, elevated walk; the Paso Corto, which has long, uncollected steps, suitable for long-distance travel; and Paso Largo, an extended four-beat gait covering up to 16mph (26k/ph).

Appearance
An attractive, compact horse, the Paso Fino has an Arab-like head, on an upright, shortish neck. The chest is muscular, and the back and hindquarters are short and strong. The limbs are fine but strongly made. Most colors are seen.

Characteristics
The Paso Fino is a very comfortable horse, intelligent, calm, and alert. It does not trot but steps in a four-beat gait (the paso). It can carry large weights.

Height
14 hands–15 hands (4ft 8in–5ft)

Peruvian Paso

The Peruvian Paso, like the Paso Fino, inherits its ambling, lateral pacing from the Spanish Jennet (see above). It is bred very selectively to keep its distinctive qualities.

Uses
The Peruvian Paso is ideal for the rocky, mountainous landscape of Peru, which is better suited to goats than to horses, and will travel long distances fast and comfortably. It is used by young Peruvians for competitive and pleasure riding, and makes a good polo pony, especially when crossed with the Thoroughbred (see p.160). It is also bred in Colombia and North America and is exported worldwide.

Appearance
Small and cob-like, the Peruvian Paso is built for comfort rather than speed. The head is wide and straight, the shoulder slopes and the limbs are strong, with dense bone and well-developed hocks. The girth is deep, the pasterns long, and the croup slopes down to the tail, carried low. The coat is fine and any color may occur.

Characteristics
The Peruvian Paso is distinguished by its lateral four-beat gait, in which the forelegs swing out in an arc, and the powerful hind legs move straight, so that the horse seems almost to be sitting on its hocks. The Paso gait divides into three "steps:" the Corto, a jog; the Fino, a slow, collected and elevated step; and the Largo, an extended, fast step. Full of stamina, the horse can travel all day at speeds of up to 16mph (26k/ph). It rarely canters. The back remains virtually rigid. The breed has a very large heart and lungs, for its size, which accounts for its great capacity for work. It also has a kind, easy temperament.

Height
Average 15 hands (5ft)

Australian Stock Horse

The first horses arrived in Australia in 1788 from South Africa and Chile. Of these, the earliest were of Dutch descent, with Barb and Spanish blood (see p.185), while most later imports were Arabs and Thoroughbreds (see pp.184 and 160). The Waler, a hardy, quality Anglo-Arab type, evolved on the vast sheep stations of New South Wales, for use under saddle or pack and also in harness, sometimes working the land in teams of up to seven horses. Despite a wiry, light frame, the Waler would willingly carry 229lb (104kg) all day in the harshest, hottest conditions. It was adopted as the mount of the Indian cavalry. In World War I, of the 120,000 Walers supplied to the allied armies, none returned. From the Waler, the Australian Stock Horse has developed but, although a definite type is emerging, it is not yet established as a true breed. Mainly larger than the Waler, it varies considerably in size and form, having mixed blood from diverse sources. Since 1954, the American Quarter Horse (see p.195) has also influenced the Stock Horse. It is now earning recognition around the world as a tough working and competition horse and is likely to be established soon as a recognized breed.

Uses

A versatile, all-round riding horse, the Australian Stock Horse is still used on large sheep and cattle stations as a hard-working stock horse. It is also gaining a reputation as a tough, sound jumping horse. In 1940, a Waler was recorded as jumping a height of 8ft 4in (2.54m). The Stock Horse tends to be faster and more refined, but with plenty of bone, while former defects of conformation are gradually disappearing as the value of this horse increases. It is popular for polo, as well as for local racing, and has the credentials of an ideal endurance horse.

Appearance

The Australian Stock Horse still varies as to type but is rapidly becoming more uniform. It is a workmanlike, practical horse, hard and wiry. The head is usually neat and fine, of Arab or Thoroughbred character.

Characteristic

The overall conformation is of a robust type of Thoroughbred, but in some the shorter, thicker head and strong physique, reveal Quarter Horse origins. With greater selectivity, there will be less variation in size.

Height

15.2 hands–16.2 hands (5ft 2in–5ft 6in)

Above: Walers and their derivative, the Australian Stock Horse, are both good-tempered horses with plenty of stamina, good legs and feet, plenty of bone and natural balance, a necessity for stock herding activities.

Left: The Australian Stock Horse is used on big cattle stations as an all-purpose mount. A versatile animal, with Thoroughbred character, it represents the largest group of horses in Australia. It is promoted by the Australian Stock Horse Society, which has had success in standardizing the "breed," although a fixity of type has not yet been fully established.

Brumby

The Australian wild Brumby may get its name from the Aboriginal word *baroomby,* meaning "wild." Thought to have originated from stock imported from South Africa and Chile in the late 18th century and then turned loose after the great Gold Rush of 1851, these horses multiplied rapidly and interbred. They deteriorated in quality, until they became scrub horses, valueless as livestock and a nuisance to farmers, since they competed with cattle and sheep for limited grazing and water supplies. Since the 1960s, the Brumbies have been systematically culled, often in their thousands. The culling methods used, chasing the animals with helicopters, motorbikes or landrovers and shooting them, or rounding them up for slaughter and transporting them, often in poor conditions, is enormously stressful. It has provoked worldwide disgust, but a better form of control has not yet been determined.

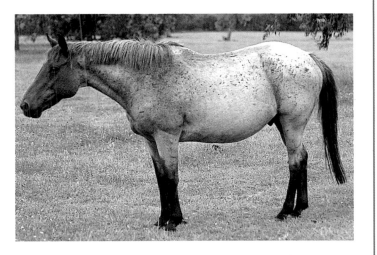

Uses
There is no demand for the Brumby as a riding horse, so its future looks bleak.

Appearance
The Brumby tends to be malnourished and, therefore, can appear poor and weedy. It has a plain head, a thin neck, short, weak hindquarters, and not much bone. Some are cow-hocked. The feet are hard and resilient enough to withstand wear from rough ground and need no attention from a farrier.

Characteristics
The wild Brumby horses are survivors. They are agile and quick and have an instinctive suspicion of humans, quite sensibly doing their utmost to avoid captivity. This makes them intractable when caught and difficult to train, so much so that few efforts have been made.

Height
Variable

Canadian Cutting Horse

The Canadian Cutting Horse is the Canadian equivalent of the American Quarter Horse (see p.195) and has similar origins. Horse breeding in Canada is a fast-growing industry, therefore their own breeds are strictly regulated and controlled. Cutting horses show a natural ability to work with cattle. They are capable of rapid bursts of acceleration and can stop abruptly, in order to match the movements of the cattle exactly as they attempt to elude the stockmen.

Uses
The Canadian Cutting Horse is used extensively for ranch and farm work in Canada, where vast distances must be covered. They are also popular at shows, rodeos and Western-style riding events, where they are used in competitions involving cutting out cattle and similar skills. The Cutting Horse crossed with a Thoroughbred (see p.160) can make an excellent competition horse for showjumping or eventing.

Appearance
The Canadian Cutting Horse is strongly made. It has powerful shoulders and hindquarters and a short, muscular back. The upper limbs are heavily muscled, and the neck, which is long, does not arch and is set quite low.

Characteristics
The Canadian Cutting Horse is intelligent and has natural "cow-sense" and herding ability. Not only is it built to go very fast over short distances, it also has the necessary staying power to work cattle all day. The horse possesses a willing nature, which makes it easy to train, and it can also jump very well.

Height
15.2 hand–16.1 hands (5ft 2in–5ft 5in)

Clydesdale

A heavy horse, the Clydesdale traces its roots back to the early 18th century, when the need for reliable, strong horses to haul coal, work the land, and carry heavy goods across country increased. As a result, heavy local mares in Lanarkshire (formerly Clydesdale), Scotland, were crossed with imported Flemish stallions to produce heavier stock. There may be Shire blood in its background, and some experts consider the two horses to be two branches of the same breed. The *Clydesdale Stud Book* opened in 1877 with 1000 stallions registered, a measure of their importance and popularity. The breed is popular worldwide and is now well established in the USA, Canada, and Australia.

Uses
Clydesdales are still used in the UK, especially Northern Ireland, for pulling work on farmland and in forests. They are also used under harness in cities for delivery or advertising work, and are popular at agricultural and county shows, where they are decoratively presented, either parading, in plowing contests, or in their own show classes. Clydesdale breeding is a thriving business, with demand for the breed from many parts of the world. In the USA and Canada, for example, they are used in teams of seven to work on the vast prairies and have also been used extensively by Australian farmers. Clydesdales cross well with the Thoroughbred (see p.160) to produce a good jumping and cross-country horse.

Appearance
The Clydesdale is a quality heavy horse. It is tall, powerful and impressive, with a dignified bearing. The head is alert, fine for its size, and it has a straight profile. The neck is arched, the wither pronounced, and the body can seem shallow against the long legs. Cow hocks are usual, a legacy from needing to turn in a narrow furrow when working the land. Nonethless, they are very strong. However, sickle hocks are unacceptable. The feet are large and round, and there is an abundance of fine silky feather on the legs and extra hair above the chin and under the stomach. Bay, brown or black are usual, with some roans and grays. All have a lot of white hair on the legs, the head and the underside of the body.

This pair of magnificent Clydesdale horses, well turned out for a plowing match, are waiting patiently to unleash their impressive power and energetic gait.

Characteristics
A horse with great presence, the Clydesdale is lighter than those bred in the past and is generally more active and spirited than horses of similar size and weight – it can weigh up to 2205lbs (1000kg). The Clydesdale is an energetic worker with a high-stepping action, making it a "singularly elegant animal among pulling horses" according to the Clydesdale Horse Society. It shuffles its feet to turn on the spot with careful precision, an important skill for turning in a furrow. The legs and feet are hard and sound. The breed has a kind nature.

Height
Average 16.2 hands (5ft 6in)

Shire

The Shire Horse derives from the medieval "Great Horse," which carried knights to war and was descended from the Norman horses brought to England in the 11th century. In the 16th and 17th centuries Flemish and Friesian imports (see p.164) influenced the native heavy horse, which became known as the English Black, and stood at about 15.2 hands (5ft 2in). The modern Shire's foundation sire is Packington Blind Horse, which stood at stud from 1755 to 1770. The Cart Horse Society, founded in 1875, was renamed the Shire Society in 1884. The Stud Book opened in 1878.

Uses
Shire horses were used for heavy haulage in town and country until the end of World War II. Today, they still work in some places and are often seen at shows in hand, or in harness, especially in pairs or teams of four or more.

Appearance
The Shire, the largest coldblood, has a long, narrow head with a Roman nose and a docile expression. It has an arched, elegant neck on well-sloped shoulders, a deep girth and broad chest. The short back is strong, the loins rounded, and the wide hindquarters muscular, with strong thighs. The forelegs are straight to the pasterns and, unlike many coldblood breeds, it does not have sickle hocks. The limbs have fine, silky feather, and massive, well-defined bone. The feet are large and wide. Black is the most popular color, although gray, bay and brown are acceptable.

Characteristics
The Shire has great presence, and is especially elegant in motion. It can haul several tons and, when mature, weighs more than 2205lbs (1000kg). Mares are smaller than stallions or geldings. Long-lived, Shires can be worked from three years old. The action is straight and powerful.

Height
16.1 hands–18 hands (5ft 5in–6ft 2in)

Suffolk Punch

The oldest British heavy breed, all registered Suffolks descend from the "Horse of Ufford," born in East Anglia in 1768, although a Suffolk breed has existed since at least the 16th century. The Stud Book opened in 1877, when demand for a horse to work the wet, heavy clay lands of East Anglia was at its peak. Also a popular coach horse, it was crossed with trotting strains, for a faster carriage horse. At fairs, in tests of strength, a good individual would go down on its knees in the effort to shift a tree trunk.

Uses
The Suffolk Punch has influenced heavy breeds in Europe and America since at least the 19th century, its prepotent genes making it a popular outcross even today. Popular in heavy horse displays, it is still used for pulling work on farms – singly, in pairs, or in a team of four.

Appearance
Weighing about 2205lbs (1000kg), the Suffolk has a broad, fine-featured head, a crested neck, a huge chest and massive 79-in (2-m) girth. This, coupled with thick bone and short cannons, makes the forelegs look short. The hindlegs are close together, enabling it to move along a 9-in (23-cm) furrow, and the hocks powerful. The quarters are huge and the large feet, rounded. The coat is fine and

there is very little feather or extra hair, an advantage in mud. It is one of seven recognized shades of chestnut.

Characteristics
The Suffolk Punch has a charming, amenable nature. It can work an eight-hour stretch well into its 20s. It matures early, is long-lived, adaptable, and economical. It has a swinging walk and, owing to its very wide chest, may dish slightly at the trot. The action is fairly rounded.

Height
16 hands–16.3 hands (5ft 4in–5ft 7in)

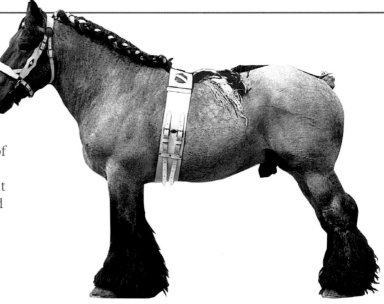

Dutch Draft

This comparatively recent breed is based on the Brabant crossed with native Dutch horses and the occasional outcross to the Ardennes horse. It was established in the Netherlands in 1914, when the Royal Dutch Draft Society was founded. With the publication of the first Stud Book in 1924, the breed became more clearly defined. The best individual horses are singled out and must pass tests of conformation, action, fertility, and true type before they can be used for breeding.

Uses
The Dutch Draft is often seen at shows and agricultural exhibitions, where it is decorated in traditional fashion. It is also a popular sight in the cities, pulling drays or other heavy carriages, as a form of advertising. Its appeal to the meat trade, too, is inevitable.

Appearance
The Dutch Draft is huge and strong. The head has a straight profile and the face an alert expression. The neck is short and thick, and the wide chest is prominent. It has heavily muscled loins and hindquarters, and the croup slopes down to the tail, which is usually docked, or tied up. The limbs are short and sturdy, with plenty of feather. Common colors are chestnut, bay, dun, gray, and black.

Characteristics
The Dutch Draft horse has a docile, willing temperament similar to that of its relation, the Ardennes horse. The breed has great stamina and considerable pulling power. It is a particularly hardy horse, which, since it is a light feeder, is also economical to keep. For such a large animal, it moves freely and easily. It is long-lived and often reaches an age of 30 years or more.

Height
Up to 16.3 hands (5ft 7in)

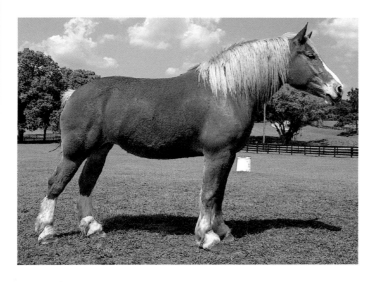

Brabant

The Brabant, or Belgian Heavy Draft, from the Brabant region, is a direct descendant of the Flanders Horse, which derives from the prehistoric Forest Horse (see p.18). The Brabant was known to the Romans and was used as a war horse in the Middle Ages. From the 16th century, it had a major influence on the Irish Draft, Shire, Clydesdale, and Suffolk Punch (see pp.162 and 200–1). Belgian breeders kept its bloodlines free of outside blood and, by the late 19th century, three main bloodlines were established based on the sires Orange I, Bayard, and Jean I.

Uses
Valued for its ancient and enduring bloodlines, this strong breed works well on the Brabant region's wet, heavy soil. Demand for its services has, however, declined with the increasing mechanization of farming. In Europe, many horses are sold for meat, but the breed is still popular in the USA, where it is bred for farm work. It has also been used to improve or found other pulling breeds, such as the Rhenish German Coldblood (see p.208).

Appearance
The Brabant is thickset, compact and heavily muscled in the back, loins and hindquarters, giving it great pulling power. The thick, rounded neck is set on short, sloping shoulders, while the head is broad, short and rather plain, with low-set pricked ears. It has a kindly nature.

Characteristics
This strong, powerful horse is still preferred to the tractor by some farmers. A willing, reliable worker, it copes in the heaviest of soils and is very patient. It has a good, free, long-striding walk. The Brabant has strongly defined characteristics that are still clear on young stock in the rare event of crossbreeding taking place.

Height
15.2 hands–17 hands (5ft 2in–5ft 8in)

Ardennes

The Ardennes heavy horse originates from the mountain plateaux of the Ardennes region bordering France and Belgium, where it is well adapted to harsh, wintry conditions. It is one of the oldest established breeds. There is evidence of a similar type of horse existing 2000 years ago, probably with prehistoric ancestors, which is referred to by Julius Caesar in the first century BC as the "Northern Gaul Horse." Much depleted during World War II, the French stock of Ardennes horses had to be replenished by foreign heavy horse imports from Belgium and the Netherlands, resulting in the heaviest of cart horses. However, remaining traces of Arab blood give the Ardennes an infusion of extra resilience and energy.

Uses

The Ardennes heavy horse provides the ideal replacement for a tractor on difficult terrain. It is still used for heavy pulling on farmland and in forests. It can be ridden, but the breed tends to be bigger than the earlier Ardennais horse, which was used in battle during the Napoleonic Wars, particularly by the artillery. It was later used as a coach horse in France, Belgium, and Sweden. Many of the Ardennes are now bred for the meat market and, sadly, their numbers are dwindling.

Appearance

The Ardennes is a heavy-boned, stocky, compact pulling horse. It has a massive body on short, stout feathered legs. The head has a straight profile, a low, flat forehead, sharp ears and bright eyes. The neck is thick and crested and set well back on powerful shoulders. It has a deep body and a short, strong back. The loins and

quarters are also very strong. The feet are neat and well shaped. The usual colors are roan, gray, chestnut, and bay.

Characteristics

The Ardennes is a hardy breed which, because of the Arabian influence, is more energetic than its heavy appearance suggests. It is a willing worker and has surprising amounts of stamina and resilience, even in severe weather conditions. A docile animal, the Ardennes horse is gentle, easy to handle and a frugal feeder, making it exceptionally economical to keep.

Height
Average 15.3 hands (5ft 3in)

Right: An Ardennes horse, often described as "built like a tractor," does the work of the machine, with less impaction to the ground, spreading fertilizer on to native soil. Gentle and docile, it can be easily handled. More thick-set than any other pulling horse, the Ardennes formed the base stock for the great horses of the Middle Ages.

Boulonnais

The Boulonnais has been an established breed since the 17th century, but was probably being bred in France for the Roman army around 55 BC. During the Crusades, finer Arab and Barb influences (see pp.184–5) were introduced to produce a lighter horse, but medieval heavy armor meant that size was still important. Of the two types of Boulonnais, the lighter Mareyeur, used to convey fish quickly from the Normandy coast to Paris, has now died out, while today's larger horse has declined in numbers because of a fall in demand for working heavy horses.

Uses
The Boulonnais is more appreciated outside France, both as a refined pulling horse and as a useful cross with riding horses. Unfortunately, now that demand for it has decreased, especially in France, it mostly sells for meat.

Appearance
The Boulonnais has a fine head, with straight or concave profile, upright ears and large expressive eyes. The neck is thick and arched, but short, and the shoulders slope well, down to a broad, deep chest. The body is deep, the back straight in outline, and the limbs strongly muscled, with well-developed joints, short cannons and hard, strong feet. The coat is silky, with light feather on the legs. The mane is long, and the tail set on quite high. Gray is the dominant color, but it can be roan, chestnut, or bay.

Characteristics
The Boulonnais is a lively, energetic heavy horse, possessing both stamina and boldness. It has straight action and can cover long distances at a trotting speed.

Height
Average 16.2 hands (5ft 6in)

Comtois

The Comtois, named after the Franche-Comté region on the Franco-Swiss border, is an ancient breed of working horse. Known in the Jura Mountains and Massif Central from the 16th century, it can be traced back to the sixth century. The Comtois was used by the army and achieved fame as Louis XIV's mount. Cross-breeding the original Comtois with the Percheron (see p.206), the Anglo-Norman, and the Boulonnais in the 19th century did not improve the breed, but using a smaller version of the Ardennes (see p.203) produced a stronger line, which proved successful in the early 20th century.

Uses
In vineyards, forests and ski resorts, where it is used to pull sleighs, the Comtois proves itself to be a genuine work horse. Like the Breton, it is exported to North Africa for agricultural uses. Sadly, as with so many heavy horse breeds today, it is also used for meat production.

Appearance
The Comtois is a light pulling horse, small and thickset. The head is broad and short, with small, alert ears and bright, expressive eyes. It has a thick, muscular, straight neck and a prominent wither. The body is broad and deep, the back strong and the quarters broad and

rounded. It has strong limbs, with ample bone and some feather. It may be cow-hocked. The feet are hardy, and the color is often bay, or chestnut with flaxen mane and tail.

Character
This active, tough heavy horse breed has survived many centuries of hardship. Sure-footed and well balanced, it adapts well to mountainous terrain and is long-lived. The paces are lively but short.

Height
14.3 hands–15.3 hands (4ft 11in–5ft 3in)

Breton

The Breton, an ancient breed of heavy horse from Brittany in northwest France, has been developed to suit the conditions of the region and the needs of its people over many centuries. When heavier horses were required for pulling work in the northern area, the early Bretons, a robust but versatile type used both in harness and under saddle, were crossed with the larger Percheron (see p.206) and Boulonnais horses. In more mountainous areas, the Breton was crossed with the Ardennes (see p.203) to produce a useful but heavy horse, the Breton Draft. The lighter Postier Breton has Hackney and Norfolk Trotter ancestry (see p.161) and faster, more active paces. The Stud Book, started in 1909, controls both divisions separately, carefully preserving the purest bloodlines since 1920.

Uses

In France, the Breton is still used on the land, for farm and haulage work, and in vineyards, while it is imported as a working horse by less-developed agricultural countries. The Postier Breton is in demand as a coach horse, often for use in teams. It is exported to North Africa, Spain, Italy, and Japan to improve lighter stock.

Appearance

Characterized by its kind expression, the Breton has a broad, straight-profiled head, wide jaw and cheek bones, bright eyes and small ears. A square-shaped horse, it has a strong, thick, slightly crested neck, a sloping shoulder with a high-set chest, and a short, wide and powerful back, loins and hindquarters. The legs are short, thick and muscular, with minimal feather, and the feet are medium sized and hard. The Breton is often chestnut, but may be roan or gray. Its tail is docked short.

Character

The Breton is a good-natured horse. It is a strong, energetic and willing worker that adapts well to varying climates and conditions. It is robust and hardy, with inherent stamina. The Breton moves freely for a heavy horse. The breed matures early, a characteristic which is exploited by the meat trade.

Height

15 hands–16.1 hands (5ft–5ft 11in)

Left: The Breton Heavy Draft is used for plowing and other farm work. It has a willing, docile temperament, as well as a light-footed action despite its size and strength. The tail is docked to prevent it from becoming entangled in the reins.

Left: These Postier Bretons in tandem demonstrate their lively trot action. They have finer limbs than the heavier Draft, but their willing temperament and coloring are similar. They are bred selectively and must have Postier parentage and pass a performance test before they can be accepted in the Breton Stud Book. These tests have become festive occasions in the locality. No outside blood has been allowed since 1920. Postiers are also used for light pulling work and other farming activities.

Percheron

The Percheron, the best-known heavy horse of France, originated in La Perche, in the northwest. The breed was founded on oriental horses of the Moors in the 8th century and heavier Flemish horses, but was further improved by Arab blood during the Crusades and later in the 19th century. Some 32,000 horses were registered at the peak of its popularity around 1900, and the breed was widely exported, but thousands were lost in World War I.

Uses

Originally famous as a warhorse, the Percheron became popular in harness, transporting the French people and their goods, and was used for agricultural work. The breed is still used for hauling and is a popular carriage horse, often seen in French shows and exhibitions. Percherons may also be ridden and can be crossed with Thoroughbred types (see p.160) to breed weight-carrying riding horses. There is a strong export trade, especially to Australia, North and South America, Britain, and South Africa, while Japan has established its own breed society.

Appearance

Handsome and well proportioned, the breed has a fine head, with wide nostrils, cheek bones and forehead, long mobile ears and a straight profile. The thick, muscular neck is long and crested, while the body is short, deep and strong, the chest wide, the shoulders sloped and the loins and hindquarters powerful and well rounded. The Percherons limbs are strong, with well-formed joints, short cannons and hard, blue-horned feet. It is clean legged, with minimal feather. It often has a full tail, which is put up for working. Usually dappled gray in color, occasionally black, the breed is fine coated.

Characteristics

The Percheron has extraordinary pulling power. It is docile yet active, intelligent and easy to handle. Its adaptability to different types of work and to alien climates makes it popular outside France. Its movement is low, straight and free, covering the ground. The hocks can be close together, but have good flexion. The Percheron usually weighs around 1 ton.

Height

Average 16.2 hands (5ft 6in).

Left: A pair of Percherons waits patiently to plough the land, as they have been doing for centuries. This pair of dappled grays are typical of the breed.

Above: The Percheron is not only extremely powerful, it is also, as a result of its distinguished bloodlines, one of the most active and versatile of the heavy breeds.

Freiberger

The Freiberger, from the mountainous Jura region of Switzerland, is a smaller working horse of mixed origins. It is a relatively new breed based on stock such as the Anglo-Norman, Brabant (see p.202), and other coldbloods. Many trace to Vaillant, a stallion of Anglo-French descent born in 1891, and since then the Anglo-Norman has remained the most successful outcross, with the occasional use of Arab blood (see p.184). Breeding is now controlled by the Swiss National Stud at Avenches, using only horses that match breeders' criteria for a docile, active horse.

Uses
The Freiberger is bred for use by Swiss farmers, especially on mountain slopes, and by the Swiss army for patrolling and artillery tasks. They are used for light pulling and often replace mechanized transport to reduce pollution and costs. The Swiss government sponsors the Freiberger's breeding and care.

Appearance
The breed's mixed ancestry may produce variation in appearance, but it is always compact, well muscled, and stocky. The Freiberger has become more standardized since breeding became more controlled and selective, with emphasis on good conformation and soundness. The neat head, with its slightly concave profile, suggests Arab blood. The overall impression is of a small cob, with clean legs with little feather.

Characteristics
Agile, active, and easy to train, the Freiberger is a reliable worker. It should have sound action and be sure-footed.

Height
14.3 hands–15.2 hands (4ft 11in–5ft 2in)

Italian Heavy Draft

The Italian Heavy Draft horse is bred throughout Italy, especially around Venice. An active working horse was needed in the 19th and early 20th centuries, so local stock was crossed with heavier imported breeds: the French Percheron and more agile Boulonnais (see p.204), and, most successfully of all, the lively Breton (see p.205). Ideal for the needs of small farmers, it has become one of Italy's most popular heavy breeds.

Uses
Although still used in agriculture and haulage, Italian Heavy Draft horses are increasingly valued only by the meat trade. The best bloodlines are preserved, however, and many stallions are exhibited at shows and horse fairs.

Appearance
Compact and balanced in outline, this breed has a long and straight-profiled head set on an upright, crested neck. The chest is deep, with the forelegs wide apart, the hindquarters powerful, the croup pronounced and the tail high set. Its upper limbs are muscular, but it sometimes lacks bone and may have rounded joints. The lower legs have some feather, while the feet can be small and "boxy." The color is usually liver chestnut, with a flaxen mane and tail, but roans and grays also occur.

Characteristics
One of the most agile work horses, the Italian Heavy Draft is energetic but has a kind, docile temper. It has a long striding walk and fast trot. The breed is quick to mature, economical to keep and has a hardy constitution.

Height
15 hands–16 hands (5ft–5ft 4in)

Rhenish German Coldblood

The Rhenish German Coldblood is a 20th-century heavy breed from the Rhine area. It was founded on Brabant (Belgian Heavy Draft) horses (see p.202), imported to establish a German draft horse. The Ardennes breed (see p.203) was also used, along with local blood lines from the Rhineland, Westphalia, and Saxony, resulting in a useful working breed. Barely surviving, even though the Stud Book remains open, it now includes some mixed, warmblood types, based on selected lighter individuals crossed with warmbloods containing Thoroughbred, Hanoverian, and Trakehner blood (see pp.160, 172, and 174). These became the Rhinelander Warmblood, a useful all-round riding horse not yet distinguished as a breed.

Uses
With mechanization, there is now little demand for the Rhenish German Coldblood as an agricultural or haulage workhorse, although horses can be found in Lower Saxony and Westphalia and a few studs still exist.

Appearance
Massive in frame, with a plain head, short, thick neck, and deep, wide, short body, the Rhenish heavy horse most resembles the Brabant. The hindquarters are muscular, and the limbs short and strong with much feather.

Although sometimes chestnut, it is usually roan in colour, with either black points or flaxen mane and tail, both thick and coarse; the latter is often docked.

Characteristics
A powerful and honest working horse, the Rhenish German Coldblood is capable of all pulling duties, having a particularly active walk. It is good-natured and matures early.

Height
16 hands–17 hands (5ft 4in–5ft 8in)

Schleswig-Holstein

Originating in the north German province of the same name, the heavy Schleswig-Holstein horse was founded in the early 19th century, when Munkedal, a stallion from Jutland in Denmark, was used on local mares containing Thoroughbred and Cleveland blood from England (see pp.160 and 163). Breeding became selective from 1860 so as to establish a definitive draft horse for use in both town and country. The Jutland influence was strong until, in 1938, the breed was improved by using a Boulonnais and a Breton stallion (see pp.204–5).

Uses
The Schleswig-Holstein was a popular draft horse for all haulage purposes until recently when mechanization replaced it. Some can still be seen performing as teams for shows, parades, or advertising companies in the city.

Appearance
The breed is medium sized and compact. The head can be fine, from the English influence, with an alert, bright expression, tapering nose and wide nostrils. It is deep-bodied with a broad chest and strongly muscled quarters. The heavily feathered legs are short but not massively boned. The color is usually chestnut, with lighter colored mane and tail; some bays and grays also occur.

Characteristics
The Schleswig-Holstein's equable temperament makes it amenable and docile. Paradoxically, by the time it was no longer in demand for pulling work, its conformation had much improved, making it better balanced and particularly sound.

Height
15.2 hands–16 hands (5ft 2in–5ft 4in)

Noriker

The Noriker is one of Europe's oldest breeds. For at least 2000 years, its ability to adapt to changing environments has enabled it to survive. It gained its name from the Roman province of Noricum, now part of Austria, at a time when packhorses were the chief form of transport. From 1565, the wealthy monasteries controlled the breed and improved it, imposing definitive standards. Neapolitan, Burgundian, and Spanish blood gave size, and in the Pinzgau area of Austria a spotted variety evolved. Strict selection is now maintained, and the breed's ability to haul weights and the quality of its walk and trot are tested against established criteria. It is also popular in southern Germany, where it is found in great numbers. The breed has four main bloodlines: the South German Coldblood (also called the Bavarian), the Steier, the Tiroler, and the Karntner (or Carinthian).

Uses
The Noriker is mainly used in forestry work and on farms as a draft horse and is exported widely. Its distinctive looks also make it popular at shows; it is a useful driving horse for competitive or display events.

Appearance
The Noriker's distinctive coloring – a dark liver chestnut with flaxen mane and tail, which are usually long, thick and flowing – makes it easy to recognize. This, and its compact and sturdy build, make it an eye-catching horse. The head is heavy and the neck thick, while the short,

strong body is notable for its depth. The hindquarters match the powerful shoulders in strength, and the legs are also strong and correctly made, with well-formed joints and some feather. The spotted variety of Noriker, the Pinzgauer, still exists.

Characteristics
With its strong inherent genes, this hardy breed is a true survivor. Adaptable, agile and very strong the Noriker is a willing and biddable workhorse, well suited to timber haulage. It is sure-footed and renowned for its soundness.

Height
16 hands–17 hands (5ft 4in–5ft 8in)

Above: The Noriker-Pinzgauer had evolved by the 18th century. Its spotted coat is a result of crossbreeding with spotted Spanish breeds. A Stud Book for this spotted strain was opened in 1903.

Left: A young Noriker is inspected at a show. It has a long, active stride for a pulling horse and will grow into a tall, strong horse for driving and haulage work.

Dales

The Dales pony from North Yorkshire, England, shares a Friesian (see p.164) and Scottish Galloway pony ancestry with its neighbor, the Fell pony. The original trotted very fast, both ridden and in harness. In the 19th century, Welsh Cob blood (see p.162) was introduced to lengthen the stride. An unsuccessful Clydesdale outcross (see p.200) was also tried to give more strength and size. The Dales Pony Improvement Society was formed in 1916, but by 1955 only four registered ponies remained. The breed was rescued by the Dales Pony Society, founded in 1963.

Uses
The Dales pony was used by the Yorkshire mining and wool industries for transporting heavy loads. Farmers used to ride it and, when roads improved, many became harness ponies for pulling, often travelling as far as London and back. It is still carries farmers over the Dales to tend their sheep and is popular for trekking, driving, and riding.

Appearance
The Dales pony has a neat head, carried on an almost upright neck, a bright, alert expression, small, inward-pointing ears, a crested neck and strong shoulders. The girth is deep, the barrel rounded and the back short and strong with powerful loins. The Dales has ample bone, very strong limbs with silky feathered heels and hard, well-shaped feet. It is more heavily built than the Fell pony. It is dark colored with few or no white markings.

Characteristics
The Dales breeds true to type, despite past crossbreeding. It is very energetic and has a strong constitution, courage, stamina, strength, and an excellent temper. It is also economical to keep. The trot action is powerful with great flexion of the fetlocks, knees and hock joints.

Height
Up to 14.2 hands (4ft 10in)

Fell

The Fell pony is native to the Border and Cumbrian regions of northern England. Like the Dales pony, it is descended from the black Friesian (see p.164) and the now extinct Galloway pony. It has been a valued packhorse since the 13th century. Travelling in droves or a pack train, ten ponies might carry one ton between them, covering about 240 miles (386km) in a week. Nowadays, they are popular both as riding and driving ponies.

Uses
The Fell was traditionally used as a packpony and on the hill farms for herding sheep and cattle. In an area where few roads existed, it also transported humans, being capable of carrying an average-sized man comfortably and safely all day. It continues to perform these tasks today. In the 18th and 19th centuries, it was used for trotting races in harness, and it is still popular in driving events.

Appearance
The Fell pony has a quality head, a broad forehead tapering to a narrow muzzle, and wide nostrils. It has small, neat ears, bright eyes, and fine jawbones. The shoulder is deep and sloping, and the back and loins strong. The round feet are of blue horn, which is naturally hard. The Fell has a long, lustrous mane and tail

and lots of fine feather around the heels. Its color is usually black, with some browns and bays. There are no white feet, but a small star is allowed.

Characteristics
The Fell has a hardy, tough constitution and is agile, quick, and sure-footed. The trot action is energetic, yet smooth, with a long, low action and good knee and hock flexion. It is courageous and willing, with a keen outlook.

Height
Average 14 hands (4ft 8in)

Highland

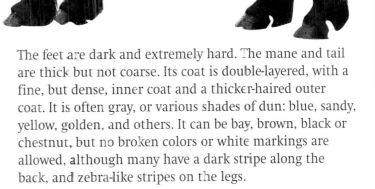

The native pony of the Scottish Highlands, the Highland pony is an ancient breed resembling prehistoric cave drawings at Lascaux, France. The Highland has been outcrossed during its known history with an Arab stallion (see p.184) and with Percherons (see p.206) given to James IV of Scotland by Louis XII of France. It is also similar to the Norwegian Fjord pony (see p.226). All Highlands are registered in one Stud Book, although those from the Western Isles tend to be finer and smaller than the mainland "Garron" type, which were bred for size for forestry work and haulage. Until recently, when machines began to replace them, the Highland was the chief form of transport in the Highlands and some other parts of Scotland. They are also famous for having been taken to South Africa by Scottish regiments fighting in the Boer War.

Uses

Throughout Scotland's history, the Highlands have excelled as packponies, carrying heavy, bulky game across steep and difficult terrain steadily and safely. As well as hauling timber, herding sheep, and pulling farm carts, they are used for pony-trekking and for riding and driving competitions. They are a popular foundation stock for riding horses, especially the Thoroughbred (see p.160).

Appearance

The Highland has a broad, short head, with wide nostrils, and a fine "beard." It has a kind eye and wise expression. The neck is strong, thick and arched on a well-sloped shoulder with a clearly defined wither. The back is short and strong, with rounded loins and powerful quarters above well-developed thighs and gaskins. It has short legs and hard, flat bone, with fine silky feather at the heels.

The feet are dark and extremely hard. The mane and tail are thick but not coarse. Its coat is double-layered, with a fine, but dense, inner coat and a thicker-haired outer coat. It is often gray, or various shades of dun: blue, sandy, yellow, golden, and others. It can be bay, brown, black or chestnut, but no broken colors or white markings are allowed, although many have a dark stripe along the back, and zebra-like stripes on the legs.

Characteristics

The Highland pony is versatile, strong, intelligent, kind and docile. It is very sure-footed and hardy and can carry great weights. It has natural good sense and can pick its way home safely through thick fog, snow, or in the dark, avoiding bogs and rocks, while carrying heavy loads. It is healthy with good longevity.

Height

Up to 14.2 hands (4ft 10in)

Left: This Highland pony is hauling timber over rough ground in a forestry area in Scotland. Haulage is also used as a good training method for harness work.

Below: A dorsal stripe is typical of many Highlands, and a characteristic of their ancient origins.

Welsh Mountain Pony (Section A)

The Welsh Mountain Pony is generally considered to be one of the world's most beautiful ponies. It has remained a true native type throughout its history. All Welsh Ponies and Cobs are registered in one Stud Book, opened in 1902. The smallest and oldest of the ancient Welsh breeds, the Welsh Mountain contains traces of an eastern equine type brought over by the Romans, as well as Thoroughbred and Arab blood (see pp.160 and 184) introduced in the 18th and 19th centuries. It is the base for all Welsh stock, and for most high-quality small riding ponies, combining pony character with oriental refinement.

Uses
The Welsh Mountain Pony is an ideal all-round riding pony for children. It jumps well, is excellent in harness, and popular with showing enthusiasts. It provides a foundation for ponies of all heights and abilities.

Appearance
The breed is compact, with a small, quality head, tapering from a broad forehead to a small muzzle with wide nostrils. It has large, beautiful eyes and slightly dished profile. The body is deep, with short, strong loins and powerful hindquarters. The limbs are short and well formed, and the feet are of hard and dense blue horn. Grays predominate, but bays, palominos, creams, and other colors also occur. No piebalds or skewbalds are registered.

Characteristics
This pony has a sound, hardy constitution and thrives on poor rations. It is intelligent and kind, but also spirited, with an attractive gaiety. Its action is powerful and it has free, ground-covering paces, which are light and airy.

Height
Up to 12 hands (4ft)

Welsh Pony (Section B)

The Welsh Pony is much sought after as a high-quality riding pony. The mix of Welsh Mountain with Thorough-bred (see p.160) has produced the best possible all-round pony for children, with athletic ability, brilliant action, versatility, stamina, and spirit. These qualities have made it a winner throughout Welsh pony history. Despite, refinement by Arab (see p.184) and Thoroughbred blood, the Welsh Pony's native character was undiminished and, until recently, many lived out on the Welsh mountains.

Uses
Early types of the pony carried Welsh farmers about the hill farms. It is now renowned as a top-class show pony that excels in all equestrian spheres. It is a valuable export worldwide and is especially popular in the USA.

Appearance
The Welsh Pony usually has excellent conformation. It has a small, quality head, large, bright eyes, and small, alert, pointed ears. It has a deep body with rounded barrel, well-defined withers and a sloping shoulder ideal for riding. The loins and hindquarters are strong and the legs fine boned with short cannons and hard feet. The tail is set high and carried proudly. All colors are acceptable, except skewbald and piebald.

Characteristics
Larger but more refined than the Welsh Mountain, the Welsh Pony can compete at higher levels. It is spirited yet biddable. Propelled by powerful hocks, the paces are low but often extravagant and impressive; straight action is almost standard to this breed. It retains its native hardiness, despite its Thoroughbred ancestry.

Height:
Up to 13.2 hands (4ft 6in)

Uses
Originally an all-round farm pony, the Section C is ideal for both riding and driving. It is a genuine all-rounder, popular as a competition pony for jumping and showing, and excelling in harness, being ideal for all driving events.

Appearance
This breed is stocky and compact, with a deep body and strong chest and loins, rounded hindquarters and well-sloped shoulder. It has short, muscular limbs, which are slightly feathered at the heels. The feet are dense and well shaped. The Welsh pony may be any color, except skewbald or piebald.

Character
Versatile, active, and strong, the Welsh pony of Cob type is friendly, with a kind temperament. It is bold, sound, and sure-footed, and is a natural jumper. Its action is free and often spectacular, and it is generally easy to handle and economical to keep.

Height
Up to 13.2 hands (4ft 6in)

Welsh Pony (Section C)

The Section C Welsh Pony was developed from crossing the Welsh Cob (see p.162) with the native Welsh Mountain Pony (A). It was bred as a useful farm pony and was used in the slate mines of North Wales during the 19th century. Most of today's Welsh Section Cs (or Welsh pony of Cob type) have registered Section C parents, although the Welsh Mountain blood is used on occasion to ensure native characteristics. Diminishing demand for working ponies and wartime disruption almost led to the breed's disappearance. To revive the breed, it was given a section

Above: The thickset neck of the Section C is arched and carried high, reflecting its Welsh Cob forebears. The head, like that of the Cob, is similar to the Mountain Pony (A) and recalls its Arab ancestry.

Right: The Section C, like the Welsh Cob, is active, courageous, and has plenty of strength and stamina, making it ideal for competitive driving, for which it is still much in demand.

Basque

The Basque, one of only three surviving native pony breeds in France, is still found in the Pyrenees and the Atlantic coastal region of southwestern France. Locally better known as the Pottok pony, it has its own registry, the *Association Nationale du Pottok*. Although semi-wild, the ponies all have owners. Every year, in January, they round up and brand the ponies and put some up for sale. In the early 20th century, Arabian and Welsh Section B pony blood (see pp.184 and 218) was introduced to the native Basque to improve its usefulness. There are three types of Basque: the Standard, the Piebald, and the Double.

Uses
The Basque has been used as a packpony for centuries. Up to World War II and probably even after, smugglers used it to carry contraband across the Pyrenees. Until recently, the Basque worked as a pit pony in both French and British coal mines. It is now useful in harness and as a good all-round riding pony.

Appearance
The Basque pony has a large, square-shaped head on a smallish body. It has small, bright eyes, short ears and a slight indentation in its forehead. The neck is short and the back relatively long, with sloping hindquarters. It has fine-boned legs, lightly feathered, and a coarse mane and tail, the latter set on high. The feet are small and hard. Most colors occur, including the piebald type, which is various colors with white.

Characteristics
This ancient breed has survived by being extremely tough and resilient. It is now more selectively bred, although still living semi-wild in its original habitat. It is quick to grow and mature. The Double, a larger version, can grow up to 14.2 hands (4ft 10in) but is often weaker. The Basque is naturally sure-footed and agile.

Height
11.2 hands–13 hands (3ft 10in–4ft 4in)

Above: As well as the accepted black and white piebald colouring, the Piebald Basque can be chestnut, white and black or chestnut and white. The head of this piebald Basque pony reflects the Tarpan (see p.228) from which it descends.

Right: A mixed herd of Basque ponies is assessed by prospective buyers. The Double and Standard Basques are generally chestnut, brown, and bay. Crossbreeding with Arabs and Welsh Section B ponies has now introduced more quality, bone, and substance to the breed, which is used as a child's pony and in harness.

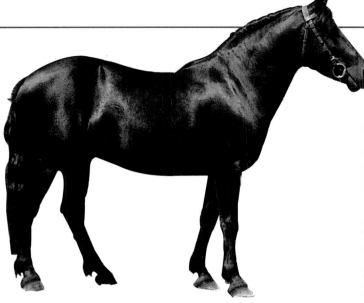

Landais

The Landais is an ancient native breed from the area bordering the Adour River of southwestern France. After the Moors' defeat by the French at Poitiers in 732, their horses were dispersed among the native ponies and their oriental blood, mostly Arabian, proved a strong influence on the Landais. In 1913, an Arab stallion was selected to improve the native ponies, then about 2000 strong. Numbers declined until, after World War II, only 150 were left. Meanwhile, Arabs were again introduced, with Welsh Section C and Connemara ponies (see pp.219–20), to rescue the breed. With the birth of the Pony Club Français, it was in demand again. A tough survivor, it still roams, semi-wild, in its original homeland.

Uses
A fast trotter, it has been used for harness racing in France for many centuries. It is better suited for driving in harness, but has proved to be a useful children's riding pony.

Appearance
This breed is sturdy, but has fine, neat Arab-type features. The profile is slightly concave, with small, pointed ears and large, widely spaced, intelligent eyes. It has a long neck, sloping but heavily made shoulders, flat withers, a short, straight back and sloping hindquarters. The mane and high-set tail, carried well raised, are thick. The limbs lack bone, and the hocks are often weak. It is fine coated and usually dark bay, brown, black or chestnut in color.

Characteristics
Tough and cunning, the Landais is able to exist on sparse rations and to withstand extremes of heat and cold. A flat wither and ill-defined shoulder make it difficult to fit a saddle, but its conformation has generally improved.

Height
Up to 13.1 hands (4ft 5in)

Avelignese

The Avelignese derives from ponies left behind at Avelengo, near Merano, by Ludwig IV and his army of Eastern Goths when they returned to Austria in 1342. Many survived and the breed became Italy's principal native pony. Descended from the coldblood Alpine Heavy Horse, it was originally bred in the Sarentino region and the Venosta Valley, but now exists in all parts of Italy. It is especially popular in the Alto Adige and throughout the northern, central, and southern mountain regions. All pedigrees go back to an Arabian foundation sire, El Bedavi XXII, born in 1837. Although larger, it is closely related in both breeding and type to the Haflinger pony (see p.225).

Uses
The Avelignese is a mountain pony by nature. Sure-footed, wise and ideally suited to negotiating difficult, rough and inaccessible terrain, it has been used for centuries as a pack and pulling animal in mountainous and forested areas. It also makes an excellent riding pony, strong enough to carry the average adult.

Appearance
Its alert, neat head reflects Arabian influence. It has a short, heavy neck and broad chest. The withers are low and the back broad and strong. Its legs are short and very sturdy, with some feather. It has a distinctive sorrel-colored coat, full mane and tail and a blaze down its face. Unlike the Haflinger, it does not have a brand mark.

Characteristics
Strongly made and resilient, the Avelignese is hardy, energetic and sensible. It is economical to keep and long-lived. It is sure-footed and has a long-striding walk.

Height
Up to 14.3 hands (4ft 11in)

Garrano

The Garrano (which means "little horse") derives from the mountainous Minho and Tras-os-Montes areas of northwestern Portugal. It is an indigenous breed of direct, primitive descent. Like most southern European breeds, it has Arab bloodlines, used deliberately and systematically to upgrade its quality and conformation, while retaining many of the distinguishing characteristics of its ancient forebears, particularly the original Barb influence. It is still popular at the famous Vila Réal and Famaliçao horse fairs.

Uses
Surprisingly strong for its small size, the Garrano was used for transport by the Portuguese army and continues to be used by foresters to haul timber and by farmers for light agricultural tasks. It was once popular for trotting races and is still purpose-bred for this in some places. It is also useful as a packpony, and for riding and trekking.

Appearance
A lightly built, quality pony, the Garrano has a fine head with a concave profile. This pony is compact, with a fairly straight shoulder, short back and sparse, but improving, hindquarters. The limbs are clean and fine and the feet are well formed. The Garrano is usually dark chestnut with a luxuriant mane and tail.

Characteristics
The Garrano is strong and hardy and has a natural resistance to extremes of heat and cold. It is sure-footed and energetic, with a sensible temperament. It moves freely and can have impressive, elevated paces. It has a quick, collected trot gait, characterized by short, high, and animated steps, which is unusual and makes it attractive to trotting-race enthusiasts.

Height
Average 11 hands (3ft 8in)

Sorraia

The Sorraia is the only native pony of the southern Iberian peninsula. The breed is a "primitive" type, similar to the original Tarpan and Asiatic Wild Horse (see pp.228 and 230). They were probably the first European horses to be domesticated and are the ancestors of the Spanish horses that were so influential from the 16th century onwards. The breed is named after the Sorraia river in Portugal where, in 1920, Doctor Ruy d'Andrade found a few survivors, which he reared naturally, with as little interference as possible, so that they bred true to the original type.

Uses
For centuries, the Sorraia was widely used for rounding up cattle and other livestock and was the main means of transport. With declining demand for its services, its numbers dwindled, but now that the breed has been revived, it has become a popular pony for children to ride.

Appearance
The Sorraia, like the Tarpan, has a black "eel stripe" along its back and stripes on the legs. The head is now smaller that that of earlier ponies, and the profile can be straight or convex. It has long, black-tipped ears, and the eyes are set high in the head. The neck is long, the shoulder upright and the back short. The hindquarters tend to be

poorly developed, with a high-set tail. The pony is compact, with fine, light-boned limbs. The usual color is dun, but palominos and some grays also occur.

Characteristics
An extremely hardy pony, the Garrano can survive healthily in extreme climates on the poorest vegetation. Improved by selective breeding, it retains its distinguishing features.

Height
12 hands–13 hands (4ft–4ft 4in)

Dülmen

The Dülmen is one of only two native pony breeds in Germany, the other being the almost extinct Senner. It has lived in a semi-wild state on the Merfelder Bruch, in Westphalia, since the 1300s, and the last Dülmen herd still survives there on the estate of the Duke of Croy. They are reared in their natural habitat and are rounded up annually to be sorted. Those that are surplus are sold. Although a small pony type, the Dülmen, with the Senner, has been credited with being partly responsible for providing the foundations of the famous German horse breed, the Hanoverian (see p.172). The introduction of various outcrosses to improve the breed has given no distinct character to today's Dülmen.

Uses
There is little demand for the pure-bred Dülmen, which, apart from its historical interest, serves no particular purpose in Germany today. However, crossed with Arabs (see p.184), they make useful children's ponies.

Appearance
The Dülmen has a small head with straight profile and small ears. The neck is short, the shoulder upright, the back short and the hindquarters poorly developed. There is adequate bone, and the feet are generally good. It is similar to Britain's New Forest pony in appearance (see p.214), but smaller. The color is mostly bay, brown, black or dun, but some are gray or roan.

Characteristics
The Dülmen has become nondescript, because of mixed bloodlines. Arab infusions have given it refinement, a free, straight action and greater stamina and spirit.

Height
Average 12.3 hands (4ft 3in)

Haflinger

The Haflinger pony is a hardy mountain breed from the Austrian Tyrol. It is named after Hafling, a village now in northern Italy. It can be traced back to both of the heavier primitive types of coldblood horse: the Alpine Heavy Horse and the Arabian, via El Bedavi XXII. This interesting and successful mixture has resulted in a distinctive breed of world renown. Once it was bred only at Austrian state stud farms and the state still owns and controls the stud stallions. To become one of these, colts undergo strict inspection and testing.

Uses
The Haflinger is popular in Austria both as a pulling and riding pony. Its excellent temperament makes it an ideal mount for children and beginners of all ages. It pulls sleds and sleighs, as well as wheeled vehicles, and is used for farm and forest work. Many are exported to Germany and the Netherlands.

Appearance
Haflingers are powerful, strongly made ponies, cob-like in appearance. They have large eyes and nostrils, small ears and a bright, lively expression. The body is deep, with a muscular back and loins, and the limbs have ample bone. The strong, rounded hindquarters are branded with the Edelweiss flower motif, enclosing the letter "H." Haflingers are always chestnut, from a golden shade to deep bronze and palomino, with a flaxen mane and tail of varying hues. The tail is full, and there are white facial markings.

Characteristics
The Haflinger is placid, intelligent, kind, and willing. Sure-footed and versatile, it has free action and a long-striding walk. It is a long-lived pony, which may start working at four years old and continue for up to 40 years.

Height
Up to 14 hands (4ft 8in)

Gotland

The Gotland pony, also known as the Skogsruss, is Sweden's oldest breed and probably descends from the Tarpan (see p.228). It may well have existed on Gotland Island since the Stone Age and is now bred throughout Sweden. Despite oriental additions in the late 19th century and a little British pony blood more recently, there are still some "pure" Gotlands running wild in the forests of Löjsta that retain their native characteristics. The Gotland also resembles the Konik and the Huçul of eastern Europe (see pp.228 and 230).

Uses
The Gotland is still an important means of transport in Scandinavia. Although small, it is used by farmers for haulage, as a packpony or in harness, and for hauling timber. It is bred selectively for trotting races, which are popular in Sweden, and its breeding is also now encouraged by the government-run Swedish Pony Association.

Appearance
Small, narrow, and lightly built, the Gotland has a medium-sized head of fine quality and a straight profile. The neck is short and the back long; the hindquarters slope to a low-set tail. The hind legs can be weakly conformed, but the feet are good. It often has a black dorsal stripe, suggesting its ancient ancestry. Its color may be bay, brown, black, dun, chestnut, gray or palomino, with a white star or blaze on the face, but no white socks.

Characteristics
The Gotland is a hardy breed, but, although usually easy to handle, can be obstinate. It is known for its endurance and is an energetic walker and a fast trotter, although its gallop is poor. It can jump well, despite its apparently weak hind legs.

Height
12 hands–12.2 hands (4ft–4ft 2in)

Norwegian Fjord

The Norwegian Fjord Pony, often called the "Viking Horse," appears on runestone carvings from the eighth century. This striking breed, with primitive features, was also known as the "Westlands pony" because it inhabited the coastal regions of west Norway. It is now found all over Scandinavia and Germany. Centuries of domestication have had little effect on its appearance. It closely resembles the original Asiatic Wild Horse from which it is believed to have descended, while also sharing many of the Tarpan's characteristics (see pp.230 and 228). In the ninth century, it was probably taken to Iceland, where it became ancestor to the Icelandic pony. Scotland's Highland pony is another probable descendant (see p.217).

Uses
In Viking times, it pulled the plow; today, it is still used in farming, especially in mountain areas. An excellent trekking pony, it is used for general riding and in harness.

Appearance
The Fjord pony has a small, neat head, with large eyes and a broad forehead, small and wide-set ears, and a concave profile. It has a thick, muscled and crested neck, heavy shoulder, and undefined withers. Its short, strong legs have dark, zebra-type markings and excellent feet.

The coarse, erect mane and thick, bushy tail are silvery. Its body color is varying shades of dun, and a black "eel stripe" runs from the forelock to the end of the tail.

Characteristics
The Fjord pony is strong and hardy. Generally kind, it can be wilful and stubborn. It is a tireless, versatile, and sure-footed worker capable, of covering long distances and difficult terrain for hours on minimal rations.

Height
13 hands–14.2 hands (4ft 4in–4ft 10in)

are used for all types of equestrian activity, including dressage. Their numbers declined as the export market dried up and some herds are now bred for the meat trade.

Icelandic

The Icelandic Horse has existed in Iceland since the ninth century, although it originated in Scandinavia and resembles the Norwegian Fjord. Imports from Scotland, Ireland, and the Isle of Man were introduced and resulted in a breed with a distinctive character and appearance adapted to its habitat. Two distinct types have been developed by selective breeding: a heavier version for pack and transport, and a lighter type for riding. Inherent genetic traits of the breed are persistant, and attempts to introduce outside blood failed and have not been repeated for 900 years. Most Icelandics fend for themselves in semi-wild conditions and it is one of the hardiest breeds in existence.

Uses

Until the mid-20th century, these ponies were the only means of transport in Iceland, and even after the advent of proper roads and mechanization continued to prove their worth in winter snow and ice. Before World War I, they were imported by British coal-mine owners as pit ponies. Since 1874, they have been popular in Iceland for races held during the summer in which they use their *tölt* gait. They can carry adults easily, despite their small size, and

Appearance

The Icelandic is a stocky, deep-bodied pony, with a large head on a thick, short neck and a straight shoulder. The back is short and the hindquarters sloping but muscular and strong, allowing the hind legs to come well under the body when travelling fast. The cannons are short and the hocks strong. The feet are excellent, with lightly feathered heels. Its mane and tail are thick. Color is important to Icelandic breeders, and 15 combinations are recognized. Various shades of chestnut, often with flaxen mane and tail, are typical, but duns and grays are plentiful, and bays, black, palominos, and mixed colors also exist.

Characteristics

The hardy Icelandic has great endurance and strength and can survive and work on a frugal diet. It is intelligent and docile, but has an independent nature that can make it stubborn. It does not canter, but has two extra gaits of its own, the *skeid*, a fast pace, and the *tölt*, a running walk that enables it to cover longer distances smoothly and briskly.

Height

Average 13 hands (4ft 4in)

Above: An Icelandic pony demonstrates the *tölt* gait for which it is renowned. It is possible to carry an egg in a spoon without dropping it, while racing along, such is the smoothness of this unique action. The pony can maintain the *tölt* for long distances, carrying a full grown man with ease.

Left: Typical Icelandics in their natural habitat show a range of colors. Despite a sparse diet and bleak climate they thrive happily, adapting to a varied life-style.

Tarpan

The Tarpan is one of the three prehistoric types from which all other horse breeds derive (see p.18–19). Its name is Russian for "wild horse," and it survived on the Russian Steppe in its original form until the late 18th century, when it was hunted almost to extinction. Its influence is thought to have extended from the Carpathian Mountains, south through Turkestan, including the Ukraine and the lands around the Caspian and Black seas, then on into the Iranian plateau. The Tarpan was officially recognized and named *Equus caballus gmelini* "Antonius" in the early 20th century. Although the original Tarpan is now extinct, a herd exist at the State reserve of Popielno in Poland, back-bred from its close descendants the Huçul (see p.230) and the Konik.

HORSE AND PONY BREEDS
Ponies

228

Uses

Formerly a working pony in its domesticated form, the Tarpan is now a protected species. It is kept in a guarded reserve, strictly monitored by scientists, yet living as in the wild. It is doubtful whether these ponies will ever have a more practical role in the equestrian world, beyond their historical and scientific interest.

Appearance

The Tarpan has a plain, long head, long ears, and high-set eyes. The profile is straight or slightly convex. It has a short, thick neck, a shallow girth, sloping shoulder, long straight back, poorly developed hindquarters, and a high-set tail. The limbs are long and fine, similar to those of horses of a more eastern character, with zebra markings on the upper limbs and sometimes on the body. It has a dorsal stripe and its dun-colored coat is wiry in texture.

Characteristics

The Tarpan has the hardiness of a native pony and is resistant to extremes of temperature. A forest browser, it is camouflaged in its surroundings and survives on low rations.

Height

Average 13 hands (4ft 4in)

Left: The Viatka is a primitive native pony, probably a descendant of the Tarpan. It is found in a modified form in the Baltic States. The largest variety, shown here, contains "klepper" blood, from cob-like ponies of mixed origins in Estonia. They range in color from golden dun to light brown, often have black markings and a dorsal stripe, and stand at 13–15 hands (4ft 4in–5ft). The original Viatka is almost extinct.

Above: The Polish Konik pony traces back directly to the Tarpan, with some Arab blood (another Tarpan relative). It is encouraged to roam free in herds and is selectively bred to maintain the traditional type. The Konik is the basis for most of Poland's horses and some Russian breeds, many of which are now extinct. Similar in conformation to the Huçul, the Konik often has Tarpan-like coloring and averages 13.2 hands (4ft 6in).

Lokai

The Lokai, from the mountains of Tajikistan, evolved in the 16th century from native Steppe horses and the horses of nomadic tribesmen from Central Asia. To increase its usefulness and versatility, it has been outcrossed with several other breeds, such as the Akhal-Teke (see p.186). It has also been refined and enlarged with Arab/Turkmene blood, but its native traits have been preserved. Young horses are still performance-tested for speed, endurance, and soundness at Tashkent and Dushanbe racecourses.

Uses
The Lokai is a tough all-rounder, with many roles as a working and ridden horse. It is still the only transport in many parts of Tajikistan and in the inaccessible Pamir Mountains, where it is used as a packhorse and for trading. It is also raced and used in the national game of *kokpar*, in which riders fight for possession of a dead goat. The mares' milk is valued as a drink, for making cream, cheese and butter, or to ferment into the alcoholic drink kumiss.

Appearance
A tall, wiry pony, the Lokai has a long head, long ears, a straight profile, and sometimes a Roman nose. The neck is short and straight, the body deep enough, the withers long and sloping, the back and loins flat, the muscular quarters slope from croup to tail. The limbs are fine boned but tough, often with poorly formed hocks. The feet are hard and the mane and tail are fine. Lokais are usually bay, gray, black, or chestnut, often with a metallic sheen.

Characteristics
A tough, enduring pony, the Lokai is fast, versatile, docile, sure-footed, and resistant to extreme heat and cold – essential features to retain when outcrossed. It is suitable for all equestrian sports, including jumping and dressage.

Height
13.3 hands–14.3 hands (4ft 5in–4ft 11in)

Caspian

The Caspian is an ancient type that was thought to be extinct until it was rediscovered near the Caspian Sea in northern Iran in 1965. Native to the Elburz Mountains and around the Caspian Sea, it has never moved far from these parts and the bloodlines have remained pure. The Caspian, possibly a descendant of the Tarpan, is accepted as the ancestor of all "hot-blooded" breeds, including the Arab (see p.184). Although pony-sized, it has a more horse-like appearance, resembling a mini-Arab, with a narrow frame and unusual physical features.

Uses
A working pony in Iran over many centuries, the Caspian is still used for light pulling work, mainly pulling small carts, and as a means of transport. It is an excellent child's riding pony and jumper. It is also used in driving events, singly or in teams, and is in demand for export, particularly to the USA, Australia, and Britain.

Appearance
The Caspian has a narrow frame and a small, fine head with Arab-like features. The chest is narrow and the shoulder well sloped, while the back is short. The wither is not clearly defined. The croup is fairly flat, and the tail high set. The limbs are fine boned, although the hind legs

may be weak and poorly formed. Gray, bay, brown, and chestnut predominate, although cream and black exist.

Characteristics
The Caspian is intelligent, kind, and easy to train. The ponies are naturally sure-footed, and have a marked talent for jumping, as well as being quick, speedy, and athletic. Like the Arab, their action is floating and comfortable.

Height
10 hands–12 hands (3ft 4in–4ft)

Asiatic Wild Horse

This horse is one of the three primitive horses that are the foundation for the world's breeds (see pp.18–19) and the only one to survive in its original form. It is also known as the Mongolian Wild Horse or the Przewalski, from its official name *Equus caballus przewalskii przewalskii* "Poliakoff." It was officially discovered by the Russian explorer, Colonel Przewalski in 1879 on the western edge of the Gobi Desert, in the Tachin Schara Nuru Mountains, although a description exists dating from 1814. Mongolian herdsmen call the horse the Taki. The Przewalski is a direct ancestor of the Mongolian, Chinese, and Tibetan ponies.

Uses
This breed no longer exists naturally in Mongolia, although zoo-bred groups have been reintroduced. It is now preserved in zoos or small reserves. It has never been domesticated.

Appearance
The Przewalski is powerfully built, with a large, short, thick-set head, of straight or convex profile, and big teeth. It has a short neck, a straight shoulder, wide chest, and no definable wither. Its short, straight back is similar to that of the asinine group (see p.19), the hindquarters poorly developed, and the fine-boned limbs short and strong, with big, hard feet. The mane and tail are coarse and sparse, with no forelock. The mane, which stands up about 8in (20cm), is a primitive feature, along with the camouflage sand-dun coat and the dorsal stripe and black legs, which are often striped.

Characteristics
Timid and suspicious of humans, this breed is aggressive in the wild. It has great endurance and stamina and, as befits a wild horse, lives on frugal rations. It is the only horse in existence to have 66 rather than 64 chromosomes.

Height
12 hands–14 hands (4ft–4ft 8in)

Huçul

The Huçul, also known as the Carpathian Pony, is a primitive type that probably descends from both the Tarpan (see p.228) and the Asiatic Wild Horse. It originates in the Eastern Carpathian mountains, and is called locally the "Hutsul," after the Hutsul range in the Ukrainian Mountains. Although some Arab influence is likely, the Huçul closely resembles the Tarpan in shape. At least one authority thinks it should be called the Forest Tarpan. Its coloring can be similar to that of the Asiatic Wild Horse. It is closely related to the Polish Konik and the Bosnian pony.

Uses
This breed is a working pony, used for pack, forestry, and agricultural purposes. It is invaluable on mountainous terrain, to work the land or as a form of transport. It is also ridden by farmers and children and used in harness. It is bred at the government-aided state studs, especially at Siary, to produce useful all-rounders to aid the economy.

Appearance
Stocky, like its neighbor, the Konik (see p.228), the Huçul has a long, broad Tarpan-like head, a compact body, with a deep girth and strong chest, but the hindquarters may be weak and poorly developed. It may also be light boned with sickle hocks, which are typical traits of many mountain breeds. The tail is set on low. It is usually a yellowish dun, but also may be gray-dun, brown-dun, bay, or chestnut. Piebald and skewbald are also common.

Characteristics
The Huçul is hardy and strong and has a willing and docile temperament. It is sensible and sure-footed.

Height
13 hands–13.2 hands (4ft 4in–4ft 6in)

Mongolian Pony

The Mongolian Pony is an ancient, prepotent breed and has been a major influence on many long-established breeds. It derives from the Asiatic Wild Horse and used to be found in large herds all over Asia and Eastern Europe. It was "domesticated" by outcrossing to other horses and ponies throughout Outer Mongolia, Tibet, and China, and has many descendants and close relations in neighboring areas such as Iran, Iraq, and Kurdestan. It is the

foundation of the Turkoman breed; the Bhutia, Spitia, and Tibetan packponies of the Himalayas; the Manipur of Assam, the first breed to be used as a polo pony; the ponies of China, which like the Mongolian are often raced; and the Japanese ponies, imported from Korea in the third century AD. The Mongolian varies in size and type, according to bloodlines, habitat, and climate. The largest distinct type is the Ili of western Mongolia, a Russian cross. Other variations include the Heiling, Wuchumutsin, Kiang, Sanho, Hailar, and the Sanpeitze. The smallest Mongolians are found on the southern edge of the Gobi Desert, where vegetation barely exists.

Uses
There are more horses and ponies per head of population in Mongolia than anywhere else in the world, where this pony is used as a hard-working animal. It is mostly used under pack and for herding and, where farming is viable, for agricultural work. In bleaker parts, tribesmen use it for tracking wolves or foxes, for clothing, or hunting food,

often with trained birds of prey. The Mongolian is expected to carry a man and his baggage all day, over steep, rough terrain, often deep in snow and ice. It is extremely fast, and is raced over distances of up to 40 miles (60km). The mares are milked, and cheese, butter, and kumiss, a fermented milk product, are produced from their milk.

Appearance
A rough-coated, muscular pony, the Mongolian is extremely strong for its size. It has a large head, small eyes, small, wide ears, short, thick neck and full, coarse mane. The shoulders are heavily built, the chest is deep, the back short, and the limbs thickset and exceptionally strong, with hard, round feet. It has a coarse, high-set tail. Colors are mostly dun, bay, and dark brown or black.

Characteristics
Mongolian Ponies are probably tougher and hardier than any other breed, including the Arab (see p.184). They are capable of surviving severe cold on frugal rations, yet have the speed and endurance to carry heavy loads over 100 miles (160km) in one day. They are natural herding animals, and have a generally docile but determined character.

Height
12.2 hands–14.2 hands (4ft 2in–4ft 10in)

Left: The Indian Spitia pony inhabits the Kangra district in the Himalayas, a similar geographical area to neighboring Bhutan. It is usually gray and resembles the Bhutia pony in both type and appearance but is smaller and lighter framed. The Spitia is mainly bred by the Kanyat tribesmen, and is traded with other Himalayan groups. It has adapted to the climate, and is often inbred to retain its small size – average 12.2 hands (4ft 2in) – and strong, hardy, frugal, sure-footed mountain character.

Bashkir

The Bashkir is an ancient indigenous breed that originated in the Ural Mountains and has been reared and used by the Bashkiri people for centuries. Unusually, it is bred mainly for its milk, a by-product of which, when fermented, is kumiss, a popular, alcoholic drink reputed to have medicinal properties. The basic breed has been upgraded, using the Budyonny, the Orlov Trotter, and the Don (see p.180–1). At the end of the 19th century, a strain of the Bashkir was also found in Nevada, USA, which had a curlier coat that it shed each summer, and a wavy mane and tail. This was confirmed as a Bashkir type, and registered as the Bashkir Curly from 1971.

Uses

The Bashkir is a valued all-rounder. It is a versatile worker, pulling a sleigh, sled, and other transport, or a farm cart, wagon or plow. It also makes a useful riding horse. Herds of Bashkirs are kept just like dairy cows, and the young mares can produce up to 6.6 gallons (30 liters) of milk per day. Cream, butter and cheese are made from the mares' milk, as well as kumiss, making the Bashkir a useful asset to the Russian agricultural economy. Surplus horses are traded as meat, and their hides are used for clothing, further aiding the economy.

Left and below: The Bashkir Curly was first discovered in Mustang herds (see p.192) in the 19th century. It has been suggested that the breed had arrived on the American continent across the Bering strait as the Native Americans did. This, however, ignores the fact that the Bering Strait became inaccessible as a land bridge during the Ice Age – about the time the horse became extinct in America – 8000–10,000 years ago.

Appearance

The Bashkir is sturdily built, with a thick head and jaw and a short neck. The body is quite shallow and tubular; the hindquarters are rounded, and the back is straight. The limbs are fairly short with good bone and lightly feathered heels, and it has a very thick mane and tail. The pony's principal colors are bay, brown, and chestnut.

Characteristics

This versatile breed must have an excellent, docile temperament. This is essential if the mares are to allow themselves to be milked continuously, often untethered where they stand. The Bashkir is strongly made and is a reliable, tractable riding horse, but equally it is also suitable for light draft and farm work, being steady and very sure-footed.

Height

Average 13.3 hands (4ft 7in)

Pony of the Americas

The foundation sire of this breed, Black Hand I, was foaled in 1954, out of an Appaloosa mare (see p.192) by a Shetland stallion (see p.221) in Iowa, USA. Outcrossed, later, to the Quarter Horse (see p.195), with the addition of Arab blood (see p.184), the Shetland features disappeared, leaving a pony with small-horse characteristics. To enter the Stud Book, a pony must conform to type and pattern and basically follow the same color requirements as the Appaloosa (see also p.242). It should have correct conformation, with both substance and quality, move freely and straight, and flex its hocks well under its body.

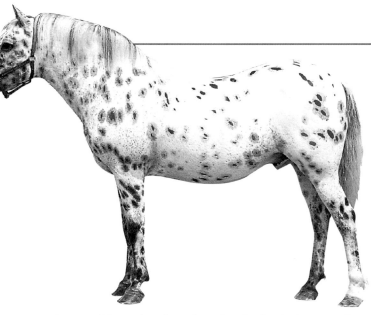

Uses
The Pony of the Americas has been purpose-bred as a useful small child's pony, a category that was lacking in the USA, where smaller ponies had always been imported. Increasingly popular, it is a useful general-purpose riding pony, under both Western and English saddles, for showing and jumping, for trekking or trail riding, and even for running in races organized for the breed.

Appearance
This pony has a small, quality head with concave profile, large intelligent eyes, often surrounded by white circles, and small pointed ears. The shoulder slopes well back to a prominent wither, the chest is wide, the back short, and the body deep with a rounded barrel and muscular hindquarters. The mane and high-set tail are fine. The limbs are strong and sound; the hooves may be striped.

Characteristics
This pony is willing, active, and versatile. It has a kind, sensible temperament and is easy to manage. Its action is straight and free, and many are long striding with an energetic hock action at the trot. They are good jumpers.

Height
11.2 hands–13.2 hands (3ft 10in–4ft 6in)

Sable Island Pony

The Sable Island Pony is named after an island 200 miles (200km) off Nova Scotia in the Atlantic Ocean. It is descended from French horses and ponies that were taken to Canada in the early 18th century via New England, where they were bred with local stock. The offspring were imported to the island. Today, many small herds remain on the island, which is just 25 miles (40km) long. Vegetation is sparse. Some ponies are rounded up and "tamed" by inhabitants, to be used in harness or under saddle.

Uses
The Sable Island Pony is respected as a native inhabitant of the island that has lived there longer than many of the families of the human population. It is preserved by careful selection to avoid inbreeding. A useful all-round pony, it is suitable for riding and can be used for light pulling, in harness or under pack.

Appearance
The Sable Island Pony has a large head with a straight profile and big ears. It has a thick neck, a fairly straight shoulder, a short back and rounded hindquarters. The limbs are fine boned and quite short, with some feather at the heels. Colors are most commonly chestnut, bay, brown, black or gray.

Characteristics
Conditioned by a bleak, wind-swept environment for over 200 years, the Sable Island Pony is hardy, tough, and wiry. Its biddable nature makes it suitable for all types of work.

Height
14 hands–15 hands (4ft 8in–5ft)

Falabella

The Falabella is the smallest equine in the world, but it is a miniature horse rather than a small pony. It stands at less than 34in (86cm). It was first bred by the Falabella family on a ranch near Buenos Aires, Argentina, and it was based on the smallest pony breed, the Shetland, crossed with a very small Thoroughbred, which was perhaps a freak (see pp.221 and 160). Consistently small in size, the early progeny were crossed with the smallest available ponies of various types and then inbred to produce a miniature version retaining the dominant genes of the miniature Thoroughbred. Now exported all over the world, it is most popular in the USA, where the Appaloosa-colored ponies are especially fashionable. It is also bred in the UK and other European countries.

Uses

The Falabella is mainly kept as a pet, being friendly and intelligent, but, because it is still unusual, it is often acquired for its novelty value. It can be driven in harness, but it is too small and fine to be ridden or carry much weight. It is able to jump, but this ability is only demonstrated when it is loose.

Appearance

A good Falabella should have fine bone and features. It has two fewer ribs and vertebrae than other horses or ponies. The head should be neat and small and, like a Shetland, should have a broad forehead, but with longer ears. The shoulder tends to be upright, but the back and hindquarters are well shaped; the limbs can be weak, lacking bone, and be bowed in front, with little muscle on the upper legs. The hind legs may be cow-hocked and the feet boxy. It has a luxurious mane and tail. Most colors occur, including appaloosa, skewbald and piebald.

Characteristics

The pony is too delicate to be ridden. It should be stabled and rugged in winter and given extra food. It has lost the hardiness and resilience of its Shetland forebears, while inbreeding has caused weaknesses in its constitution and its ability to breed. Most of the breed move correctly and can go well in harness.

Height

Up to 8.2 hands (2ft 10in). Some mature at 5 hands (1ft 8in).

Above: A mature Falabella pony demonstrates its agility, loose jumping. Although this is little more than a spectacle, it is to be encouraged for the soundness and toughness of a delicate breed.

Left: This Falabella foal is put into perspective by its handler. The pony now has horse characteristics, but has use only as a pet. The Falabella should be a companion to small, gentle horses or ponies since it cannot defend itself easily against bullying.

Australian Pony

The Australian pony should be a well-balanced, conformed child's mount with a good temperament, tough enough to live out all year and athletic enough for most activities, including jumping. A Stud Book was formed in 1929. The breed comprises South African blood, imported in 1788, and Indonesian lines, derived from the Mongolian (see p.231) and improved with Arab blood (see p.184), which were imported increasingly after 1803. Most of these had the ability to adapt to the fierce extremes of heat or cold of the Australian climate. Further outcrosses to Thoroughbreds (see p.160) and Exmoor and Shetland ponies (see pp.215 and 221) produced performance ability and character. The greatest contribution was made by the Welsh Mountain Pony stallion Dyoll Greylight imported to Australia in 1911 and recognized as the breed's foundation sire. The Australian pony serves a large and enthusiastic Pony Club all over Australia.

Uses
Primarily an all-round child's pony, the Australian is suitable for all equestrian pursuits, including mounted games, showing, showjumping and eventing, long-distance riding and trekking, and driving and harness events. It is also often expected to be a ranching pony, herding cattle and sheep, as well as performing at shows.

Appearance
The Australian pony has a fine head with concave profile, large, dark eyes, and broad forehead, tapering to the muzzle. It has a long, often crested, neck, sloping shoulder, well-formed withers, a deep body, short back, and strong hindquarters. It is mostly gray or chestnut, but any color may be seen, apart from piebald or skewbald.

Characteristics
Versatile, generally docile, and intelligent, this pony is easy to manage and train. It has a smooth, free-moving action.

Height
12 hands–14 hands (4ft–4ft 8in)

Basuto

The Basuto pony is derived from the Cape Horse, a fine type based on Arabs and Barbs (see pp.184–5) that were imported to the Cape Province from Java in 1653 and then crossed with increasing amounts of Thoroughbred blood (see p.160). However, in 1808, stocks of the Cape horse were raided and taken to Basutoland where conditions were harsher. The Capes soon lost their refinement in their fight to survive – the smallest adapted best. Mixed with native scrub ponies, the resulting Basuto is a wiry, tough, famously strong, pony-sized horse. The British bought 30,000 Basutos for use in the Boer wars. They gave the army greater mobility and proved crucial to their victory.

Uses
Used in war, the Basuto has also proved popular for polo and racing. They are suitable for most riding activities, by all ages, for pleasure or for herding cattle and sheep. They can carry a big man on long treks, or be heavily laden as a packpony. They are also used for light pulling work.

Appearance
The Basuto is thickset. It has a quality head, a legacy of its Arab and Thoroughbred forebears. The neck is quite long and thin, the shoulder rather upright, and the back lengthy, but the chest is wide and the body deep on short, very strongly made limbs. The feet are hard. The most usual colors are bay, brown, gray and chestnut.

Characteristics
The Basuto pony is tough, hardy, and sure-footed. It has great endurance for its size and will carry adults over long distances. Although not fast, it is agile and wiry and is still raced at country meetings in South Africa.

Height
14.2 hands (4ft 10in)

PART 6

THE
NOBLE
HORSE

A unique relationship has existed between horse and humankind for thousands of years. To humans, the horse is a mystical creature but also a partner and friend. It has plowed fields and brought in the harvest; hauled goods and conveyed passengers; followed game and tracked cattle; carried soldiers into battle and adventurers into unknown lands; and helped shape history. It has provided recreation in the form of jousts, tournaments, hunting and modern equestrian sports. Its noble influence is expressed in the English language in a term like "chivalry" (from the French, *chevalerie*, meaning horsemanship) with its connotations of honor. A beautiful and well-trained horse – "the proudest conquest of man" – has been a status symbol for centuries across the entire horse-owning world.

Horses & the Imagination

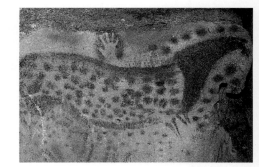

From the moment Palaeolithic man first drew horses on the walls of the caves in which he lived, the horse has been an inspiration in all forms of art, literature and, today, film. A creature appealing to the imagination, it played a magical role in the mysterious beliefs and rites of Stone Age man. Later, it was deemed to be involved in the movement of the seas and the sun, capable of flying through the air. It has inspired poetry and in some mythologies even accompanied the dead to their final rest. It has also played an essential role in the history of humankind, facilitating war, migration and the shaping of empires. It transcends its role as a beast of burden or means of transport and enters the spheres of culture, religion and politics, holding a special significance for each succeeding generation. Few interpretations reveal the horse to be anything less than powerful, beautiful, noble, loyal and true, reflecting these qualities upon its less-than-perfect human master. It has rightly held a secure place in the mind and affections of humankind for centuries.

Spotted Horses

Spotted horses, as shown by these French cave paintings made more than 20,000 years ago, have long been admired. They appear in Chinese and Persian art 2,000 years before Christ and by the 8th century AD were shown on artifacts from Turkey to Spain. Spanish spotted horses influenced the US breeds and were a major influence in Europe until the end of the 18th century.

MYTHICAL HORSES

❖

As human beings developed their relationship with the horse, it was perhaps inevitable that their gods and heroes would be mounted on superhorses. Parallel tales appear in different cultures – the sun god pulled in a horse-drawn chariot across the sky is a common example. Extraordinary horse-creatures, such as centaurs and unicorns, also evolved in the human imagination, possibly based on ancient interpretations of unexplained phenomena.

✦ Cyllaros and Harpagos were the white steeds of Castor and Pollux, twin sons of the Greek god Zeus, by Leda, a mortal.
✦ Hades, Greek god of the Underworld, was drawn in a chariot by four black chargers; the Greek sun god Apollo (or Helios) and the Hindu sun god both crossed the sky pulled by white horses; Poseidon, the Greek sea god, was regarded as the creator and "embodiment of all horses," to whom valuable white horse were sacrificed. On Rhodes each year, at the end of winter, a chariot pulled by a white horse was driven into the sea to "revive the sun." In English, the white tops of waves on a rough sea are called "white horses."
✦ The immortal horses Xanthus and Balios belonged to the Greek hero Achilles. They were the sons of Zephyrus, the West Wind.
✦ Sleipnir was the eight-legged steed of Odin, the chief Norse god, who was also responsible for war and care of poets. Sleipnir journeyed to the Underworld, and myth tells how he will die with Odin at Ragnarok, the battle that will mark the death of the gods and a new cycle of time.
✦ A black horse, Hrim Faxi (Frost Mane, so named because of the rime which

The Trojan Horse

The Trojan Horse was not a living horse, but a huge wooden statue that was left outside the gates of Troy by the Greeks at the end of the Trojan War. The Trojans, assuming that the Greeks had surrendered and left the horse as an offering, wheeled it into the city. That night, the Greeks hidden inside it, leapt out, led by the hero Odysseus (Ulysses), and sacked the city. The story is told in Virgil's *Aeneid*, written in the first century BC.

The mare goddess is a recurring theme in European mythology and is usually an earth, or corn, goddess. In Gallic folklore she was called Epona (left), the Welsh called her Rhiannon and in Irish mythology she was known as Macha. In the early Celtic world she was depicted with a mare's head but was later shown in human form accompanied by horses. The Greek earth goddess, Demeter, was represented by a black mare's head.

clung to its mane and bit) drew the dark chariot of Nott, the Scandinavian goddess of the night.

◆ Unicorns were mystical white horses possessed of a magical spiral horn in the center of their foreheads.

◆ Centaurs were mythical Greek creatures with the torso of a man and the trunk of a horse. Apart from the wise and gentle centaur Cheiron, who tutored many of the Greek gods and heroes, centaurs were wild, dissolute creatures who were depicted as the savage, drunken and lustful followers of the wine god Dionysus, whose chariot they drew.

Pegasus, the Greek flying horse, sprang from his mother Medusa's blood when she was beheaded by the hero Perseus. As he took flight, one hoof struck the ground on Mount Helicon and Hippocrene, a spring sacred to the Muses and regarded as a source for poetic inspiration, sprang forth. Tamed by the prince Bellerophon (left), the two had many adventures, including killing the Chimaera, a terrible monster. Later, Pegasus carried thunderbolts for the god Zeus.

Heavenly Horses

From the middle of the second century BC, the Chinese began to buy and breed horses in order to challenge the marauding nomadic horsemen who harried their frontiers. Trade missions were sent to Bactria, Turkestan and Ferghana, where horses descended from the famous Nisean stock that had belonged to Alexander the Great were acquired. The Chinese called these beautiful, powerful creatures "Heavenly" or "Celestial" horses.

Gods and heroes are depicted on well-trained horses.

XENOPHON (C.430–355 BC)

Horses & the Imagination

Horses of the Apocalypse

Horses are mentioned in several places in both the Bible and the Qur'an, the Islamic holy scripture. One of the most famous biblical examples, illustrated above in the woodcut *The Four Horsemen of the Apocalypse* by the German artist Albrecht Dürer (1471–1528), is in St John the Divine's description of the end of the world in Revelation, 9:17: 'And thus I saw the horses in the vision, and them that sat on them, having breastplates of fire, and of jacinth, and brimstone: and the heads of the horses were as the heads of lions; and out of their mouths issued fire and smoke and brimstone.'

When God had created the horse,
he spoke to the magnificent creature:
I have made thee unlike any other.
All the treasures of this earth lie
between thine eyes.
Thou shall cast mine enemies beneath
thine hooves,
But thou shall carry my friends
on thy back.
THE QUR'AN

FAMOUS HORSES IN FICTION

Many writers of books, television programs and film have made horses the protagonists or secondary characters in their works. Some of the most famous are listed below.

✦ Black Beauty, from the book (1877) by Anna Sewell. The book aroused public concern about cruelty to animals especially horses in the 1890s and was made into a film in 1946, 1971 and 1994.

✦ Black Bess was immortalized in legend as the mare that belonged to the famous English highwayman Dick Turpin.

✦ The Black Stallion, a wild Arab crossbred, survived a shipwreck and made friends with the boy hero of *The Black Stallion* (1941) by Walter Farley.

✦ Bree and Hwin were the talking horses in C.S. Lewis's *The Horse and his Boy* (1954).

Flicka was a wild filly tamed and cared for by 10-year-old Ken McLaughlin on his father's ranch in Wyoming in the books *My Friend Flicka* (1941), *Thunderhead* (1945), and *Green Grass of Wyoming* (1947) by Mary O'Hara. They were made into popular films in 1943, 1945 and 1948.

HORSES IN PAINTING AND SCULPTURE

The horse has been an inspiration in art for centuries, as a creature of beauty and also as a means of ennobling royal and political figures.

✦ Lyssipus (3rd/4th century BC), Greek sculptor, designed and probably cast the four bronze horses of St Mark's, Venice. Over life-size, they originally adorned the Byzantine city of Constantinople.

✦ Donatello (1386–1466), revolutionary Italian sculptor, created the *Gattamelata*, the first life-size triumphal equestrian statue since antiquity. It is in Padua.

✦ Sir Anthony van Dyck (1599–1641), Flemish painter famed for his portraits of court personages, gave the small, unimposing Charles I of England nobility and height by painting the king seated on a beautifully represented horse.

✦ George Stubbs (1724–1806), English painter and engraver, became much sought after for his horse 'portraits'. Passionate about anatomy, he published *Anatomy of the Horse* in 1766.

✦ Edgar Degas (1834–1917), French artist, sculpted and painted racehorses, fascinated by their power and the way in which they moved.

✦ Frederic S. Remington (1861-1909), American artist, sculptor and writer, immortalized the Wild West horses in hundreds of paintings and scultures. His chosen epitaph was, 'He Knew the Horse'.

✦ Alfred Munnings (1878–1959), English artist, was famous for painting horses, particularly hunting horses. Son of a miller, he was knighted and became President of the Royal Academy.

✦ Franz Marc (1880–1916), German painter, believed in the spirituality of animals, using colour symbolically as in *The Blue Horse*, 1911. He helped to found the group of German artists known as *Der Blaue Reiter* (The Blue Rider).

✦ Peter Corling (1955–) British artist, is well known for atmospheric, technically correct, lively scenes with horses.

Race Horses at the Grandstand, by Edgar Degas, 1879. Musée d'Orsay, Paris.

◆ Brigadore, the 'loftie steed', was lost and found by Sir Guyon in *The Faerie Queene* (1590) by Edmund Spenser.

◆ Brigliadoro was the steed belonging to the hero Orlando (known as Roland in the French epic) in Carolingian legend.

◆ Champion the Wonder Horse belonged to the cowboy-actor Gene Autry and starred in film and on television. Over the years, Autry owned more than one horse called Champion.

◆ Fury, a Saddlebred horse originally called Highland Dale, starred in many films (winning several acting awards) but became famous as the star of the television series *Fury* (1955–60).

◆ Gabilan was the pony tamed by a boy in *The Red Pony* (1933) by John Steinbeck.

◆ The Houyhnhnms, a kind and intelligent race of talking horses, ruled a mythical South Sea island in *Gulliver's Travels* (1727) by Jonathan Swift.

◆ The Maltese Cat, a heroic polo pony, saved his rider from injury, badly hurting

Silver was a wild stallion tamed and ridden by the Lone Ranger, a masked cowboy star of comics, books, radio show and television series (1948–60). It was spurred on by the cry 'Hi-ho Silver, awa-a-ay!' The Lone Ranger's companion, an American Indian named Tonto, rode a Pinto called Scout.

himself in the process, in Rudyard Kipling's story, *The Maltese Cat*, (1898).

◆ Misty, from the book *Misty of Chincoteague* (1947) by Marguerite Henry. Filmed in 1961.

◆ Rakhsh was the brave, spotted steed belonging to the Persian hero Rustam, whose adventures are recounted in *Shah-nameh* (Book of Kings), an 11th-century epic poem written by the poet Firdausi. Rakhsh's exploits included killing a lion. The horse is also featured in Matthew Arnold's poem *Sohrab and Rustam* (1893).

◆ Rocinante was the ridiculous and tubercular old stallion that belonged to Don Quixote in *Don Quixote de la Mancha* (1605) by Miguel de Cervantes.

◆ Shadowfax was the noble horse ridden by Gandalf the Grey in *The Fellowship of the Ring* (1954–5) by J.R.R. Tolkien.

◆ Silver Blaze was a racehorse that mysteriously disappeared in Arthur Conan Doyle's Sherlock Holmes story, *The Adventure of Silver Blaze*, published in 1892.

The Wild West

The horse had been extinct in the Americas for 8,000 years when the Spanish invaded Mexico in 1519. Within 60 years wild herds had spread north into what is now the United States. The Pueblo Indians of Mexico were among the earliest to ride; the northern tribes took longer. By 1720 the Pawnee, from modern Nebraska, owned hundreds of horses; ten years later the Snake in modern Wyoming rode against the Blackfoot in southern Alberta.

The Sioux, from Lake Superior, were the last "canoe" Indians to ride, starting in about 1770, after they were driven into Minnesota by the Ojibwa and forced to adopt a plains way of life. The introduction of the horse had a profound impact on Plains life, revolutionizing the buffalo hunt, travel and warfare and providing a valuable commodity for both trade and theft.

They buried the dark chief; they freed
Beside the grave his battle steed
HENRY WADSWORTH LONGFELLOW,
BURIAL OF THE MINNISKINK

The First Horses

The modern horse first arrived in the New World with Hernán Cortès, a soldier in the pay of the Spanish king. He landed in Mexico in 1519, bringing with him 16 horses. The local people were terrified and, at first, believed Cortès and his horse-riding men to be fantastical centaur-like creatures. The reintroduction of the horse altered the course of the life and welfare of the indigenous peoples throughout the continent.

Petroglyphs, Arizona

Plains Indian rock paintings, known as petroglyphs, usually depict sacred images or historical events. The earliest date from c.2500 BC. This petroglyph showing Spanish soldiers in capes, hats, and carrying guns, is among the first to show the Indians' contact with the Spanish. It dates from c.1805.

INDIAN HORSES

The Indian horse was more of a pony: tough, wiry, with endless stamina and the ability to perform on low rations. His masters became skilled riders, with the simplest equipment, such as a rawhide loop round the jaw as a bridle. The Indians gelded their horses, but only the Nez Percé plateau tribe of Idaho understood selective breeding. Their legacy is the Appaloosa (see p.192), a spotted horse that conforms to one of five basic coat patterns, although a number of variations occur within each category.

Leopard: white base, black spots all over the body

Snowflake: dark base, white spots all over the body

Blanket: dark forehand, white blanket over the back, spotted rear

Marble: dark base that fades with age, leaving darker marks on the head and legs

Frosted: dark base, white spots or patches over the loin and hip areas

Buffalo Hunt by George Catlin

The horse gave the culturally and linguistically different Arapaho, Apache, Kiowa, Cheyenne, and Comanche tribes similar lives as mounted buffalo hunters. Before the mid-1600s, hunting was done on foot. The Indians killed enough for their needs, hunting in the autumn when the animals were fat and had thick coats. The herds died as a result of overhunting by whites who, between 1872 and 1874, killed over four million buffalo on the southern plains alone. Diseases caught from imported cattle and competition with the cattle and wild mustangs for grazing land were other factors in the buffalo's tragic decline.

Horse Travois

The travois, a horse-borne sled comprising two long poles joined by a frame, was the preferred mode of transport of Plains Indians families. With no moving parts, it was ideally suited to rugged terrain and was largely used by womenfolk for domestic travel.

HORSES AS STATUS AND WEALTH

Horses were very important to 19th-century Native American life. Vital for hunting buffalo, they also became the standard of value, especially for such transactions as buying a wife. A man's status, wealth, mobility, and position as warrior and hunter became based upon the horses he owned. Horse raids on other tribes and white settlers were common. Unlike other European introductions, the horse was beneficial to the Plains Indians of the American West and became an important part of their culture and self-image.

The Wild West

Go West, young man

The West represented the land of opportunity where lives could be staked out and begun afresh. Without the horse, this would have been virtually impossible – it drew the wagons of the pioneers, plowed the plains and was a means of communication with home. Incursion into the West, beyond the Appalchians, was underway by 1763.

Hell, ma'am, what's the point in giving a name to something you might have to eat?

ALLEGEDLY, COWBOY TO LADY FROM EAST,

REGARDING THE NAME OF HIS HORSE

THE PONY EXPRESS AND THE WELLS FARGO STAGECOACH

The frontier spirit was perhaps epitomized by the Pony Express, which provided communication between East and West before the coming of the telegraph. The service covered the 1,966 miles (3,164km) between St. Joseph, Missouri, to San Francisco, California, in 10 days, using a relay of 400 ponies; much of the journey was through hostile Indian territory. The riders were tough, wiry young men ("orphans preferred"), but the Express lasted for only two years, 1860–61, because of the losses incurred. The Pony Express was superseded by the Wells Fargo Overland Stagecoach, which was heavily armed against attack, and also carried passengers.

Cowboys

The cowboy's mount was his essential tool, each type prized for different qualities. Cutting horses, quick of mind and action and regarded as the elite, were used to isolate a particular cow from the herd. With roping horses, which braced against a lassoed animal even with the rider dismounted, they were the most highly trained of the herd, and the best would work with the lightest touch. The favored pace was the lope, an easy canter – rising to the trot was seen as effeminate. The modern cowboy and his horse are as skilled as their forebears.

The Wild West still holds a special place in the American imagination. The early cowboys worked in largely unsettled, unpoliced territory and had to ensure the safety of their employers' cattle. The herds had to be driven long distances to shipping points, and the cowboy needed great strength, endurance, and ingenuity to complete the treks. The hard life tended to develop rough-

and-ready virtues, as well as great skill in horse- and marksmanship. The responsibilities gave rise to the romantic notion of the courageous, chivalrous cowboy on a huge glossy creature; Silver, Champion, or Fury. The reality, however, was usually a tough, hardy pony from the herd, often changed several times a day. In the early years, this was little more than a semi-feral, half-broken mustang, the loss of which, in these vast plains, meant certain death.

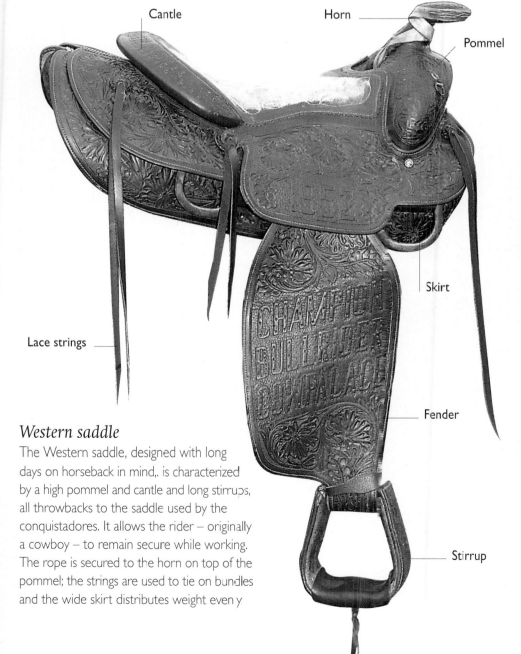

Cantle · Horn · Pommel · Skirt · Fender · Lace strings · Stirrup

Western saddle

The Western saddle, designed with long days on horseback in mind, is characterized by a high pommel and cantle and long stirrups, all throwbacks to the saddle used by the conquistadores. It allows the rider – originally a cowboy – to remain secure while working. The rope is secured to the horn on top of the pommel; the strings are used to tie on bundles and the wide skirt distributes weight evenly

War Horses

*I*t is ironic that, despite being a timid animal species, whose every instinct is to flee from any danger, real or imagined, the horse has had a profound effect on warfare and, consequently, the shaping of history. It has carried rulers and their armies, pulled chariots, guns and baggage trains and shared comradeship in both glory and – more often – horror, misery, privation, and death.

The story of warfare has always been the story of the balance between mobility, firepower, and protection. Thus, while the chariot was the first vehicle of war – appearing *c*.1500 BC – it was the cavalry that became the elite military unit (see page 20–1).

Surprisingly perhaps, cavalry and horse transport survived into World War II, and more recently native ponies have been used in conflicts in the mountains of Afghanistan and in Bosnia. But in general, the role of the horse in war is now little beyond the ceremonial.

The Mongol Hordes

The skills needed to use a bow from the back of a galloping horse were probably best exemplified by the Mongol hordes who, under Genghis Khan, carved an empire from the China Sea to the Baltic during the 13th century AD. Riding small, sturdy, well-trained ponies possessed of legendary stamina, they easily covered 80 miles (130km) a day, with no need of a bridle, and virtually lived in the saddle; not even bothering to dismount to eat, drink, sleep or answer the call of nature. In general, each man would ride several horses, perhaps as many as ten, in a day, switching mounts as each tired.

> *Their's not to make reply,*
> *Their's not to reason why,*
> *Their's but to do and die:*
> *Into the valley of Death*
> *Rode the six hundred . . .*
>
> ALFRED, LORD TENNYSON, THE CHARGE OF
> THE LIGHT BRIGADE, *1854*

Boudicca, Warrior Queen

Boudicca, Queen of the British Iceni tribe in Norfolk, revolted against the Romans in AD 60 and sacked the Roman towns of Colchester, London and St. Albans. Her armies used the ancestors of the native ponies (see pp.212–19) and followed in the British tradition of light cavalry and effective chariots, allegedly with scythes on the wheels. This was the combination that had foiled Julius Caesar's first attempt to invade Britain in 55 BC when the ships carrying his cavalry were blown off course. Learning their lesson, the Romans successfully invaded in 54 BC, backed up by 2,000 heavy horsemen from Gaul.

The Charge of the Light Brigade

The full-scale cavalry charge was the ultimate dream of every mounted soldier and none is more famous – or infamous – than the Charge of the Light Brigade during the Crimean War. Owing to a gross military blunder, on October 25, 1854, five British regiments – 673 men and their horses – launched a suicidal attack on the enemy Russian guns at the head of a flat valley at Balaclava in present-day Ukraine. In ten minutes 113 men and 513 horses died in a needless waste of life. The arrogant commanding officer, Lord Cardigan, was unharmed. His charger, Ronald, whose only injury was a superficial gash, was one of the few horses to survive both the action and the rigors of the Crimean winter. On his return to England, he became a public idol.

Horses in World War II

In November 1941, near the village of Musino, northwest of Moscow, the 44th Mongolian Cavalry Division took on the German artillery and infantry in probably the last cavalry charge in history. To the astonishment of the German soldiers, they were attacked by 2,000 horsemen brandishing sabres at a gallop. Every horse and rider was killed; there were no German casualties.

HORSE CASUALTIES

◆

Throughout history, up to the early days of World War II, horses have died in battle. However, it is less obvious that the "civilian" horse population, like its human counterpart, should also have suffered severe, far-reaching damage. Many important lines have been lost.

◆ The US Civil War claimed the lives of over a million and a half horses and mules. The vast majority of the equine casualties were not the cavalry mounts, who made up only a small part of the armies' overall horse population, but were the working animals that moved the armies and their supplies in and out of battle.

◆ The Trakehner stud in Lithuania was evacuated five times between 1812 and 1945 because of invasion, with inevitable loss of equine life (see p.174).

◆ Thoroughbred breeding in Normandy, France, suffered badly during the Allied invasion after D-Day in 1944. Famous horses lost from studs include the stallion Plassy, winner of the 1936 Coronation Cup at Epsom, burned in his stable; the Belgian champion Prince Rose, killed by bombing; and the mare Corrida, brilliant winner of the 1936 and 1937 Prix de l'Arc de Triomphe, which disappeared from Fresnay-le-Buffard, quite possibly eaten by starving soldiers.

Heroic Horses

The concept of the horse as an aggressor, teeth bared and hooves flailing, is erroneous – equines put flight before fight. But such is their nature, and perhaps the nature and perception of human beings, that in some extraordinary partnerships of horse and rider, the horse's patience, endurance, and apparent loyalty and nobility have been celebrated. In some instances, these qualities have been perceived to have made the difference between failure and success, especially in war. Occasionally such horses have become heroes in their own right, identified with an influential leader or as part of a defining moment or period, acting as potent symbols of courage, friendship and loyalty under fire.

SEFTON

◆

A black troop horse, Sefton, became a modern symbol of defiance and courage after an IRA bomb killed two guardsmen and seven horses of the Blues and Royals in Hyde Park, London, on June 20, 1982. The 19-year-old Irish-bred gelding was horribly injured in the attack, but survived to return to army life after less than a year. He retired at the age of 21 to the Home of Rest for Horses in Buckinghamshire. He lived peacefully for seven more years and was buried at the Animal Defense Center, Melton Mowbray, UK.

Bucephalus

Bucephalus belonged to Alexander the Great (356–323 BC), who brought the known world from Egypt to India under Greek influence. Bucephalus, of a sturdy Thessalonian strain, was bought in 343 BC by Alexander's father for 13 talents – about $15,000 today. But he proved unmanageable until Alexander, aged 12, who had already been to war, turned him from the frightening spectacle of his own shadow and leapt upon his back. Thereafter, the pair were inseparable until Bucephalus died at the battle of Hedaspes in India in 327 BC. A now-defunct city was founded on the site and named Bucephalia in his honor.

Babieca

Babieca, meaning "stupid" was an Andalucian and the mount of the soldier Rodrigo Diaz, called El Cid, "the lord", famed in 11th-century Spain for his efforts in driving out the Moors. El Cid died in Valencia in 1099 with the Moors at the gate. Before he died, he arranged for his corpse, in full armor, to be sat up in Babieca's saddle to lead one last mission. Babieca played his part perfectly, leading the white-clad army from the city walls at midnight. The superstitious Moors believed El Cid had returned from the dead and fled in terror.

Comanche

On June 25, 1876, General Custer and his 7th Cavalry attacked 3,000 Cheyenne and Sioux warriors near the Little Big Horn river in Montana. The result was the worst defeat ever suffered by the US Army at the hands of Indians; 263 soldiers were slaughtered, along with 319 horses. The battle became known heroically as "Custer's Last Stand", and the only survivor was a bay gelding, Comanche. But although he was badly wounded, he recovered and became America's most revered horse. He was never ridden or worked again until his death 15 years later, at the age of 29, at Fort Riley, Kansas, in November 1891. His stuffed body is on display at the University of Kansas.

COPENHAGEN AND MARENGO

◆

The horse played so vital a part in war that some, often those belonging to famous leaders, also became famous. Copenhagen, the Duke of Wellington's favorite horse, for example, was loved as much by the troops as by his master, and when he died was buried with full military honors. When Napoleon's favourite horse – a white Arab named after the battle of Marengo in 1800 – died, his skeleton was put into the army museum at Sandhurst. Marengo and Copenhagen carried their masters on June 18, 1815 at the Battle of Waterloo.

Copenhagen saved his master from French dragoons at Waterloo by clearing a fence and ditch full of the 92nd Highlanders in one leap. He died on February 12, 1836 and was accorded an obituary in *The Times*.

Marengo was captured at Aboukir in 1798. He was wounded eight times and carried Napoleon in many battles. He was also one of Napoleon's mounts in the French retreat from Moscow in 1812 (right).

Glossary

Action The movement of the skeletal frame with regard to locomotion.
Aids Signals given to the horse via the rider's legs, hands, seat etc.
Articulation Where two or more bones meet to form a joint.
Balance Distribution of weight between the horse and the rider.
Barrel The body of the horse between the forearms and the loins.
Bone The measurement around the leg, just below the knee or hock. The amount of bone determines a horse's ability to carry weight. Common bone is bone of inferior quality.
Boxy feet Narrow, upright feet with a small frog and a closed heel.
Breed A group of equines selectively bred for consistent characteristics, which are accepted within a Stud Book.
Brushing When the hoof or shoe of one foot strikes the opposite leg at or near the fetlock when in motion.
By Used to indicate the sire of a horse.
Cadence How a horse moves with reference to the rhythm, impulsion and elasticity of its steps.
Cob A stocky, short-legged weight-carrying horse up to 15.1 hands in height – a type rather than a breed.
Coldblood Used to describe heavy European breeds, descended from the Forest Horse.
Collection Shortening of the pace. The horse should flex its neck, relax its jaw and bring the hocks well under the body while being properly balanced.
Cowhocks Hocks that turn inwards.
Crossbreeding Breeding between two breeds or families of equine. Selective crossbreeding aims to reproduce certain characteristics of dam and sire in the resultant offspring.
Dam The mother of an equine.
Desert horse A breed that originated in eastern desert conditions and has a light skeleton and fine, thin skin.
Dished profile A concave profile.
Dishing When the front hooves are thrown out in a circular motion.
Dock The area around the tail where hair grows. Also the hairless underside.
Dorsal stripe A dark stripe along the spine from the neck to the tail.
Economical Used to describe a horse or pony that survives and remains in condition on minimal rations.
Extension Length of stride in motion.
Feather Hair on the fetlocks and lower limbs, typical of heavy horses.
Flexion Full bending of the hock joints.
Floating Used to describe the trotting gait of the Arab horse.
Forearm The forelegs above the knee.
Forehand The head, neck, shoulders, withers and forelegs.
Frog Triangular, rubbery part on the hoof base, which absorbs shock when the horse or pony is in motion.
Frugal *see* Economical.
Gelding A castrated male horse.
Girth The measurement around the barrel from behind the withers.
Gymkhana Amateur horse event in which horses and riders show skill and aptitude in races and contests.
Handy Used to describe the agility and flexibility of a horse or pony, especially with reference to ponies participating in gymkhana games.
Haute école The classical form of High School or advanced riding.
Heavy horse Any large draught horse.
High school see *Haute école*.
Hotblood Used to describe desert-horses and also the Thoroughbred.
Inbreeding Breeding sire/daughter, dam/son, brother/sister, to fix a particular characteristic.
Light horse A horse used for riding, as opposed to pulling or hauling.
Mare A female horse of four or over.
Mealy nose Oatmeal coloured muzzle.
Near side The left side.
Nicked Used to describe a tail that has an artificially high carriage – an effect achieved by dividing and resetting the muscles underneath.
Nicker A vocal sign made with a closed mouth. A neigh, given with the mouth open, is louder and a different pitch.
Off side The right side.

Out of "Born from" (a mare).
Outcross To introduce unrelated blood to a breed.
Pace Another term for gait.
Packhorse A horse that carries heavy loads in packs, on both sides of its back.
Plaiting When the feet cross over each other in motion.
Prepotency The ability to pass on characteristics consistently.
Purebred Any horse with both parents of the same breed.
Quality A refinement often found in horses influenced by the Arab or Thoroughbred.
Registry An official breed organization that maintains records of all horses catalogued within it.
Roman nose A convex profile.
Scope Capability for freedom of movement with maximum extension.
School To train a horse for whatever purpose or discipline it is required.
Sickle hocks Weak, crooked hocks that are "sickle"-shaped.
Sire The father of an equine.
Stallion An entire (ungelded) male horse of four or over.
Stud Book The registry for each breed that indicates a horse or pony's pedigree. Only top-class pedigrees may be entered in a Stud Book.
Submaximal work Athletic activity where the horse is working below its maximum physiological capacity.
Substance The physical quality of the body in terms of its overall build and musculature.
Type A horse that fulfils a particular purpose, but does not necessarily belong to any particular breed or has not been accepted into a Stud Book.
Unsound A horse with any condition that stops it from being able to move or function properly.
Warmblood A horse with Arab or Thoroughbred blood, crossed with another blood or bloods.
Whicker A vocal signal, less pronounced than a neigh, made with the mouth slightly open.

Useful Addresses

American Association of Horsemanship
Safety, Inc.
PO Drawer 39
Fentress, TX 78622-0039
Phone: (512) 488-2220
Fax: (512) 488-2319

American Association of Riding Schools
8375 Coldwater Road
Davison, MI 48423
Phone: (810) 653-1440
Fax: (810) 658-9733
Website: www.ucanride.com

American Horse Council
1700 K Street, NW, Suite 300
Washington, DC 2006-3805
Phone: (202) 296-4031
Fax: (202) 296-1970
Website: www.horsecouncil.org

American Horse Protection Association, Inc.
1000 29th Street NW, #T-100
Washington, DC 20007-3820
Phone: (202) 965-0500
Fax: (202) 965-9621

American Horse Shows Assocation, Inc.
220 E. 42nd Street, #409
New York, NY 10017-5876
Phone: (212) 972-2472
Fax: (212) 983-7286
Website: www.ahsa.org

American Veterinary Medical Association
1931 N. Mecham Road, #100
Shaumberg, IL 60173-4360
Phone: (800) 248-2862
Fax: (847) 925-1329
Website: www.avma.org

Animal Transportation Association
10700 Richmond Ave., Suite 201
Houston, TX 77042
Phone: (713) 532-2177
Fax: (713) 532-2156
Website: www.npscmgmt.com/AATA

Animal Welfare Council
209 N. Main Street
PO Box 2007
Weatherford, TX 76086
Phone: (817) 598-1581
Fax: (817) 598-1582
Website: www.animalwelfarecouncil.org

Equestrian Training Center Horse Rescue
600 NW 117th Street
Ocala, FL 34475
Phone: (352) 369-9300
Fax: (352) 369-9301

National Equine Safety Association
PO Box 1090
Spotsylania, VA 22553
Phone: (800) 643-3760
Fax: (505) 373-4655

Thoroughbred Retirement Foundation, Inc.
1050 State Highway 35, Suite 351
Shrewsbury, NJ 07702-4308
Phone: (732) 957-0182
Fax: (802) 767-4912

United States Animal Health Association
PO Box K227
8100 Three Chopt Road, #203
Richmond, VA 23288
Phone: (804) 285-3367
Fax: (804) 285-3367

United States Equestrian Team (USET)
Headquarters and Olympic Training Center
Pottersville Road, Gladstone, NJ 07934
Phone: (908) 234-1251
Fax: (908) 234-9417
Website: www.uset.org

United States Pony Clubs, Inc.
4071 Iron Works Pike
Lexington, KY 40511-8462
Phone: (606 254-PONY
Fax: (606) 233-4652

Western and English Manufacturers
Association
451 E. 58th Ave., #4625
Denver, CO 80216-1411
Phone: (303) 295-2001
Fax: (303) 295-6108
Website: www.waema.org

Further Reading

The Anatomy of the Horse
Robert F. Way, DVM, MS
and Donald G. Lee DVM
Breakthrough Publications

Dr. Kellon's Guide to First Aid For Horses
Elenor M. Kellon, DVM
Breakthrough Publications

Equine Drugs and Vaccines
Elenor M. Kellon, DVM, and
Thomas Tobin, MBV, MRCVS
Breakthrough Publications

For the Good of the Horse
Mary Wanless
Trafalgar Square

*Horse Care Health Care: A Step-by-Step
Photographic Guide*
Cherry Hill
Storey Books

Horse Diseases: Causes, Symptoms, and Treatment
HG Belschner, DVM
Wilshire Book Company

*Horse Handling and Grooming: A Step-by-Step
Photographic Guide*
Cherry Hill
Storey Books

Horse Selection and Care for Beginners
George H. Conn
Wilshire Book Company

*The Illustrated Veterinary Encyclopedia
for Horsemen*
Equine Research
Equine Research

*The Lame Horse: Causes, Symptoms,
and Treatments*
James Rocney, DVM, MS
Wilshire Book Company

UC Davis Book of Horses
UC Davis
HarperCollins Publishers

*Veterinary Notes for Horse
Owners (17th Edition)*
Horace Hayes, FRCVS

Index

Credits

Photography sources

Abbreviations
b bottom
c center
l left
r right
t top

1 Kit Houghton; 2–3 Ardea/Jean-Paul Ferrero; 4–5 Bob Langrish; 6–7 Only Horses; 8–9 Tony Stone/K Lamm; 10 t Robert Harding/Paolo Koch, cl Stockmarket, cr Ardea/Jean-Paul Ferrero, b Stockmarket, ; 10–11 Tony Stone/Eastcott/Momatiuk; 11 Ardea/M Watson; 12 tl FLPA/P Perry, bl Bob Langrish, r Tony Stone/K Lamm; 13 t FLPA/P Reynolds, c Stockmarket/D Stoecklein, b Only Horses; 14–15 Bob Langrish; 18 tl & br Bob Langrish, tr Ardea/Jean-Paul Ferrero, bl Ardea/ H D Dossenbach; 19 l Corbis/S Kaufman, r FLPA/ E & D Hosking; 20 t Animal Photography, b C M Dixon; 21 t AKG London, b Peter Newark's Pictures; 24 Bob Langrish; 26 Kit Houghton; 30 Bob Langrish; 31–34 Kit Houghton; 35 t FLPA, b Bob Langrish; 36 t & br Bob Langrish, bl Ardea/Jean-Paul Ferrero, bc Kit Houghton; 37 Bob Langrish; 38 Kit Houghton; 39 tl Kit Houghton, tr FLPA, b Ardea/Jean-Paul Ferrero; 40–2 Kit Houghton; 42–43 Bob Langrish; 44 l Ardea/Jean-Paul Ferrero, c Only Horses, tr & b Bob Langrish; 45–46 Kit Houghton; 48–49 Bob Langrish; 50 Kit Houghton; 51–52 Bob Langrish; 53 t & b Bob Langrish, c Kit Houghton; 54 Bob Langrish; 55 Kit Houghton; 56–59 Bob Langrish; 60 Bob Langrish 61 tl & b Kit Houghton, r Bob Langrish; 62 Kit Houghton; 63 Bob Langrish; 64 t & c Bob Langrish, b Kit Houghton; 65–69 Bob Langrish; 71–72 Bob Langrish; 73 t Bibliotheque Nationale, Paris/e.t. archive, b Bob Langrish; 74–75 bl Bob Langrish, 75 br Kit Houghton; 76–87 Bob Langrish; 88 t Ardea, b Bob Langrish; 89 t Bob Langrish, b Kit Houghton; 90–91 t Bob Langrish, 91 b Sylvia Cordaiy/Graeme Buchan; 92 t University of Liverpool/Dr D Knottenbelt, b Bob Langrish; 93 t University of Liverpool/Dr D Knottenbelt, b Bob Langrish; 94 Bob Langrish; 95 t Only Horses, b Bob Langrish; 96 Bob Langrish; 96–7 Bob Langrish; 97 University of Liverpool/Dr D Knottenbelt; 98 Bob Langrish; 99 t University of Liverpool/Dr D Knottenbelt, b Bob Langrish; 100 t Bob Langrish, b Ardea/John Daniels; 101 Kit Houghton; 102 Only Horses; 102–3 Bob Langrish; 103 bl University of Liverpool/Dr D Knottenbelt, br Bob Langrish; 104 t Bob Langrish, b Kit Houghton; 105 t University of Liverpool/Dr D Knottenbelt,

bl Bob Langrish, br University of Liverpool/Dr D Knottenbelt; 106 t Bob Langrish, bl University of Liverpool/Dr D Knottenbelt, br Bob Langrish; 107 tl University of Liverpool/Dr D Knottenbelt, tr Ardea, b FLPA/R P Lawrence; 108 Russell Lym; 109 t Bob Langrish, c & b University of Liverpool/Dr D Knottenbelt; 110 University of Liverpool/Dr D Knottenbelt; 110–111 Kit Houghton; 111 l Bob Langrish, r Kit Houghton; 112-113 Bob Langrish; 114–115 Kit Houghton; 116 t Trevor Jones, b Kit Houghton; 117 l Trevor Jones, r Kit Houghton; 118 l Bob Langrish, r Kit Houghton; 119 Bob Langrish; 120 t Bob Langrish, b Peter Newark's Pictures; 120–121 Kit Houghton; 122 Bob Langrish; 123 t Ardea/John Daniels, b Corbis/J Cooke; 124 t Bob Langrish, b Kit Houghton; 125 Kit Houghton; 127 t Elisabeth Weiland, bl Deidre Davie, br Bob Langrish; 128 Kit Houghton; 129 l Allsport, r Bob Langrish, bl Cheryl Bender; 130 Aachen-Laurensberger/Avia-Luftbild, Aachen; 132-133 Bob Langrish; 134 t Bob Langrish, b Brant Gamma; 135 l Ardea/M Putland, r Bob Langrish; 136 Bob Langrish; 138 t Bob Langrish, bl Ardea/J Van Gruises, br Kit Houghton; 139 t & b Bob Langrish; 140 t FLPA, b Kit Houghton; 141 t Bob Langrish, b Kit Houghton; 142 Ronald Grant Archive; 142–43 Bob Langrish; 143 b Corbis/K R Morris; 144 Kit Houghton; 145 Bob Langrish; 146 t & br Bob Langrish, bl Kit Houghton; 147 Bob Langrish; 148 FLPA/L West; 149 tl Bob Langrish, tr & b Kit Houghton; 150 Hughes Photography; 151 tl Kit Houghton, tr & br Bob Langrish; 152–153 Bob Langrish; 154 t Bob Langrish, bl Popperfoto/R Boyce, br Corbis/Z Icknow; 154–155 Bob Langrish; 155 t Robert Harding, b Elisabeth Weiland ; 156 Bob Langrish; 156–57 Robert Harding/Elisabeth Weiland; 157 t Stockmarket, b Corbis/J McDonald; 158–59 Ardea; 160 t Bob Langrish, b Kit Houghton; 161 t & bl Kit Houghton, br Bob Langrish; 162 t Ardea/Jean-Paul Ferrero, b Bob Langrish; 163 Kit Houghton; 164 Bob Langrish; 165 t Kit Houghton, b Ardea/M Watson; 166 t Kit Houghton, b Ardea/H D Dossenbach; 167 t Kit Houghton, bl Only Horses, br Ardea/Jean-Paul Ferrero; 168 Bob Langrish; 169 t Bob Langrish, c & b Kit Houghton; 170 Bob Langrish; 171 t Kit Houghton, b Bob Langrish; 172 t Kit Houghton, b Bob Langrish; 173 Kit Houghton; 174 t Kit Houghton, b Ardea/H D Dossenbach; 175 t Bob Langrish, b Dr N Zalis; 176 Kit Houghton; 177 t Kit Houghton, b Bob Langrish; 178 t Bob Langrish, b Kit Houghton; 179 t Sally-Anne Thompson, 179b-181t Bob Langrish; 181b-183 Kit Houghton; 184 t Only Horses, bl Bob Langrish, br FLPA/Sunset/ Weiss; 185 t & c Kit Houghton, bl Ardea/Jean-Paul Ferrero; 186-187 t Bob Langrish, 187 b Sally-Anne Thompson/

V Nikiforov; 188 Kit Houghton; 189 Bob Langrish; 190 t Bob Langrish, b Kit Houghton; 191 t Kit Houghton, b Bob Langrish; 192 t Kit Houghton, b Ardea/Jean-Paul Ferrero; 193 Bob Langrish; 194 t Bob Langrish, b Kit Houghton; 195 t Kit Houghton, b Bob Langrish; 196 t & bl Bob Langrish, br Kit Houghton; 197 t Kit Houghton, b Bob Langrish; 198 t & c Bob Langrish, b Kit Houghton; 199 Bob Langrish; 200 t Bob Langrish, b FLPA/M Walker; 201 t Bob Langrish, b Ardea/Jean-Paul Ferrero; 202 Bob Langrish; 203 t Bob Langrish, b Kit Houghton; 204 Bob Langrish; 205 Kit Houghton; 206 t & br Bob Langrish, bl FLPA/M Walker; 207 Bob Langrish; 208 b Kit Houghton; 209 t Bob Langrish, bl Elisabeth Weiland, br Ardea/H D Dossenbach; 210-211 Bob Langrish; 212 t E Hanbury, b Bob Langrish; 213 Kit Houghton; 214 t Bob Langrish, bl Ardea/Jean-Paul Ferrero, br FLPA/A Wharton; 215 t Kit Houghton, b Bob Langrish; 216 t Kit Houghton, b Bob Langrish; 217 t Bob Langrish, bl Kit Houghton, br Ardea/Jean-Paul Ferrero; 218 t Kit Houghton, b Ardea/Jean-Paul Ferrero; 219 t Ardea/Jean-Paul Ferrero, bl Bob Langrish, br Kit Houghton; 220 t & br Ardea/Jean-Paul Ferrero, bl Kit Houghton; 221 t Only Horses, b Bob Langrish; 222 Ardea/Jean-Paul Ferrero; 223-224 Bob Langrish; 225 t Stockmarket, b Bob Langrish; 226 Bob Langrish; 227 t Bob Langrish, c Kit Houghton, b Ardea /P Morris; 228 t Oxford Scientific Films/J B Blossom, c Kit Houghton, b Bob Langrish; 229 Bob Langrish; 230 t FLPA/E & D Hosking, b Bob Langrish; 231 t Ardea/H D Dossenbach, b Elisabeth Weiland; 232 t Ardea/H D Dossenbach, c & b Bob Langrish; 233 Bob Langrish; 234 t Only Horses , bl Ardea/F Gohier, br Bob Langrish; 235 t Bob Langrish, b Ardea/ M Dossenbach; 236–37 e t archive/ National Gallery, London; 238 R. Delon/Casteiet; 238–39 AKG/Cameraphoto; 239 tl e t Archive/National Gallery, London tr Bridgeman Art Library /Lauros-Giraudor/ Musée des Antiquitées Nationales, St Germain-en-Laye, b Werner Forman Archive/Idemitsu Museum of Arts, Tokyo; 240 l AKG London, r 20th Century Fox/Ronald Grant Archive; 241 t The Legend of the Lone Ranger/ITC/Wrather Productions/Kobal Collection, b Musée d'Orsay, Paris/e t archive; 242 t Museum of America, Madrid/e t Archive, b Hulton Getty; 243 t Private Collection Bridgeman Art Library, b Peter Newark's Pictures; 244 l Peter Newark's Pictures, r Bryan & Cherry Alexander; 244-245 AKG London; 245 l Bob Langrish, r Hulton Getty; 246 t e t archive, b Hulton Getty; 246-247 Peter Newark's Pictures; 247 National Archives, USA/Corbis; 248 Portfolio Pictures; 249 tl Ronald Grant Archive, tr & b Peter Newark's Pictures; 256 Kit Houghton

Team Media would like to thank Linda Allen, the showjumping course designer for the Atlanta Olympics, for helping with the showjumping artwork on page 131; Aintree and Badminton for supplying artwork reference material; David Girling for editorial assistance; Rita Wüthrich for design assistance; Gwen Rigby for proofreading and Hazel K. Bell for the index.